Still Standing?

Praise for this book

'Still Standing? fills a major gap in the literature on housing reconstruction following disasters. The text examines five critical issues that surround the subject: 'user satisfaction', 'beneficiary targeting', 'replication by users', 'technical performance' and 'livelihood generation'. Thus it is essential reading for all involved in holistic recovery policy and practice, since it is crammed full of practical advice and rich case studies from international leaders in the field.'

Ian Davis, Visiting Professor in Disaster Risk Management in Copenhagen, Kyoto, Lund and Oxford Brookes Universities

'In the complex world of post-disaster housing reconstruction, this excellent book addresses an important and often-overlooked gap: how we learn from past projects to inform future actions.'

David Sanderson, Professor, Norwegian University of Science and Technology, Trondheim

'Which post-disaster reconstruction and recovery programmes have been truly successful? What are the critical elements that turn humanitarian shelter assistance into sustainable homes and communities? This much-needed publication provides the missing longer term analysis of what works and what does not, valuably informing the response to future disasters.'

Graham Saunders, Head, Shelter and Settlements, International Federation of Red Cross and Red Crescent Societies

Still Standing?
Looking back at reconstruction and disaster risk reduction in housing

Edited by Theo Schilderman and Eleanor Parker

PRACTICAL ACTION
Publishing

Practical Action Publishing Ltd
The Schumacher Centre
Bourton on Dunsmore, Rugby,
Warwickshire CV23 9QZ, UK
www.practicalactionpublishing.org

ISBN 978-1-85339-839-1 Hardback
ISBN 978-1-85339-840-7 Paperback
ISBN 978-1-78044-839-8 Library Ebook
ISBN 978-1-78044-840-4 Ebook

Schilderman, Theo, and Parker, Eleanor (eds), (2014) *Still Standing?
Looking back at reconstruction and disaster risk reduction in housing*
Rugby, UK: Practical Action Publishing.

Since 1974, Practical Action Publishing has published and disseminated
books and information in support of international development work
throughout the world. Practical Action Publishing is a trading name of
Practical Action Publishing Ltd (Company Reg. No. 1159018), the wholly
owned publishing company of Practical Action. Practical Action Publishing
trades only in support of its parent charity objectives and any profits
are covenanted back to Practical Action (Charity Reg. No. 247257,
Group VAT Registration No. 880 9924 76).

Cover photo: Post earthquake rehabilitation
through user participation at Gandhi nu gam, Ludiya, India; reintroducing
the vernacular with aspects of continuum and change.
Credit: Abhijeet Singh Chandel
Cover design by Mercer Design
Indexed by Liz Fawcett
Typeset by Allzone Digital
Printed by CPI Antony Rowe

Contents

List of Figures and Tables   vii
Acknowledgements   xi
Foreword   xiii

1   Introduction: What do we really know about
    the impact of reconstruction?   1
    Theo Schilderman

2   Emerging stronger? Assessing the outcomes
    of Habitat for Humanity's housing reconstruction
    programmes following the Indian Ocean tsunami   21
    Victoria Maynard, Priti Parikh, Dan Simpson, and Jo da Silva

3   Looking back at agency-driven housing
    reconstruction in India: Case studies from
    Maharashtra, Gujarat, and Tamil Nadu   39
    Jennifer Duyne Barenstein with Akbar Nazim Modan,
    Katheeja Talha, Nishant Upadhyay, and Charanya Khandhadai

Part I Asian Case Studies

4   A market-based programme to improve housing in the
    mountains of northern Pakistan:
    Addressing seismic vulnerability   59
    Nawab Ali Khan and Charles Parrack

5   India: Gandhi Nu Gam, an example of holistic
    and integrated reconstruction   77
    Yatin Pandya with Priyanka Bista,
    Abhijeet Singh Chandel, and Narendra Mangwani

6   Challenges for sustainability: Introducing
    new construction technologies in post-tsunami Sri Lanka   97
    Eleanor Parker, Asoka Ajantha, Vasant Pullenayegem,
    and S.Kamalaraj

7   Reconstruction in Vietnam: Less to lose!
    Examples of the experience of Development
    Workshop France in Vietnam   115
    Marion MacLellan, Matthew Blackett,
    Guillaume Chantry, and John Norton

8   Integrated people-driven reconstruction in Indonesia   137
    Annye Meilani, Wardah Hafidz, and Ashleigh King

http://dx.doi.org/10.3362/9781780448398.000

Part II Latin American case studies

9   Guatemala: Knowledge in the hands of the people   153
     Kurt Rhyner

10   Honduras: 'La Betania', resettlement of a
     flooded neighbourhood   171
     Kurt Rhyner

11   Nicaragua: reconstruction with local
     resources in an isolated region   187
     Kurt Rhyner

12   A roof for La Paz: reconstruction and development
     in El Salvador after the 2001 earthquakes   201
     Claudia Blanco, Alma Rivera,
     Jacqueline Martínez, and Jelly Mae Moring

13   Peru: building on the vernacular   217
     Theo Schilderman and Max Watanabe

14   Conclusions: How does our approach to
     reconstruction need to change?   233
     Theo Schilderman, Eleanor Parker, Matthew Blackett,
     Marion MacLellan, Charles Parrack, and Daniel Watson

Appendix   247
Index   253

List of Figures and Tables

Figures

2.1 Flooded houses in Indonesia at the time of the assessment 24

2.2 Typical core home designs: Indonesia, Sri Lanka, India, Thailand 25

2.3 HFH's core home design (far right) in one community in Indonesia which incorporates the re-use of a timber transitional shelter as a kitchen (right) and later extensions using a combination of timber and other materials (centre and left) 26

2.4 Some households in Indonesia had chosen to re-locate within their community so that they could set up a small shop or cafe near to the road 31

3.1 Plans of agency provided houses in Malkondji 43

3.2 Village map of Malkondji, 1996 44

3.3 Village map of Malkondji, 2011 44

3.4 Example of extensions carried out to a core house in Malkondji 45

3.5 Transformed houses in new Malkondji 45

3.6 Transformed houses in new Malkondji 45

3.7 Village map of old and new Fadsar 48

3.8 Empty agency-built houses in Fadsar in 2004 49

3.9 A transformed large house in Fadsar in 2012 49

3.10 A typical self-built traditional house in coastal Tamil Nadu 50

3.11 Example of house built by one of the agencies involved in the reconstruction of Seruthur 53

3.12 Example of extensions of an agency-built house in Seruthur 54

4.1 Heavy roof construction held up by wooden posts 61

4.2 Plan of traditional house construction 61

4.3 A BACIP enterprise that is selling stoves, water warming facility 64

4.4 Traditional building with wooden tie beams 67

4.5 BACIP galvanized wire technology (GWR) for new construction 67

4.6 Shahbaz Khan, a disabled person and the original owner of the house, with his wife outside their improved house 69

4.7 External view of Shah Raise's house which was reconstructed using seismic-resistant technology, thermal insulation, and illumination techniques 69

4.8 Principles of seismic resistance and thermal efficiency have been adopted in Faizabad School 70

4.9   Internal view of Noor Shah's house, where the family is using
      the energy-efficient stove to cook food   72
5.1   The traditional settlement layout of the region
      with *bhungas, chowki,* and a plinth   79
5.2   After the earthquake, Ludiya, 2001   80
5.3   Consultation with the community   82
5.4   Simulation kit showing the layout of
      plots as described by the inhabitants   82
5.5   Painting of the façade of the *bhunga* indicating
      high sense of belonging   83
5.6   Personalized interior of a household showing
      its socio-cultural appropriateness   83
5.7   Site plan of Gandhi Nu Gam, 2001 as created
      in consultation with inhabitants   84
5.8   View of Gandhi Nu Gam, 2001 after rehabilitation   84
5.9   Site plan of Gandhi Nu Gam, 2013   85
5.10 Exterior of the house, 2013   86
5.11 Site plan of House # 1   87
5.12 Puna Bhai's house (L-shaped form)   87
5.13 Site plan of House #2   88
5.14 Women working in semi-open space   88
5.15 Site plan of House #3   89
5.16 Textile work   93
5.17 Woodworking   93
5.18 Carpentry   93
6.1   Rat-trap technology, used in India and introduced by Practical Action
      post-tsunami after an earlier trial in north-western Sri Lanka   103
6.2   Rat-trap technology topped with a
      tile roof (house on the left)   104
6.3   With a flat roof showing ventilation
      holes in white below (house on the right)   104
6.4   Galle house extension constructed with concrete blocks   107
6.5   Galle house with boarded extension   107
7.1   Map of Vietnam with provinces discussed herein highlighted   116
7.2   The ten key principles of cyclone-resistant construction   119
7.3   Dwelling under concrete plinth, reinforced concrete frame and
      cement block retaining wall, with the interior filled with sand
      up to the raised floor level   122
7.4   A risk-reduction slogan on a chin strap   128
7.5   Schoolchild's painting of a house blowing away during a storm   128
8.1   Spacious kitchen in the back part of the house,
      made from materials recycled from temporary house   142
8.2   House abandoned by owner since he remarried and
      now lives with his new spouse outside the village   143
8.3   Uleelheu, 2006, immediately after reconstruction   144

8.4	Uleelheu, 2013, seven years after reconstruction	144
8.5	A porch has been added to the front of the house	146
8.6	Wooden wall covered with metal sheeting to protect it from rainwater	146
8.7	Stilt house modified into a restaurant, 2013	148
9.1	On the day of inauguration at the priest's model house	156
9.2	Dual education for builders was ongoing over the whole project cycle	156
9.3	The project dynamics in Salamá brought improvements to the community	158
9.4	Celso building his house in Salamá, 1977	162
9.5	Celso's house and carpentry shop, 2013	163
9.6	Her grandfather built the house in 1977	163
9.7	Domingo, now 70 years old, in front of the house he built 36 years ago	164
9.8	Fabian and Amalia in front of their house, 2013	165
9.9	Raquel Moya and her house, 2013	167
9.10	Demetrio's house in San Miguel, 1977	168
9.11	Demetrio, 2013	168
10.1	Guided self-help construction	173
10.2	Roof construction	173
10.3	Building the house is a family task	174
10.4	A lively well-kept neighbourhood	178
10.5	Illegal but apparently tolerated, 'soft invasion' with low-cost housing	181
10.6	People have made additions but the architectural unity is preserved	183
10.7	Several owners have made additions, up to three storeys	183
11.1	Drawing of house plan showing the design principle of having the same floor plan but different roof shapes	192
11.2	Aerial view of the houses showing the variety of design	192
11.3	Typical rural scene with the houses after a few years	194
11.4	Some families try to make some extra cash by setting up shop from their homes	194
11.5	Fatima in her house, 2013	196
11.6.	A well-maintained house	197
11.7	Houses are in good repair	197
11.8	Community buildings are well maintained and their tile roofs are in good shape	198
12.1	Concrete block housing	204
12.2	Concrete panel housing	204
12.3	Removable steel structure housing	204
12.4	A concrete block house in San Miguel Tepezontes municipality that was extended in the back with the construction of a	

covered patio and the main room was modified to put up
a shop as a means of livelihood   206

12.5 Concrete panel houses in the Edin Martinez
community: house on the left – no changes made
since its handover; house on the right – painted
façade, doors and floor changed   208

12.6 Unmodified removable steel structure house
in San Miguel Tepezontes municipality   209

12.7 ASPODEPAZ lobbying for decent housing
for low-income families   212

13.1 People living amongst the remnants of their
adobe houses, putting up reed mats as
temporary walls for shelter   218

13.2 Traditional *quincha* house under construction
in the Alto Mayo of Peru   220

13.3 Interior of a temporary shelter   221

13.4 *Improved quincha* houses during construction   222

13.5 Extension of a well-finished *improved
quincha* house with one part made of bricks
and a structural frame of concrete   225

13.6 Painted *improved quincha* house, including
an 'imitation-brick' lower part   225

13.7 Several houses in a row that have been
well finished, the farthest with 'imitation-brick'
paint and metal windows   227

Tables

5.1   Changes in spatial typology   85
5.2   List of materials used in extensions, 2013   91

Acknowledgements

This book has been developed through collaboration between the Building and Social Housing Foundation, Coventry University, and numerous research partners: the Aga Khan Planning and Building Service, Footprints E.A.R.T.H., Practical Action, Development Workshop, Uplink, Grupo Sofonias, Fundasal, Habitat for Humanity, and the World Habitat Research Centre. It reflects the contributions of many people within those organizations, including the authors whose names are indicated on the respective chapters, and draws together the experience and reflections of many more academics, community members, and practitioners. The collaborators and editors would like to thank each one of the named and unnamed writers, contributors, researchers, peer reviewers, and organizers who have helped to bring this book to fruition. We are also grateful to the Tony Bullard Trust for financing its publication.

About the editors

Theo Schilderman is a Senior Researcher at the Building and Social Housing Foundation, UK. He is an architect with over 40 years' experience of low-cost housing and reconstruction in developing countries.

Eleanor Parker is a Principal Lecturer in the Department of Geography, Environment and Disaster Management, Coventry University, UK.

Foreword

Each year, hundreds of thousands of houses are damaged or totally destroyed as a result of natural disasters – earthquakes, cyclones, landslides, flooding. Millions of people are left homeless. They must wait for flood waters to recede, rubble to be removed, houses to be repaired or reconstructed, services to be reinstated, and the trauma of a disaster to subside, so that they can return home and start to rebuild their lives. For some, resettlement may be the only option. Land which was previously occupied may have become uninhabitable due to topographical changes. Or, planning legislation, such as the introduction (or reinforcement) of a protective coastal-zone, may prevent families rebuilding.

Without durable housing, families are vulnerable in multiple ways. They have limited protection, are at greater risk from natural hazards, and their ability to pursue their normal household duties, resume their livelihoods or re-establish social networks is compromised. Consequently, both emergency shelter and longer-term housing assistance has been recognized as a primary need in the aftermath of disasters for decades. Immediate life-saving shelter (blankets, plastic sheeting, and tents) is not enough. Ongoing assistance from humanitarian agencies or government is necessary in order to catalyse the process of recovery and reconstruction – or, if necessary, resettlement.

In this context, the term 'reconstruction' does not just refer to building houses that have been damaged or destroyed, but to re-establishing communities that not only survive, but go on to thrive. In *Shelter after Disaster*, published in 1982, Ian Davis emphasized the importance of understanding housing as a 'process' rather than a 'product'; a house being 'merely the end-product of social, economic, technological, environmental, political and other interactions'. Nevertheless, the role of donors and humanitarian agencies is frequently misconstrued as being to provide houses, rather than to provide assistance that enables communities and local government to identify and overcome issues that prevent families – particularly the most vulnerable families – from accessing decent, durable, and affordable housing. This means housing that enables them to go about their day-to-day business with dignity, as well as reducing their vulnerability to future disasters.

Although ensuring the housing needs of the most vulnerable households are met remains a priority, many of the critical issues associated with housing play out at the community level. Land tenure, access to utilities (water, electricity, sanitation, roads, etc.), lack of construction skills, or the cost of building materials are best addressed by community-based interventions including: micro-finance, cadastral mapping, training in safe construction techniques, bulk purchase of materials, construction of 'core' houses or upgrading neighbourhood infrastructure. Meanwhile, interventions at a household level must take account of the cultural norms that govern day-to-day interactions and activities. For example, whether families cook inside or outside, require internal partitions for privacy, or wish to use their house for livelihood activities (sewing, growing vegetables, opening a shop, or mending fishing nets). In short, housing programmes are complex. In post-disaster situations even more so, as a balance must be struck between addressing the immediacy of needs and ensuring solutions are sustainable. This can prove particularly challenging when there are very large numbers of people affected resulting in intense political or media pressure.

Following the Indian Ocean tsunami in 2004, the phrase 'build back better' coined by UN Special Envoy, President Clinton, was intended to highlight the opportunity reconstruction affords to improve living standards and to reduce vulnerability. Nevertheless, for many implementing agencies including the government, the overwhelming driver was to construct as many houses as quickly as possible. In Aceh, considerable efforts were made by some agencies to integrate disaster risk reduction (DRR) into housing programmes, but the investment in raising awareness of natural hazards and promoting safe (or safer) construction practices has not had a lasting impact. The majority of reconstruction was un-confined charcoal-fired masonry reflecting local building practices. Post-tsunami, concrete ring beams, careful reinforcement detailing, and small panel sizes were introduced. These are essential to avoid collapse in an earthquake but are still not common practice. One agency attempted to introduce reinforced concrete blocks which are more suitable in seismic areas and are used elsewhere in Indonesia, but faced resistance as the technology was unfamiliar. Meanwhile, several manufacturers supplied pre-cast concrete or steel panel systems which enabled large numbers of houses to be built quickly, but did not necessarily take account of either seismic risk or future adaptability. Notably, there was a reluctance to construct vernacular timber frame houses, due to a lack of skilled carpenters and perceptions that timber houses are inferior. Building back better, even simply building back safer, is easier said than done; yet, remains a goal worth aspiring to.

Substantial evidence exists to suggest that developmental approaches founded on community participation and integrated programming which provide assistance over several years, are more likely to create sustainable settlements in the long term. However, community engagement takes time and multi-sector programming (including shelter, wat-san and livelihoods, DRR) adds complexity which may not be compatible with donor priorities and timescales, or the mandates or skillsets of individual agencies. Despite this, the case studies in Theo Schilderman's previous book *Build Back Better* (co-authored by Michal Lyons who sadly passed away last year) makes a strong case for owner-driven construction even for large-scale post-disaster programmes. Whilst, the experiences of eleven agencies captured in *Lessons from Aceh*, suggests that the most successful programmes combined expertise in community engagement with construction management skills typically found in the private sector.

Typically, funding for reconstruction is limited, and the timeframe when funding is available demands immediate action. Consultation with affected communities is essential to understand the needs and priorities of those affected, but these are likely to change over time. Humanitarian agencies are left with difficult choices: to provide limited assistance to many, or target the most vulnerable; to support the reconstruction of four hundred houses which are designed and detailed to withstand a significant earthquake, or a larger number built to a lower standard which may then collapse if a significant earthquake occurs; to focus on immediate needs or invest in the future by providing communities with knowledge and skills. The amount of funding available in the aftermath of the Indian Ocean tsunami (2004), which enabled humanitarian agencies to construct hundreds of thousands of houses, was unprecedented. Moreover, it is unlikely to be repeated given current predictions of reduced funding for humanitarian assistance in the future.

In contrast, the numbers of people affected by flooding three years in a row in southern Pakistan (2010–2012) dwarfed the capacity of humanitarian agencies. Recognizing their limited resources and that severe flooding is becoming an annual event in this region, increasing emphasis has been placed on assisting families to adapt vernacular construction to include flood-resistant features (plinths, roof overhangs, rendered walls), as well as providing training so that they are able to maintain and repair their houses themselves. This recognizes the importance of building local capacity, and enhancing existing building practices. Moreover, it exemplifies a necessary shift from responding to disasters towards creating more resilient communities that are better able to withstand multiple shocks and stresses.

Earlier this year, I had the privilege of listening to presentations of each of the case studies on which this book is based. I was struck by the commonality of lessons, despite the diversity of contexts. The choice of technology is critical, as is active community participation at every stage of the process. Not only to ensure programmes are culturally appropriate and relevant, but to generate awareness, skills, and knowledge that have a lasting impact. From a community's perspective, a secure living environment in terms of tenure as well as safety is fundamental, likewise affordability (including the cost of maintenance) and adaptability, whilst investment in local institutions and markets is necessary for replication and scale. I was left with no doubt that there are long-term benefits in adopting more integrated and inclusive approaches to housing programmes, but also limitations as to what can really be achieved directly as the result of a reconstruction programme taking place over a few years.

There is no shortage of experience to draw on in designing and implementing post-disaster programmes. Yet, to date there is surprisingly little evidence or exploration of the efficacy of housing programmes either in promoting long-term recovery, or creating resilient communities that are better able to withstand and adapt to future shocks or stresses. *Still Standing?* addresses this gap by looking back at reconstruction programmes globally, specifically reflecting on the extent to which they have resulted in safer and more resilient communities. In doing so, it identifies key factors that contribute to the effectiveness and long-term impact. Above all, it encourages us to think more holistically and with longer-term horizons, in order for the limited funding that is available for reconstruction to be considered as an investment in the future, as well as a response to a disaster.

Jo da Silva OBE FREng, Director, Arup International Development
28 May 2014

CHAPTER 1

Introduction: What do we really know about the impact of reconstruction?

Theo Schilderman

The need for a longer-term approach to reconstruction and recovery

The Philippines were hit by a typhoon in November 2013, the intensity of which they had not experienced before. According to the International Disaster Database, EM-DAT (2014), the number and intensity of hydro-meteorological disasters is increasing steadily. Financial damage attributed to disasters also shows an upward curve. Disasters and development are closely interlinked. On the one hand, disasters regularly wipe out years of development (Schilderman, 1993; IEG, 2006), an impact we strive to reduce. On the other, development gone wrong creates the vulnerabilities that turn natural hazards into disasters (Wijkman and Timberlake, 1984; Grunewald et al., 2000; IEG, 2006). Even in recovery, people sometimes end up struggling more with underlying development problems such as a declining economy or poor governance, rather than simply rebuilding houses (Cosgrave et al., 2009).

Disasters are not neutral; they are known to affect the poor more (Guha-Sapir et al., 2013; Arnold and Burton, 2011). Reconstruction and recovery can be very difficult for the poor and may further increase pre-disaster inequalities; those longer-term impacts, though, often remain hidden from the outside world because the attention of donors and the media has shifted elsewhere (IEG, 2006; Arnold and Burton, 2011), and can vary hugely. A recent report by a special rapporteur to the United Nations (2011) concluded that reconstruction and recovery too often focus on physical structures (houses), whereas for those affected the recovery of livelihoods, social networks, or services is frequently a higher priority than houses. Predominant approaches to reconstruction and recovery seem to be short-term and reactive, where they ought perhaps to take a longer-term view and pro-actively seek to reduce pre-existing and post-disaster vulnerabilities, not just of houses, but of affected people.

The full impact of recovery and reconstruction on people's livelihoods and resilience can only be truly understood in the longer term. Yet, agencies rarely return to locations where they were supporting projects. Much of our knowledge about impact comes from project evaluations or end-of-project reports produced shortly after projects ended. There have been far fewer longitudinal studies of impact. This chapter is largely based on a literature review that aimed to take stock of such longitudinal studies. Of the 99 documents reviewed, only 15

http://dx.doi.org/10.3362/9781780448398.001

were written more than five years after the end of reconstruction, 40 within four years; the remaining often covered several projects and a more variable timespan, but were rarely found to include long-term lessons.

For us to be able to develop more effective long-term approaches to reconstruction and recovery in the housing sector which consider their contribution to general development and to a reduction of vulnerabilities, especially of the poor and marginalized, we need to learn more lessons from the past. That is why the Building and Social Housing Foundation (BSHF) and its partners undertook the research that forms the basis for this book.

Developing the research

BSHF was established to identify innovative housing solutions with a proven track record, through research and a competition, and to promote their transfer to potential users worldwide. Its sources of funding are limited. We, therefore, could not opt for a quantitative approach, e.g. interviewing hundreds of households. Instead, we adopted a more qualitative method, interviewing small numbers of people as individuals and in groups, but verifying the reliability of their answers through triangulation. Our aim was to begin to understand what issues and factors had the greatest impact on the long-term resilience of people in disaster areas and their houses, illustrate them with some real-life examples, and communicate these to reconstruction agencies. Hopefully, this would then help them to design better projects in the future, identify indicators to measure success during and after the life of projects, and identify gaps in understanding to be addressed by additional research.

Through its annual World Habitat Award (WHA) competitions, BSHF has developed resources, including databases of excellent projects dating back to 1985, and of professionals involved in housing, many of whom have been involved with us in networking, exchanges, or collaborative research. A number of these dealt with reconstruction or disaster mitigation of housing. For most, we also had a project summary that had adequate information on the end-of-project situation and the lessons and impacts at that stage, which we could use as a 'baseline' with which to compare the current situation of each project. Fieldwork could provide evidence not only for changes in housing and livelihoods over time, but also stakeholder perspectives on factors influencing those changes. The 'baseline' and the fieldwork could then be used to write a story of change for each project, ultimately becoming chapters in this book. We contacted a number of agencies who had implemented reconstruction and mitigation projects that had either previously won a WHA or were finalists and asked them whether they would like to partner with BSHF in looking back to establish the projects' impact over time; seven were happy to do so. Three agencies then offered to investigate additional projects: in one case, a reconstruction project was added to a mitigation project in the same country; in another case, two more projects were investigated in neighbouring countries; and in the last case, a different office of the same international agency, on another continent, offered another study. None of these were on our database, but we believed all to be good projects, of which we were able to obtain 'baseline' information and could draw lessons. That produced 11 case studies with a good worldwide spread: five in Latin America; three in South Asia; and three in South-east Asia.

In order to focus the research we first discussed the information all of us wanted to get out of it with the research partners involved. This was summarized into broad themes with a series of questions under each, that were subsequently discussed with around 150 members of the broader relief and reconstruction community, including practitioners, researchers, and donor agencies, at the UK Shelter Forum in Oxford and the Shelter Centre in Geneva. Those involved in all those discussions broadly agreed on five thematic areas of investigation:

- User satisfaction – what matters to beneficiaries, and how do projects achieve it? Is it a factor in people assuming 'ownership' of their house which could be an important indicator of the sustainability of the houses built?;
- Beneficiary targeting – do projects reach the right people, and are the solutions they offer appropriate in the long term? Do beneficiaries continue to benefit from their reconstructed home, particularly exploring why some did not occupy or abandoned their houses?;
- Replication – of the housing technology and implementation approach, by individuals or agencies, which is an even stronger indicator of appropriateness.
- Technical performance – assessing whether houses were durable in the environment and stood up to subsequent disasters, the weather and other external factors.
- Livelihoods – the link between livelihoods which generate a reliable income, vulnerability reduction, gender equality and future resilience to disasters, is well proven. The research sought to explore whether projects had increased the resilience of people through integrated livelihood activities, rather than focusing on building more resilient houses.

The full research methodology is provided in Appendix 1.

All research partners reported back to BSHF under the above thematic headings. They subsequently presented the main outcomes and lessons of their cases to each other and representatives of the broader reconstruction community at an international conference at Coventry University on 15–16 January 2014. This provided a true opportunity to share lessons from across the world and hear personal stories come alive from people able to revisit their projects. The discussions there and the people who contributed to them were influential in the formulation of the ideas developed in this book.

What do we know from past experience?

Most of what we know about the outcomes and impact of reconstruction was written shortly after the end of projects; documentation of their longer-term impact is much rarer. This chapter summarizes the available information on the identified themes, and may, therefore, be rather biased towards immediately visible lessons.

Over time the mistakes made by projects in their design or implementation become more apparent: leaking roofs or walls being affected by humidity, poorly cured concrete showing damage and rusting reinforcement, kitchens or toilets being in the wrong place, unused or moved. Outcomes that seem positive at the end of projects can seem less so later on, for instance because an agency has stopped supporting the activity or a temporary post-disaster construction boom has subsided. When that happens, people's opinions about their rebuilt house may worsen. Conversely, as reported by Duyne Barenstein (2013; Chapter 3 of this book), when residents have the skills and means to improve their houses at a later stage, their satisfaction may improve as well as the houses' performance.

Contextual changes over time can also affect people's opinions and desires. Rules, policies, and public opinion will evolve, for example, with people becoming more conscious of their environment and saving energy. Economic growth and related increases in income, coupled with advertising of a 'modern' way of life, can create a desire to change. Guzmán Negrón (2010) reports that people in rural areas of Alto Mayo, Peru are still happily replicating the improved *quincha* (mud-and-pole) houses built after the 1990 earthquake, but in urban areas that had benefited more from Peru's economic boom, about a third of those were replaced by 'modern' concrete frame technology.

Looking back at projects, therefore, it is important to consider that not every change that occurred in housing or beneficiaries' livelihoods can be attributed directly to decisions made by the relevant reconstruction project teams; external influences may also impact people's opinions.

User satisfaction

If beneficiaries and those around them are happy with the housing solutions provided, they are more likely to replicate them. We have to bear in mind, though, that happiness is subjective, and may vary between residents and, as we have seen above, over time. Many researchers have indicated factors that contribute to the satisfaction or dissatisfaction of residents. They do not always agree with each other, but important trends exist.

Some sources maintain that owner-driven reconstruction (ODR) leads to greater user satisfaction than donor-driven reconstruction (DDR); e.g. Duyne Barenstein (2006) in post-earthquake Gujarat, and Lyons (2007, 2010) in post-tsunami Sri Lanka. But in a large survey of reconstruction approaches in Aceh, UN Habitat (2009) generally found little difference in satisfaction between these approaches, though some projects stood out, either positively or negatively. A key factor that distinguishes them is the degree of participation beneficiaries had in decision-making. Where they had little say, it often led to inappropriate houses (Sadiqi et al., 2011) and 'one-design-fits-all' solutions (Barakat, 2003). Lack of participation frequently produces culturally inappropriate house designs or settlements (Jigyasu, 2000; Kelly, 2010) or climatically unsuitable houses. Participation tends to promote some flexibility in design and, by considering beneficiaries' expressed needs, leads to more appropriate design and greater functionality (Wilches-Chaux, 1995; Duyne Barenstein, 2006; da Silva and Batchelor, 2010) and ultimately greater satisfaction.

Well intentioned post-disaster risk reduction initiatives have imposed land zoning and otherwise required relocation of communities. Studies have shown that often relocation affects, and may become a source of, dissatisfaction (Grunewald et al., 2000; IEG, 2006; Fallahi, 2007). Relocation has particular challenges but such projects are not universally causes of dissatisfaction for beneficiaries, e.g. Cronin and Guthrie (2011) report on an often flooded slum in Pune being relocated and inhabitants being happy with the result.

A major contributor to beneficiary unhappiness with relocation sites was the tardy installation of infrastructure (Grunewald et al., 2000; Hidellage and Usoof, 2010). At times, insufficient infrastructure can also cause problems to those reconstructing in-situ. If water or energy supplies are absent, building becomes difficult. Other components, like toilets, may be absent altogether when the focus of a reconstruction project is solely on the provision of permanent shelter. The review found a minority of beneficiaries were unhappy with some infrastructure in their projects, but where it was improved when lacking before that was appreciated (Basin South Asia, 2008; Cronin and Guthrie, 2011).

Good quality and durable materials and construction are highly valued (Wilches-Chaux, 1995), and the absence thereof regretted (Duyne Barenstein, 2006; UN Habitat, 2009; Guzmán, 2010). That appreciation can extend to the use of vernacular materials or technologies (Schilderman, 2004; Stephenson, 2008; Jha et al., 2010) and is often linked to achieving good disaster resistance (Barakat, 2003; van Leersum, 2008; Razavi and Razavi, 2013). An unfortunate consequence of quality improvement is sometimes that size is reduced to remain within budget. It is important to residents to have an adequately sized house and plot to accommodate household and livelihood activities, particularly to allow for future extensions (Wilches-Chaux, 1995; Duyne Barenstein, 2006; Maynard et al., 2013).

Both quality and size relate closely to affordability: beneficiaries like housing solutions that are affordable to them (IEG, 2006; van Leersum, 2008), even if these are based on vernacular technologies. Over time, residents do adjust to things they do not like. They will replace leaking roofs, or alter them to adjust better to the climate (Guzmán, 2010). They alter inappropriate designs (D'Souza, 1986), or change rooms into shops, kitchens, or areas of worship (Wilches-Chaux, 1995; Maynard et al., 2013). Some will add rooms (Wilches-Chaux, 1995; Schilderman, 2010). Where houses or toilets were inappropriate, some were turned into stores (Jigyasu, 2000; Salazar, 2002). If they cannot afford the resistant technologies implemented during reconstruction, they may revert to poor quality vernacular technologies that may make them vulnerable again (Jigyasu, 2000, 2004).

The choice of project staff can be crucial in determining the options beneficiaries have. Professionals involved often lack the experience and the education suited to traditional contexts, e.g. they may have a strong bias toward modern technologies over the vernacular, with which they are often unfamiliar and are, therefore, not confident to apply (Jigyasu, 2000, 2004); they may value quality and perceived greater disaster resistance over appropriateness and affordability; and they often view reconstruction from the narrow perspective of their own sector only, such as housing, which may explain the lack of integration in projects (United Nations General Assembly, 2011). A lack of consideration for people's livelihoods, e.g. in how houses are designed or where they are located, is a major contributor to user dissatisfaction.

Reconstruction can lead to health improvements, but the opposite happens more often. Evidence of improvement can be vague (Duyne Barenstein, 2006); Cronin and Guthrie (2011) claim it to 'have somewhat improved'. It may also be circumstantial, with authors stating that health risks are reduced due to the provision of better water, sanitation, and hygiene or occasionally because projects also built health facilities (Basin South Asia, 2008; Deprez and Labattut, 2010; Jha et al., 2010). More frequently though, residents' health is put at risk, particularly because of sanitation that is poorly built and maintained (Duyne Barenstein, 2006), leaking into the groundwater (Maynard et al., 2013), inappropriate and, therefore, not used (Salazar, 2002; Maynard et al., 2013) leading to reversion to open defecation (Jigyasu, 2000; Duyne Barenstein, 2006). In Aceh, inefficient drains cause health risks (Deprez and Labattut, 2010).

Beneficiary targeting

This review found many examples of beneficiaries not occupying houses allocated to them, or abandoning them after a while. Is this because projects did not target the right people? Or is it because inappropriate houses and locations were offered to the 'right' beneficiaries?

Whether the right people are always reached remains debatable. In the case of DDR, there often are complaints that the housing provided is so expensive, that only a fraction of disaster victims can be reached because the number of houses that can be constructed is limited by funds available, as in most cases complete houses are donated to those affected by disasters. Less frequently, beneficiaries are given a core house, which they are expected to expand over time, or a minimum amount of cash for shelter to which they add their own resources; this allows more people to be reached. Occasionally, money is made available as a reconstruction loan only; this can lead to repayment problems. One of the main criticisms of ODR is that it solely focuses on those who owned a house prior to the disaster, and, therefore, provides no solutions for victims who cannot prove their ownership, are tenants, or informal settlers. There is also evidence that the more powerful and richer victims often achieve better access to reconstruction aid than those more marginalized (Lyons and Schilderman, 2010b). Some argue that the aid available for reconstruction and recovery ought to be equally divided amongst all victims. That could mean that households might only get a core house, and that adequate size may have to be achieved over time after the reconstruction project is complete, as is most often the case when people realize their own housing. Compromise may also have to be made in terms of quality, durability, and the resistance of the buildings, so houses provided may only withstand hazards of lesser magnitude. Whether aid agencies should provide everything to some or something to all remains a question with no easy answer.

Whether or not the right people have been targeted, the housing solutions offered seem to be frequently inappropriate. That is closely related to the theme of user satisfaction, treated above. One might say that many cases of households not occupying their houses, or abandoning them after a while, are evidence of extreme user dissatisfaction; but not all cases are, sometimes people leave their house for other reasons.

In Gujarat, Duyne Barenstein (2006) found that far fewer households abandoned or did not occupy their allocated houses in ODR than in DDR. That was confirmed by Hidellage and Usoof (2010) in Sri Lanka. Participation of beneficiaries in the design and implementation of housing projects appears to be key. Major factors for non-occupancy included inappropriate design, the lack of livelihood opportunities – particularly following relocation – and poor quality construction. Where radically different technologies are offered in a traditional context, problems often occur with construction quality or with residents not having the skills to maintain houses. Consequently, Jigyasu (2000) and Salazar (2002) found that in Maharashtra about half of houses had fallen into disrepair and were empty or used for storage. Where households do not occupy or abandon their allocated house, they often return to their old site and rebuild a house in traditional ways, which leaves them as vulnerable to disasters as before. A lack of infrastructure can also be a major factor in non-occupancy; too often, agencies provide only houses, and leave it up to local authorities or utilities to provide related infrastructure, but the latter are often too stretched to do so immediately, e.g. after hurricane Mitch in Honduras (Telford et al., 2004), in Afghanistan (Kelly, 2010), and in Aceh (da Silva and Batchelor, 2010).

Households who do not use their allocated houses may rent them out or sell them, as found by the IEG (2006) in seven out of 30 World Bank-funded reconstruction projects involving relocation. In Colombia, Wilches-Chaux (1995) noticed this happened more frequently with households on lower incomes struggling to keep up loan repayments. This raises an issue about the affordability of solutions offered to them. Occasionally, poor people appear to move on because better-off households make them an offer they cannot refuse, but that does not equate with them being unhappy with the houses provided. The opposite may also happen; there are cases where the better-off are disappointed with houses offered to them. This occurred in Aceh, where the authority established to deal with reconstruction (BRR – *Badan Rehabilitasi dan Rekonstruksi*), proposed 36 m² standard plans, leading to fairly monotonous settlements (Deprez and Labattut, 2010). This was below expectations, particularly of the urban better-off, and many of them did not occupy the houses offered.

Replication

If owners are able to expand their house or construct another one in the same way as one built in a reconstruction project that confirms their appropriateness, and is an indicator that the same level of disaster resistance is being maintained. The same applies when others copy those examples. A requirement for replication is that original designs and technologies are of adequate quality and affordability; where that is not the case, people will change them.

Poverty is a key factor in replication. Where original solutions are only affordable with aid, poor beneficiaries will be unable to replicate them (Schilderman, 2010). They will then choose different designs and technologies for future construction, or try to 'cut corners', for example dilute mortar or concrete mixes, resulting in poorer quality and greater long-term vulnerability to disasters (D'Souza, 1986; Cory, 1995; Barakat, 2003; Twigg, 2002/2006).

Several authors (Schilderman, 1993, 2004; Duyne Barenstein, 2006; Stephenson, 2008) found that replication is made easier, and happens more frequently, when it involves familiar materials and technologies. In such cases, many residents will quite quickly begin to add and change elements of the original structure (da Silva and Batchelor, 2010; Maynard et al., 2013). Others nearby will start to replicate (Schilderman, 1993; Wilches-Chaux, 1995). But where projects introduce alien technologies, they will often build vernacular extensions (Aysan and Oliver, 1987; Salazar, 2002). After a disaster, there is often an emphasis on rebuilding safely, resulting in a preference for modern reconstruction technologies, but these may be inappropriate in a local context and hamper replication (Jigyasu, 2000; Duyne Barenstein, 2006). Vernacular approaches, perhaps with some adaptation for greater resistance, can be as safe as modern methods. What may limit wider use of vernacular technologies is that they are often not covered by building regulations and, therefore, may be refused in certain locations or by some agencies. If relevant, authorities can approve them quickly, that can stimulate their uptake (Stephenson, 2008; Duyne Barenstein and Iyengar, 2010).

Another factor promoting replication is a greater feeling of ownership, often a result of active participation in decision-making and construction (Maskrey, 1995; Deprez and Labattut, 2010). A lack of skills even in vernacular technologies can make replication difficult (Jigyasu, 2000; Guzmán, 2010); this happens where projects make insufficient efforts to build capacities (Maskrey, 1995). DDR generally develops few skills locally (Barakat, 2003). ODR often does, but not always; where projects focus on providing cash for shelter, with little additional support, this can limit replication (Schilderman, 2010).

Technical performance

It is difficult to judge how houses will perform after the end of a project; whether they will stand up to future hazards, or the effects of climate and wear, will only become clear in the longer term. User satisfaction with quality just after beneficiaries have occupied their houses, therefore, is a poor indicator of technical performance. This is one theme for which a longitudinal assessment is particularly important.

Disaster resistance and quality can be imposed by building codes, or they can be encouraged where codes do not apply, are inadequate or inappropriate. Disaster resistance is not always required by law for non-engineered or one-storey buildings, nor may codes apply in rural areas (UN Habitat, 2009). This was the case in Aceh, sometimes resulting in a need to retrofit later (da Silva, 2010). Where housing is informal, safer building may need to be disseminated differently (IEG, 2006). Where codes are applied and properly inspected, resulting houses can be disaster-resistant (Duyne Barenstein, 2006), but this does not always happen (Barakat, 2003; Powell, 2011), e.g. problems may occur if codes are imposed, but beneficiaries are unaware of them or do not know how to comply. This may lead to cash instalments for reconstruction to them being halted, or retrofitting being required (Jigyasu, 2004; Davis, 2007) before further assistance is provided. Even in Sri Lanka, where ample aid was available after the tsunami, disaster-resistant features required by authorities were often omitted by ODR beneficiaries, who did not always see the need for them, though overall construction quality was acceptable (Hidellage and Usoof, 2010); the same was noticed at times in Gujarat (Powell, 2011). Where codes are being neglected or inspection is lax, vulnerability remains high (Davis, 2007). In some locations, quality control is virtually absent, or inadequate (Telford et al., 2006).

A lack of knowledge and awareness, not just of codes, but of risks and quality, can maintain vulnerability. Jigyasu (2004) reports on repairs of houses that remained standing after the Gujarat earthquake of 2001, where inhabitants filled and plastered over cracks without retrofitting, leaving them at risk of future hazards. Houses may be rebuilt on the same risky sites, and even in relocation, risks may be ignored or not well known, e.g. in Honduras (Telford et al., 2004) and Aceh (da Silva and Batchelor, 2010). Some projects provide houses only, but the drainage that is essential to reduce risks may receive insufficient attention (Maynard et al., 2013).

Poor workmanship during the reconstruction phase also reduces quality and increases risk (D'Souza, 1986; da Silva, 2010). This is often due to inadequate training, supervision, and support (Jigyasu, 2000; Fallahi, 2007; Guzmán, 2010). In some cases, e.g. Maharashtra (Jigyasu, 2000; Salazar, 2002), modern construction was performed badly due to poor implementation of unfamiliar technologies, or lack of funds for maintenance or repair (World Bank, 2010). Radical changes of technology can often lead to lower quality, e.g. because concrete is insufficiently cured, or to errors in placing the reinforcement (da Silva and Batchelor, 2010; Guzmán, 2010; Powell, 2011).

Authors like Schilderman (2004), and Mantel (2013) argue that future repair and maintenance are more likely to be done in a disaster-resistant way if good or improved vernacular practice is integrated into reconstruction, which also reduces the cost of training and support during reconstruction. Others maintain that since modern technologies are so often unaffordable, there is a need to promote more vernacular technologies (Reddy, 1995). In some locations vernacular skills have declined, though, because poverty and changing aspirations reduced demand (Salazar, 2002; Barakat, 2003). Where they can be maintained or improved, vernacular technologies have proven to stand up to natural hazards (Schilderman, 1993, 2004; Stephenson, 2008; World Bank, 2010).

DDR does not guarantee better quality construction than ODR, though it is often assumed to. Contractors used in DDR may value profits over quality, but the owners involved in ODR do try to maintain quality, either whilst doing the work themselves or through strict supervision. Insufficient supervision of contractors by inexperienced agencies can add to the problem (Jayawardena, 2011).

The quality and disaster resistance of houses also depends on the amount of money invested in them, something that affects satisfaction and replication equally. It will vary with agency budgets for reconstruction, and can differ considerably between agencies, as noticed e.g. after hurricane Mitch in Central America (Telford et al., 2006) and in post-tsunami Aceh and Sri Lanka (UN Habitat, 2009). Agencies face difficult choices between reaching more beneficiaries with some housing support and targeting fewer with more complete housing. Where the beneficiaries have resources of their own, they can add these to those received from agencies, either directly or later, and achieve adequate quality incrementally. The poorest, though, may be unable to do so. The same applies where extensions happen later on (van Leersum, 2008; Guzmán, 2010), or when repairs or maintenance need to happen (Graf, 2013). This can increase vulnerability, sometimes even of a core originally designed to withstand disasters (da Silva and Batchelor, 2010; Guzmán, 2010). Even where money is available, necessary investments in better housing are not always made, e.g. when insecurity of tenure puts owners at risk of losing their investment (Twigg, 2002/2006; World Bank, 2010).

Livelihoods

Reconstruction offers the opportunity to build back more safely, and where agencies invest sufficient money and subsidize beneficiaries, safer homes are provided. This, however, does not necessarily address the factors that made pre-disaster houses unsafe nor the lack of capacity and resources residents frequently face when building, extending, and maintaining houses. Poverty and lack of skills are key factors in this; others include poor access to information and the lack of voice that often accompanies poor governance. Under the general heading of livelihoods, this section explores how reconstruction has helped people – and not just houses – to become more resilient, that is to resist, cope with, and recover from the effects of hazards.

Reconstruction can stimulate the local economy, particularly the construction sector, by generating jobs and incomes in materials production, building, transport, and related services. The extent to which this happens depends on choice of designs, technologies, and builders. We must be aware that traditional trades lose out where more modern technologies are preferred (Jigyasu, 2000;); the import of pre-fabricated houses precludes local jobs (D'Souza, 1986); large contractors prefer bringing in their own labour over hiring locally (Duyne Barenstein, 2006), which may even put local companies out of business (Barakat, 2003; Twigg, 2002/2006). Providing cash for reconstruction often encourages beneficiaries to buy materials and labour locally (Lizarralde, 2010), but occasionally such materials are of low quality or scarce, causing agencies to buy them elsewhere and missing the opportunity to promote local economic development (Twigg, 2002/2006; da Silva and Batchelor, 2010). Da Silva (2010) found in Aceh that training provided in the context of reconstruction did help local people find jobs. However, overall, the post-tsunami reconstruction process did not evaluate potential long-term benefits to the local economy, and 60 per cent of investment in reconstruction ended up outside the region (Deprez and Labattut, 2010). Cosgrave et al. (2009) argue that one job in housing creates at least one to two jobs elsewhere in the economy, and reconstruction may even be significant enough to promote more general economic recovery, as happened in Yogyakarta, Indonesia, and in India, where the economy remained strong (Basin South Asia, 2008; Duyne Barenstein, 2013), and elsewhere (Jha et al., 2010; Maynard et al., 2013). In other cases, though, the construction sector reverted to its pre-disaster level after the reconstruction boom, e.g. in Sri Lanka. Additional jobs created initially may then not be sustained (Cory, 1995; Lyons and Schilderman, 2010b).

Relocation to other sites removes people from previous income-generating opportunities, and may not create new employment options (Jigyasu, 2000; Cosgrave et al., 2009; Jha et al., 2010) with obvious negative impacts on livelihoods. Relocation may also impact livelihoods through increasing the cost of services (Grunewald et al., 2000; Duyne Barenstein, 2006), or weakening social networks. If agencies focus too much on housing alone (Grunewald et al., 2000; UN General Assembly, 2011) and people are relocated to sites detrimental to their livelihoods, they often move back to the original sites and rebuild in traditional ways, maintaining their vulnerabilities (Duyne Barenstein and Iyengar, 2010).

A lack of consideration for beneficiaries' livelihoods not only appears in relocation, but also in the design of many in-situ projects. Few truly embrace livelihood activities (Lizarralde, 2010). It is more common where ODR allows real flexibility in design (Duyne Barenstein, 2006; Hidellage and Usoof, 2010). Many people would like to have a shop at home, but they are rarely accommodated (Deprez and Labattut, 2010). The same applies to other home-based enterprises (Cosgrave et al., 2009). Many houses also lack sufficient storage space, impeding livelihood development (Duyne Barenstein, 2006). With plots frequently being too small, artisans and others are left with insufficient space to practice trades (Jigyasu, 2004; Grunewald et al., 2000).

Reconstruction can benefit and ultimately empower some people over others. Often those who were more powerful before a disaster end up gaining more than others in their communities, e.g. getting the best houses or plots, sometimes even several houses; owners being targeted over renters or squatters; or richer villages over poorer ones by contractors (Duyne Barenstein, 2006; Hidellage and Usoof, 2010; Schilderman and Lyons, 2010b). Others then lose out and get disempowered and become more vulnerable (Jigyasu, 2004; Lyons, 2007). Women's voices are often less heard in post-disaster decision-making (Sadiqi et al., 2011). They also lost out following changes in building technologies. Hidellage and Usoof (2010) noticed that women's ownership rights were reduced in Sri Lanka. The same happened to older people in Tamil Nadu (Duyne Barenstein and Trachsel, 2013). Men are often favoured over women in general aid delivery (Jayasuriya and McCawley, 2009) or where it comes to livelihood support (Cosgrave et al., 2009). Where beneficiaries are supposed to contribute their own resources to reconstruction as an integral part of a project or are forced to by inflation, the poorer or less able households frequently lose out, which can lead to spirals of debt or incomplete houses (Hidellage and Usoof, 2010). Commercial interests may also use disasters as an opportunity to remove poor people from prime land, e.g. coastal strips with tourism potential or inner cities (UN General Assembly, 2011).

Particular groups, often viewed as disadvantaged, often need particular support in reconstruction, for example the Mexican government specifically targeted tenants, an economically less well-off group, after an earthquake (Jha et al., 2010). The disabled often lose their support systems after disaster, but these should and can be restored (Arnold and Burton, 2011). The position and rights of women can be strengthened when reconstruction is used as an opportunity (Grunewald et al., 2000; Cosgrave et al., 2009; Jha et al., 2010), and they can be specifically targeted with livelihood support (IRP, 2009). The less advantaged can be accommodated by integrating them into groups with more able households (Schilderman, 2010; Maynard et al., 2013), or by securing help from others, resulting in greater social capital benefits (Barakat, 2003).

The urgency of recovery causes many agencies to limit consultation, which disempowers all, but especially the vulnerable (Schilderman, 2010; Arnold and Burton, 2011). Too often, the focus is solely on physical reconstruction, and welfare, livelihoods and equity receive insufficient attention (Lyons and Schilderman, 2010b; Arnold and Burton, 2011; UN General Assembly, 2011). Housing reconstruction projects rarely include cash for livelihoods. Consequently, where cash is given for housing, some may be siphoned off to restart income generation, hampering or occasionally halting housing development. Projects with a more integrated recovery approach, however, can be very successful (Basin South Asia, 2008; Lizarralde, 2010).

There is only sporadic evidence in the literature reviewed of empowered, well-organized communities going on to undertake other activities after reconstructing their houses, e.g. community facilities or infrastructure (IRP, 2009; Lyons, 2010; Guzmán Negrón, 2010), or livelihood activities (Régnier et al., 2009; IRP, 2009). This may be due to the scarcity of longitudinal impact studies, but could equally be a sign of insufficient empowerment and social capital developed during reconstruction eroding over time (Lyons, 2010). Local governance often is not good enough to facilitate this (Jigyasu, 2004).

Disasters not only increase people's short-term vulnerabilities, but also affect their capacity to deal with future shocks (Arnold and Burton, 2011). Many poor people have a range of livelihood strategies that provide some resilience and can help them overcome changes and shocks. Livelihood support should aim to rehabilitate and extend a diverse range of livelihood options (Vishwanath, 2011), but rarely does. The vast majority of disaster responses have been short-term and reactive, rather than long-term and pro-actively seeking to reduce vulnerability (IEG, 2006).

What do our case studies add to this knowledge?

Chapters 2 and 3 in this book look across a range of cases in Asia. In Chapter 2, Maynard et al. reflect on post-tsunami work by a large international NGO, Habitat for Humanity, in four Asian countries. They stress the importance of participation, long-term thinking, and the adoption of a more holistic approach helping to build communities rather than just houses. In Chapter 3, Duyne Barenstein and others look back at DDR involving relocation, following three different disasters in India. Key to long-term success there was the involvement of professionals in a participatory approach, leading to much more appropriate house and settlement designs facilitating future adaptations by owners. The cases also showed that even where beneficiaries initially disliked the housing offered, they often managed over time to make improvements of their own, and become happier with the result.

The five chapters on Asian projects in this book overlap partially with these previous two. In Chapter 4, Parrack and Khan describe a long-term disaster mitigation programme in the extreme North of Pakistan. The project proposed a range of relatively small and affordable home improvements, focusing not only on disaster resistance, but importantly also on energy efficiency. It foresaw an important role for the market in producing building components and offering construction skills. The project has made some real contributions to improving the quality of life over the longer term, making people safer and reducing the cost of reconstruction and energy. In Chapter 5, Pandya looks at a case of people-centred reconstruction (or Participatory Housing Approach as defined by Duyne Barenstein, 2006) involving relocation in Gujarat that adds to what Duyne Barenstein concluded on DDR. They argue for a holistic, participatory and long-term approach to reconstruction building on what is good in vernacular construction, and incorporating livelihood development.

The result is a village that is much better off and self-reliant than before the disaster. Chapter 6 covers a case of in-situ reconstruction by owners in Sri Lanka, described by Parker et al. They conclude that whilst user participation in design led to the desired flexibility, the same was not applied to technology choice. Innovative technologies were introduced that required a more stringent quality control during reconstruction than was occasionally available. The approach was hardly replicated, because of costs, and lack of local skills and long-term agency support. In Chapter 7, MacLellan et al. discuss two case studies: a long-term approach to disaster mitigation as well as a one-off reconstruction project in Vietnam. This case highlights the importance of disaster risk reduction (DRR) in the face of climate change. In order to achieve that, agencies have to commit to a long-term presence. Following a successful demonstration in one province, this work has now expanded to over a dozen, and to other South Asian countries. And the Vietnamese Government is becoming convinced too, asking the agency to help define reconstruction guidelines. Finally, reconstruction in Aceh is covered in Chapter 8 by Meilani et al. This is another case where participation and an inclusive approach were key to successful long-term outcomes, including housing designs, small enterprise development, and empowerment of women. However, some of the innovations introduced did not work, and the community organization established did not continue. A lesson here is that agencies need to plan for a presence over time to build more capacity and achieve longer term recovery.

The five chapters on Latin American cases offer a mix of corroborative and divergent different perspectives. In Chapter 9, Rhyner describes a 35-year old self-built reconstruction project in Guatemala. Improvements to vernacular adobe construction made houses safer. Success here was thanks to a decentralized approach that put knowledge in the hands of people and their local builders. Unfortunately, growing repression in the country did not allow this empowerment to scale up. In Chapter 10 the same author describes another case of reconstruction in Honduras involving relocation after a hurricane, in Chapter 10. Here, strong community participation ensured the project got the design and technologies right. Moreover, it helped to bring communities together and gain the capacity they needed to grow and develop long-term. In Chapter 11, he goes on to assess a self-built reconstruction project with relocation after the same hurricane in neighbouring Nicaragua. The agency being part of a strong network helped to attract expertise and ensure project experience spread elsewhere. Whilst this worked well in planning and design, the technology was less successfully replicated, partly because the production equipment required was removed from the area after the end of the reconstruction period. In Chapter 12, Blanco et al. discuss a much larger mutual aid project in El Salvador, building core houses. Strong participation ensured appropriate design, and the promotion of a range of technology options, rather than a single imposed approach. In contrast to Nicaragua, the agency continued to support its building materials centre in the region, which stimulated replication and was crucial to enable safe extension of core houses. Participation, mutual aid, and capacity building all contributed to the generation of strong CBOs and an umbrella organization that went on to advocate for changes in national housing policies. The continued presence of the agency after reconstruction was crucial to long-term success. Finally, in Chapter 13, Schilderman and Watanabe assess a recent self-build project of core houses in Peru, using a relatively cheap improved vernacular technology that proved to be earthquake resistant. Extension was made easy by astute positioning of the cores on plots, and much training. However, whilst the technology was replicated elsewhere, it was not amongst beneficiaries. Whilst central and local authorities praised the technology, they did not include it as an option in financial support programmes that were funding extensions.

The concluding chapter draws together key lessons learned from these projects reviewed over a longer timeframe than many previous projects. It confirms a majority of the findings from the literature, discussed under the five themes above. But it also discovered that, over time, such findings can change, for example some beneficiaries seem to be able to overcome the negative consequences of relocation, or to make changes to an inappropriately designed house. And it adds a number of new findings, for example on the importance of producing houses that are adaptable, making it easier for beneficiaries to change or extend them or incorporate home-based enterprises, as well as the importance of aesthetics and ease of maintenance, and to have more holistic projects and pay more attention to DRR if resilience is to be achieved. Finally, it questions whether true transformation can be achieved within the typical two-to four-year timespan of the average reconstruction project.

For reconstruction to have a more positive long-term impact, agencies need to think more holistically and in the long term, and start considering reconstruction as a process towards re-development in which beneficiaries and their communities play the prime roles. Relief and reconstruction are only the first steps in that process, but they are crucial to put in place the components, methods, and skills that enable this to happen.

References

Arnold, M. and Burton, C. (2011) 'Protecting and empowering vulnerable groups in recovery' *Proceedings of the World Reconstruction Conference*: 210–240, The World Bank, Washington DC, and UN-ISDR, Geneva.

Aysan, Y. and Oliver, P. (1987) *Housing and Culture after Earthquakes*, Oxford Polytechnic Press, Oxford.

Barakat, S. (2003) 'Housing construction after conflict and disaster' *HPN Paper 43*, Overseas Development Institute, London.

Basin South Asia (2008) *Tsunami, Lessons for Habitat Development*, UNDP India, New Delhi.

Cory, A. (1995) 'The Dhamar building education project, Yemen', in Aysan et al. *Developing Building for Safety Programmes*, Intermediate Technology Publications, London.

Cosgrave, J. with Brusset, E., Bhatt, M., Fernandez, L., Deshmukh, Y., Immajali, Y., Jayasundere, R., Mattson, A., Muhaimin, N., and Polastro, R. (2009) *A Ripple in Development. Document Review*. SIDA, Stockholm.

Cronin, V. and Guthrie, P. (2011) 'Community-led resettlement: From a flood-affected slum to a new society in Pune, India' *Environmental Hazards* 10: 136–161.

da Silva, J. (2010) *Lessons from Aceh – Key Considerations in Post-disaster Reconstruction*, Practical Action Publishing, Rugby.

da Silva, J. and Batchelor, V. (2010) 'Indonesia: Understanding agency policy in a national context' in M. Lyons and T. Schilderman (eds) *Building Back Better: Delivering People-centred Reconstruction at Scale*, pp. 135–161, Practical Action Publishing, Rugby.

Davis, I. (editor, 2007) *Lessons from Disaster Recovery: Guidance for Decision Makers*, International Recovery Platform, Geneva and Kobe.

Deprez, S. and Labattut, E. (2010) *Après le Tsunami, Reconstruire L'habitat en Aceh*, Karthala, Paris and Groupe URD, Plaisians.

D'Souza, F. (1986) 'Recovery following the Gediz earthquake: A study of four villages of western Turkey' *Disasters* 10(1): 35–52.

Duyne Barenstein, J. (2006) 'Housing reconstruction in post-earthquake Gujarat – A comparative analysis' *HPN Paper 54*, Overseas Development Institute, London.

Duyne Barenstein, J. (2013) 'Communities' perspectives on housing reconstruction in Gujarat following the earthquake of 2001' in J. Duyne Barenstein and E. Leemann (eds) *Post-disaster Reconstruction and Change – Communities' Perspectives*, pp. 215–239, CRC Press, Taylor & Francis Group, Boca Raton.

Duyne Barenstein, J. and Iyengar, S. (2010) 'India: From a culture of housing to a philosophy of reconstruction' in M. Lyons and T. Schilderman, *Building Back Better: Delivering People-centred Housing Reconstruction at Scale*, pp. 162–188, Practical Action Publishing, Rugby.

Duyne Barenstein, J. and Trachsel, S. (2013) 'The role of informal governance in post-disaster reconstruction and its impact on elderly people's social security in coastal Tamil Nadu' in J. Duyne Barenstein and E. Leemann, E. *Post-Disaster Reconstruction and Change – Communities' Perspectives*, CRC Press, Boca Raton.

EM-DAT (2014) <http://www.emdat.be/natural-disasters-trends> [accessed 28 May 2014].

Fallahi, A. (2007) 'Lessons learned from the housing reconstruction following the Bam earthquake in Iran' *The Australian Journal of Emergency Management*, 22(1): 26–35.

Graf, A. (2013) 'Unaffordable housing and its consequences: A comparative analysis of two post-Mitch reconstruction projects in Nicaragua' in J. Duyne Barenstein and E. Leemann, *Post-Disaster Reconstruction and Change: Communities' Perspectives*, pp. 195–212, CRC Press, Boca Raton.

Grunewald, F., de Geoffroy, V. and Lister, S. (2000) 'NGO responses to Hurricane Mitch: Evaluations for accountability and learning' *HPN Paper 34*, Overseas Development Institute, London.

Guha-Sapir, D., Santos, I. and Bord, A. (eds, 2013) *The Economic Impacts of Natural Disasters*, p. 1, OUP, New York.

Guzmán Negrón, E. (2010) 'The long-term impact of short-term reconstruction work' in M. Lyons and T. Schilderman, (eds) *Building Back Better: Delivering People-centred Housing Reconstruction at Scale*, pp. 307–343, Practical Action Publishing, Rugby.

Hidellage, V. and Usoof, A. (2010) 'Scaling up people-centred reconstruction: Lessons from Sri Lanka's post-tsunami owner-driven programme', in M. Lyons and T. Schilderman, *Building Back Better: Delivering People-centred Housing Reconstruction at Scale*, pp. 77–112, Practical Action Publishing, Rugby.

IEG (2006) *Hazard of Nature, Risks to Development: An IEG Evaluation of World Bank Assistance for Natural Disasters*, The World Bank, Washington DC.

IRP (2009) *Gender Issues in Recovery* (draft, V1) International Recovery Platform.

Jayasuriya, S. and McCawley, P. (2009) *The Asian Tsunami: Aid and Recovery after a Disaster*, Asian Development Bank Institute, Manila and Edward Elgar Publishing, Cheltenham.

Jayawardena, S. (2011) *Turning around the Tsunami: UN Habitat Working in Partnership with Sri Lanka*, UN Habitat, Nairobi.

Jha, A., with Duyne Barenstein, J., Phelps, P., Pittet, D., and Sena, S. (2010) *Safer Homes, Stronger Communities – A Handbook for Reconstructing after Natural Disasters*, The World Bank, Washington DC.

Jigyasu, R. (2000) 'From "Natural" to "Cultural" Disaster: Consequences of Post-earthquake Rehabilitation Process on Cultural Heritage in Marathwada Region, India', *International Conference on the Seismic Performance of Traditional Buildings*, Istanbul.

Jigyasu, R. (2004) 'Sustainable post disaster reconstruction through integrated risk management: The case of rural communities in South Asia' *Second International Conference on Post-Disaster Reconstruction: Planning for Reconstruction*, Coventry Centre for Disaster Management, Coventry.

Kelly, J. (2010) 'Afghan project failing in a town called AliceGhan' *The Australian*, June 15, 2010. Available from: http://www.theaustralian.com.au/news/nation/afghan-project-failing-in-a-town-called-aliceghan/story-e6frg6nf-1225879656418 [accessed 20 November 2013].

Lizarralde, G. (2010) 'Decentralizing (re)construction: Agriculture cooperatives as a vehicle for reconstruction in Colombia' in Lyons, M. and Schilderman, T. *Building Back Better: Delivering People-centred Housing Reconstruction at Scale*, pp. 191-213, Practical Action Publishing, Rugby.

Lyons, M. (2007) 'Building Back Better: Large-scale impacts of small-scale approaches to reconstruction' *IDEAR Working Paper Series 2007/1*, London South Bank University, London.

Lyons, M. (2010) 'Can large-scale participation be people-centred? Evaluating reconstruction as development' in M. Lyons and T. Schilderman (eds), *Building Back Better: Delivering People-centred Reconstruction at Scale*, pp. 39–61, Practical Action Publishing, Rugby.

Lyons, M. and Schilderman, T. (eds) (2010a) *Building Back Better: Delivering People-centred Reconstruction at Scale*, Practical Action Publishing, Rugby.

Lyons, M. and Schilderman, T. (2010b) 'Putting people at the centre of reconstruction' *PCR position paper*, Practical Action, Rugby, and London South Bank University, London.

Mantel, C. (2013) 'Ownership, control and accountability in post-tsunami housing reconstruction processes in Aceh, Indonesia' in J. Duyne Barenstein and E. Leemann, *Post-Disaster Reconstruction and Change – Communities' Perspectives*, pp. 55–70, CRC Press, Boca Raton.

Maskrey, A. (1995) 'The semiotics of technological innovation – introducing safe building technologies in housing in Peru' in Y. Aysan et al., *Developing Building for Safety Programmes*, pp. 112–121, Intermediate Technology Publications, London.

Maynard, V., Parikh, P., Simpson, D., and da Silva, J. (2013) 'Emerging stronger? Assessing Habitat for Humanity's housing reconstruction programme following the Indian Ocean Tsunami' *i-Rec Conference 2013: Sustainable Post-Disaster Reconstruction: From Recovery to Risk Reduction*, Ascona.

Powell, P. (2011) 'Post-disaster reconstruction: A current analysis of Gujarat's response after the 2011 earthquake' *Environmental Hazards* 10: 279–292.

Razavi, H. and Razavi, S. (2013) 'Housing reconstruction after disasters in Iran: A case study of Gavarzin after the earthquake of November 2005' *i-Rec Conference 2013: Sustainable Post-Disaster Reconstruction: From Recovery to Risk Reduction*, Ascona.

Reddy, Shri A. (1995) 'The cyclone-prone coastal region of the State of Andra Pradesh, India: A state-government approach' in Aysan, Y. et al. *Developing Building for Safety Programmes*, Intermediate Technology Publications, London.

Régnier P., Neri, B., Scuteri, S. and Miniati, S. (2009) 'From emergency relief to livelihood recovery: Lessons learned from post-tsunami experiences in Indonesia and India' *Disaster Prevention and Management* 17(3): 410–429.

Sadiqi, Z., Colley, V., and Trigunarsyah, B. (2011) 'Post-disaster housing reconstruction: Challenges for community participation' *Proceedings of the International Conference on Building Resilience*, Heritance Kandalama, Sri Lanka.

Salazar, A. (2002) 'The crisis of modernity of housing disasters in the developing countries: Participatory housing and technology after the Marathwada (1993) earthquake'. Available from: http://www.grif.umontreal.ca/pages/papersmenu.html [accessed 21 November 2013].

Schilderman, T. (1993) 'Disasters and development: A case study from Peru' *Journal of International Development* 5(4): 415–423.

Schilderman, T. (2004) 'Adapting traditional shelter for disaster mitigation and reconstruction: Experiences with community-based approaches' *Building Research and Information* 35(5): 414–426.

Schilderman, T. (2010) 'Putting people at the centre of reconstruction' in M. Lyons and T. Schilderman, *Building Back Better: Delivering People-centred Reconstruction at Scale*, pp. 7–37, Practical Action Publishing, Rugby.

Schilderman, T. and Lyons, M. 'Resilient dwellings or resilient people? Towards people-centred reconstruction' *Environmental Hazards* 10: 218–231.

Special Rapporteur on Adequate Housing (2011) *Right to Adequate Housing*, United Nations General Assembly, New York.

Stephenson, M. (2008) *Notes from Experience in Post-earthquake Rural Housing Construction in Pakistan*, UN Habitat, Islamabad.

Telford, J., Arnold, M., and Harth, A., with ASONOG (2004) 'Learning lessons from disaster recovery: The case of Honduras', *Disaster Risk Management Working Paper Series 8*, The World Bank, Washington DC.

Telford, J., Cosgrave, J., and Houghton, R. (2006) *Joint Evaluation of the International Response to the Indian Ocean Tsunami: Synthesis Report*, Tsunami Evaluation Coalition, London.

Twigg, J. (2002/2006) *Technology, Post-disaster Housing Reconstruction and Livelihood Security*, Benfield Hazard Research Centre, London.

UN Habitat (2009) *Post Tsunami Aceh Nias Settlement and Housing Recovery Review*, UN Habitat, Nairobi.

van Leersum, A. (2008) *A Socio-Economic Impact Study of a Post-disaster Housing Program: A Case Study of a Red Cross Housing Program in Vietnam*, The Netherlands Red Cross, The Hague and University of Technology, Eindhoven.

United Nations General Assembly (2011) *Report of the Special Rapporteur on Adequate Housing as a Component of the Right to an Adequate Standard of Living*, United Nations, New York.

Vishwanath, T. (2011) 'Reviving livelihoods and local economy' in *Proceedings of the World Reconstruction Conference, Geneva*, pp. 272–296, The World Bank, FDRR and UN ISDR.

Wijkman, A. and Timberlake, l. (1984) *Natural Disasters: Acts of God or Acts of Man?* Earthscan, London.

Wilches-Chaux, G. (1995) 'The SENA Self-Help Reconstruction Programme following the 1983 Popayan Earthquake, Colombia – A Governmental Vocational Training Centre Approach', in Y. Aysan et al., *Developing Building for Safety Programmes – Guidelines for Organising Safe Building Improvement Programmes in Disaster-probe Areas*, pp. 69–76, Intermediate Technology Publications, London.

World Bank (2010) *Natural Hazards, UnNatural Disasters: The Economics of Effective Prevention*, The World Bank, Washington DC.

About the author

Theo Schilderman is a Senior Researcher at the Building and Social Housing Foundation (BSHF), a consultant and lecturer. He is a Dutch architect with 40 years of experience in low-income housing and post-disaster reconstruction who has worked for Practical Action, COOPIBO, and the IHS in the past, both in developing countries and in management. He was the editor, with Michal Lyons, of *Building Back Better* in 2010.

CHAPTER 2

Emerging stronger? Assessing the outcomes of Habitat for Humanity's housing reconstruction programmes following the Indian Ocean tsunami

Victoria Maynard, Priti Parikh, Dan Simpson, and Jo da Silva

Abstract

Habitat for Humanity (HFH) built, rehabilitated or repaired homes for 25,000 families in four countries in the five years following the Indian Ocean tsunami in 2004. As part of a broader organizational and learning review in 2009-2010, HFH commissioned Arup International Development to carry out an assessment of its post-tsunami housing reconstruction programmes in India, Sri Lanka, Thailand, and Indonesia. The purpose of this assessment was to investigate the extent to which HFH's tsunami-response housing reconstruction programmes had contributed to the development of sustainable communities and livelihoods. Arup International Development undertook the assessment using the ASPIRE tool they had developed with Engineers Against Poverty. Basing their assessment on programme documentation and key informant interviews, household questionnaires and workshops with communities in each country, they completed one assessment for each country and a fifth assessment covering all four countries. This enabled comparison of both the impact of these four programmes and how the outcomes varied as a result of varying approaches and contextual issues.

The assessment found that HFH's programme had made a significant contribution to the development of sustainable communities and livelihoods. The provision of high quality core homes had reduced household vulnerability and increased the standard of living, while HFH's participatory process had increased community cohesion and developed positive relationships between communities and a range of external actors. There were also areas for improvement such as: the incorporation of hazard assessment, settlement planning and infrastructure at settlement level; greater community participation in decision-making regarding settlement planning, house design and the choice of appropriate construction techniques and technologies; greater focus on livelihood support and diversification both during construction and after completion of the housing programme; and complementing HFH's experience in housing construction with the specialist expertise of other actors to maximize the impact of its work.

http://dx.doi.org/10.3362/9781780448398.002

Keywords: Disaster; Tsunami; Asia; Reconstruction; Housing; Impact

Introduction

Habitat for Humanity (HFH) built, rehabilitated or repaired homes for 25,000 families in Indonesia, Thailand, Sri Lanka, and India in the five years following the Indian Ocean tsunami in 2004. This represents 7 per cent of the total housing need of approximately 440,000 houses across the four countries (International Recovery Platform, 2011). In response to one of the worst natural disasters in recent history HFH's approach emphasized:

- community-based strategies involving local people in decision-making;
- encouraging families to rebuild their homes in-situ;
- a preference for a simple core house design that could be extended later;
- working with partners to reach more families;
- a focus on the poorest and most vulnerable families;
- mobilizing HFH's network of volunteers to assist; and
- assisting others in need in neighbouring areas who had not been directly affected by the tsunami and those likely to be affected by future natural disasters (Habitat for Humanity, 2009).

In 2009, HFH commissioned Arup International Development (Arup ID) to carry out an assessment of its housing reconstruction programmes in India, Sri Lanka, Thailand, and Indonesia after the tsunami based on their previous experience in post-disaster reconstruction (da Silva, 2010; Batchelor and da Silva, 2010). The purpose of this assessment was to investigate the extent to which HFH's housing reconstruction programmes had contributed to the development of sustainable communities and livelihoods (Chambers and Conway, 1992; DFID, 1999), namely their contribution to increased human, social, physical, economic, and environmental assets as well as more enabling institutional structures and processes.

This chapter describes the methodology for undertaking the assessment. It then describes common strengths and weaknesses of the programmes evaluated in terms of houses and settlements as 'products' (or outputs), as well as the process of housing construction through engagement with households, communities, governments, and other actors. In conclusion, the authors reflect on the findings from the assessment, highlight key strengths and recommend areas for improvement in future programmes.

Methodology

This research was completed between November 2009 and March 2010; roughly five years after the disaster and fewer than three years after the completion of construction. The assessment was based on programme documentation provided by country offices and one week of fieldwork per country which included: key informant interviews; workshops with HFH personnel; visual observation of four or five communities; participatory workshops using standard Participatory Rapid Appraisal (PRA) techniques; and completion of questionnaires by 30 households. This provided a range of quantitative and qualitative data on which to base the assessment.

The data was analysed using the ASPIRE tool Arup ID had developed previously with Engineers Against Poverty (2009a). This tool provides a holistic appraisal framework which generates a qualitative assessment based on 96 indicators under four key dimensions. Three of ASPIRE's dimensions (society, environment, and economics) incorporate the human, social, natural, and financial assets from DFID's Sustainable Livelihoods Framework (DFID, 1999) 'assuming that the fifth dimension of physical assets is the project itself' (Arup and Engineers Against Poverty, 2009b). The fourth key dimension (institutions) assesses the project's relationship with and contribution to the development of enabling institutions, organizations, policies, and legislation–the 'transforming structures and processes' aspects of DFID's Sustainable Livelihoods approach.

Arup ID made one assessment for each country (Arup, 2010a, 2010b, 2010c, 2010d) and a fifth assessment covering all four countries (Arup, 2010e). This enabled comparison of both the outcomes of the four programmes and how these varied as a result of different approaches and contextual issues. The results of Arup ID's assessments fed into HFH's broader organizational and learning review of their tsunami-response programme in 2009-2010. In writing this chapter, the authors have also returned to the original data to review the key findings and broader themes emerging from the assessment. Thus the findings presented below both reinforce the initial assessment and add additional insights where these have been identified through the review process.

Housing as a product

Site selection and settlement planning

All of HFH's programmes after the tsunami had a strong focus on in-situ housing reconstruction which meant that households maintained access to existing social networks, employment opportunities, and social infrastructure such as schools, health centres, places of worship, community meeting places, etc. (where these had not been destroyed by the tsunami). However, responsibility for reinstating social infrastructure typically resided with government or other humanitarian organizations so this produced varying levels of service.

While in-situ reconstruction had many benefits to communities, it also meant that they remained in coastal locations vulnerable to flooding, storm surges, and cyclones. Although HFH engaged with the whole community as part of the process of housing reconstruction, its approach to the built environment focused on the reconstruction of individual houses: for example, HFH's programmes sometimes included the provision of community facilities (such as schools) but rarely included settlement-level infrastructure, such as roads or stormwater drainage. The assessment found that lack of consideration of hazard assessment, settlement planning, and infrastructure at a settlement level was a significant contributing factor to continued levels of risk within the communities. Households interviewed in all four countries continued to feel at risk from flooding (this varied from 28 per cent in Thailand to 79 per cent in Sri Lanka) with several households in Indonesia reporting that they had already experienced flooding within their new houses one or more times a year.

Despite the focus on in-situ reconstruction, resettlement programmes did occur in all four countries. This was particularly rare in Thailand and Indonesia but a necessary reality in India and Sri Lanka after the governments introduced 'buffer zones' – minimum distances from the coastline within which houses and communities could not be reinstated. Relocated communities were less vulnerable to natural hazards, with community members stating that they felt safer as they were at a greater distance from the sea. However, relocated communities in India and Sri Lanka reported reduced access to education and employment opportunities as well as less community cohesion.

Figure 2.1 Flooded houses in Indonesia at the time of the assessment

HFH worked pragmatically to resolve - land-tenure issues in all four countries, but different policy environments meant this had mixed levels of success. In Indonesia, HFH supported communities in community-driven tenure adjudication through the government Reconstruction of Aceh Land Administration System (RALAS) programme, while (at the time of the assessment) land tenure for relocation communities in India and Sri Lanka was yet to be clearly resolved. HFH's tsunami-response programme in Thailand worked with Muslim and Morgan (nomadic sea-based) communities–both of which are minority groups in Thailand. In several communities where land ownership was unclear, HFH Thailand worked with local government to gain security of tenure for households before beginning construction of houses; enabling them to build permanent housing and invest in their homes.

House design and construction

HFH programmes in all four countries provided a simple single-storey core home which could later be extended (see Figure 2.2). Core homes in Sri Lanka and India were smaller (around 30 m^2) and contained two rooms (a living room and a bedroom) while core homes in Thailand and Indonesia were larger (40–45 m^2) and typically included a living room with one or two bedrooms. Households interviewed were generally satisfied with the size of their core homes, but HFH had not included space or facilities for cooking, leaving more than 50 per cent of households dissatisfied with this aspect of the design. In India, Indonesia, and Thailand, 45–60 per cent of households had already extended their houses at the time of the assessment (only 28 per cent in Sri Lanka), while more than 60 per cent of households planned to do so in the future. In India and Sri Lanka many households had changed their room layouts and converted the smaller rooms into pujas (worship areas) or kitchens, while in Indonesia the majority of extensions were to accommodate a large kitchen suitable for entertaining guests. While this provides positive evidence that HFH's core home design enabled people to easily adapt or extend their houses, so many extensions or alterations being undertaken for the same purpose, less than three years after completion of the core home, may also indicate that families were making these changes out of necessity because of limitations in the original core home design.

Figure 2.2a Indonesia

Figure 2.2b Sri Lanka

Figure 2.2c India

Figure 2.2d Thailand

Figure 2.2 Typical core home designs

Core homes were typically masonry construction with a flat (India) or pitched roof with tiles or metal sheeting. In Indonesia, where confined brick masonry was commonly used for housing, HFH introduced concrete block construction and established its own block production facility. This significantly increased the speed of construction and reduced both cost and environmental impact (as local timber was not used for burning bricks). Although communities initially did not believe that concrete blocks were suitable for housing, HFH staff reported that once the blocks had been proven they were well accepted. However, despite concrete blocks continuing to be manufactured by local suppliers after the completion of the programme, the majority of extensions had been completed in timber and where extensions had been completed in masonry, they did not include the key seismic details included in HFH's core home designs (see Figure 2.3). HFH's core home designs in Thailand were based on small improvements to traditional housing typologies. For example, where people had traditionally lived in timber houses on stilts, HFH introduced concrete stilts and concrete board cladding (which can be used like timber). Thus, while the overall quality of core homes provided by HFH in Thailand was lower than in other countries (for example, concrete board cladding is less robust than masonry), the construction materials and techniques were closer to the vernacular and families found it easier to maintain and adapt their houses using similar techniques.

Figure 2.3 HFH's core home design (far right) in one community in Indonesia which incorporates the re-use of a timber transitional shelter as a kitchen (right) and later extensions using a combination of timber and other materials (centre and left)

Although physical disaster risk reduction measures at a settlement level were not typically part of HFH's tsunami-response programme, house by house hazard assessment and mitigation was undertaken. Typical disaster risk reduction aspects of HFH core homes included: rebuilding houses in different locations within the settlement because of unsuitable soil conditions for foundations (Indonesia); raising the ground floor slab of houses in flood-prone areas (Indonesia, India, Sri Lanka); building houses on stilts (Thailand); ensuring robust earthquake-resistant design and construction (Indonesia); and incorporating cyclone resistant features such as concrete roofs (India and Sri Lanka).

In hot, humid climates minimizing internal temperatures and ensuring adequate ventilation make a significant contribution to individual health and well-being. Across all four countries more than 60 per cent of the households interviewed felt comfortable with the temperature inside their home but there were significant variations in house designs and levels of thermal comfort between countries. In Indonesia, overhanging eaves provided some shading to windows and walls, a ventilated pitched roof with ceiling reduced heat transmission through the roof, while ventilation bricks were provided above windows and doors in each room. Pitched roofs and ventilation bricks were also a feature of HFH's core home design in Sri Lanka and while ceilings were not included to reduce heat transmission, HFH staff felt that sufficient ventilation was provided through gaps in the roof tiles. HFH's core homes in India typically had concrete walls and roofs with no insulation to reduce heat transmission into the house, limited shading of external windows or walls, and little or no ventilation other than windows. In contrast, the lightweight construction of HFH's core homes in Thailand – often raised on stilts – maximized the potential for ventilation through having several windows which either fully open or have glass louvres depending on the preference of the household.

Access to services

Communities in all four countries had high water tables and households typically sourced water from rivers or shallow wells. In general, HFH did not include the provision of water supplies in their tsunami-response programme because these were typically provided by government or other NGOs. Notable exceptions are in Indonesia, where HFH provided water supply systems (either boreholes or water filtration) in six villages and established small committees to manage the systems and in Thailand, where HFH partnered with another NGO to provide rainwater harvesting equipment (guttering and large ceramic pots) to some, but not all, households.

HFH provided toilets to each household assisted in India, Sri Lanka, and Indonesia, often to families who had not previously had access to improved sanitation at a household level. In Thailand, HFH's earlier projects did not include toilets as part of their core house design but these were included in later projects. HFH Thailand supported families indirectly affected by the tsunami through the provision of micro-loans for housing repairs/upgrades – many of these households also used their loan to build toilets and kitchen extensions onto their houses.

The provision of improved sanitation was particularly successful in Sri Lanka where septic tanks meet national standards and so could be emptied by the local government. HFH also worked with public health inspectors to promote hygiene awareness and 97 per cent of households interviewed felt that their new facilities met their needs. In contrast, HFH India provided leach pits with the toilets in some houses, and in areas with high water tables these posed a potential source of ground water contamination. The assessment also noted that in some communities only women used the toilets. In Indonesia, water, sanitation and hygiene training was only provided in the six communities where HFH had provided water supply systems and this left many communities unaware of the importance of using their new toilets, with some families not understanding how to maintain them or how to empty their septic tanks once full. Consequently 37 per cent of families interviewed were no longer using the bathrooms for a variety of reasons including leaks, closeness of the toilet to the living area, and their preference to continue using traditional practices.

While some of the sanitation challenges experienced in India and Indonesia were related to the physical design and construction of facilities, they were primarily a result of programme design which did not adequately respond to communities' existing knowledge, attitudes, and practices. This highlights the importance of an integrated approach to water, sanitation and hygiene, with improvements in future programmes needed to ensure understanding at a household level and a strategy for long-term operation and maintenance of the facilities provided.

In India, Indonesia, and Thailand, HFH worked with the government to provide electricity connections to all HFH families; in India and Thailand only a few households had not previously had electricity connections, but in Indonesia this had increased coverage from 60 to 100 per cent of the households interviewed. In Sri Lanka, the number of households with electricity connections had decreased from 21 per cent before the tsunami to only 10 per cent after the HFH programme. HFH Sri Lanka struggled to find sites for relocation settlements with access to electricity, and lack of clarity on land tenure for these communities further delayed the provision of electricity connections. In response to the challenge of providing mains grid electricity, HFH Sri Lanka supported the use of solar technology. Forty-eight per cent of households interviewed understood and used solar energy for lighting and small appliances (compared to 31 per cent before the tsunami). HFH Sri Lanka also introduced the use of solar cookers. However, the evaluation noted that solar technology was not fully understood by communities and further support was required for it to be fully successful.

Although HFH's tsunami-response housing programme did not specifically target fuel consumption, 10-25 per cent of households interviewed in Indonesia, Thailand, and India had stopped using wood or charcoal for cooking since the tsunami. The assessment did not directly investigate the reasons for this change in behaviour but households in India cited the new housing as an incentive to switch over to gas. This may also be the case in Indonesia and Thailand, as HFH 'homepartners' typically expressed significant pride in their new houses, but it may also be attributed to raised environmental awareness (as a result of HFH's gardening programmes), increased access to electricity (particularly in Indonesia), or improved living standards more generally as a result of HFH's programme or the activities of government or other NGOs. If attributable to the HFH housing programme, this is potentially an important outcome as reduced use of wood or charcoal for cooking both reduces the use of local timber for fuel and improves indoor air quality, with long-term benefits to health.

While HFH's programmes did not include the construction of educational facilities (except in isolated cases), 60–90 per cent of the households interviewed felt that HFH's programme had increased access to education and this was reinforced in the interviews with community leaders. Households cited various factors for this improvement including: increased disposable income to spend on uniforms/books (because of reduced spending on housing); better conditions for studying, including private rooms for children and increased electric lighting; and increased motivation and a sense of well-being. This was a significant positive finding of the assessment, despite the fact that some of the relocation communities did not have schools located within the community.

Housing as a process

Community engagement

HFH typically established a project management committee in each community which included beneficiaries, community representatives, and local government officials. Households and community leaders in all four countries felt that all sections of the community were able to participate in the project, that beneficiary selection criteria had been transparent and equitable, and that there was little corruption throughout the process. However, 10–20 per cent of households interviewed in Indonesia and Sri Lanka did not find the HFH process easy to understand. In Indonesia, this was in communities where they spoke predominantly the local language of Acehnese, rather than Indonesian, and in Sri Lanka, this was in migrant communities where the high mobility of individuals and families reduced effective community engagement.

In several instances, HFH targeted their assistance on the most vulnerable groups such as Morgan communities (Thailand), remote, lower caste, or migrant communities (Sri Lanka), and households with disabled family members (India). Households and community leaders in all four countries emphasized that the HFH programme had increased community cohesion through integrating vulnerable groups into society (India), increasing community spirit through providing 'sweat equity' on each other's houses (Thailand), and bringing members of diverse religious groups to work together (Sri Lanka). In Indonesia where the cash for work programmes of other agencies had sometimes reduced the tradition of *gotong royong* (community self-help) (Thorburn, 2007), this had been maintained in the communities where HFH worked, with communities working together to construct roads to enable materials to be delivered, cleaning drains, etc.

In theory, HFH developed a standard core home design in each country to suit the local culture and climate and this was further adapted following consultation with specific communities or households. In practice, more than 70 per cent of households interviewed reported being consulted regarding the location and design of their house; but it was less clear if changes were made as a result of the consultation. Many households commented that changes were not allowed as HFH had a standard house design, while Arup ID's evaluation of the programmes in India and Sri Lanka noted that programmes 'are primarily driven by donor objectives and government guidelines'. Positive evidence of design changes made by HFH in response to household and community needs included adaptation of the core home design for the needs of fishing communities, households with a larger than average number of members, or those with disabled family members (India), and positioning of the toilet within the bathroom so that it was not orientated towards Mecca (Indonesia). However, the possible limitations of the core home design and challenges experienced by HFH introducing new construction materials and techniques, seismic detailing, sanitation and solar technologies suggest that the level of engagement might be considered 'consultation' over minor details, rather than real 'partnership' in decision-making (Arnstein, 1969) which built upon local knowledge, skills, attitudes, and practices to co-develop appropriate designs.

Very different approaches to community involvement in housing construction were taken across the four countries leading to diverse outcomes on the development of skills and employment opportunities:

- There was very little involvement of beneficiaries in construction in India (either through 'sweat equity' or as paid labourers) with the majority of construction being undertaken by national contractors or international volunteers. Although these fishing communities had not traditionally built their own houses, this was a missed opportunity for both short-term employment opportunities (while livelihoods were disrupted during recovery) and skills transfer to communities so that households could supervise paid labourers to maintain and extend their houses safely in the future. Very few households interviewed stated that the HFH programme had generated employment for communities or local suppliers at any point during or after the reconstruction process.
- In Sri Lanka, few households could contribute 'sweat equity' during construction because they could not afford to take time away from their work but 45 per cent of households interviewed took part as paid unskilled labourers. Beneficiaries and community members also had significant involvement in the selection of material suppliers resulting in 38 per cent of households interviewed feeling that the HFH programme had generated employment opportunities for local suppliers and 17 per cent stating that it had provided continuing employment opportunities after the completion of the programme.
- Construction in Indonesia was undertaken by professional labourers, sometimes from as far afield as Medan or Java, because of the shortage of skilled labour closer to hand. HFH encouraged communities to establish good relationships with their labourers and while the beneficiaries did not take part in construction directly, they were responsible for monitoring the quality of materials and workmanship on their own home. This encouraged a high degree of ownership, but although HFH provided training for local supervisors (one per ten houses), the households interviewed felt that they had not had specific training on how to monitor the quality of construction. As a result, by the time of the evaluation, households had already started to extend their houses without incorporating the key features of seismic-resistant design.

- HFH achieved the greatest involvement of communities in construction in Thailand. There, both beneficiaries and other community members were involved in all aspects of construction and 24 per cent of households interviewed also felt that it had benefited local suppliers. The use of 'sweat equity' and international volunteers supported rather than competed with local labourers (as local capacity was exceeded in the aftermath of the tsunami) and households reported that working with international volunteers was a positive experience. So much involvement of households and communities during construction had significant benefits for these communities. Many learnt new skills during the process, and of the households interviewed 90 per cent felt that they had the skills and tools required to repair and maintain their home (compared with 30–50 per cent in other countries). At the time of the assessment, many households had begun supplementing their income through construction employment during the rainy season when they were unable to fish.

HFH did not typically provide specific livelihood support programmes but sometimes: encouraged NGOs providing livelihood support to work in HFH communities (Thailand); partnered with other NGOs to provide livelihood training, tools or access to credit (Sri Lanka and India); or developed their own small-scale livelihood support programmes (Sri Lanka). HFH's programmes in India, Sri Lanka, and Indonesia often included the support of household or community gardening after the completion of the housing programme while some households in Indonesia had also used the opportunity of a new house to purchase land close to the road and invest in opening a small business or shop. Despite localized instances of livelihood support and some short-term benefits during the reconstruction programme, the long-term reliance on low-paid employment, subject to seasonal or climatic disruption, remained a key concern of most communities visited in the assessment. Thus, while there were positive examples of livelihoods support to some communities through HFH's programmes, the lack of a systematic strategy to support livelihood development within these vulnerable coastal communities was a significant missed opportunity.

Figure 2.4 Some households in Indonesia had chosen to re-locate within their community so that they could set up a small shop or cafe near to the road

Relationships with other actors

A disaster on the scale of the tsunami required local and national governments to rapidly establish policy guidelines on eligibility criteria, reconstruction standards, land tenure, etc. HFH managed the risk of undertaking reconstruction programmes in a rapidly changing policy environment through close liaison with local government officials, government reconstruction agencies and other humanitarian organizations. HFH's reconstruction programme in both Sri Lanka and Indonesia took place within complicated conflict or post-conflict situations. In both instances HFH worked sensitively with the government, military and police (in addition to communities and partner NGOs) to ensure that HFH were aware of the security situation and that HFH's programmes responded appropriately. In all countries, the Head of the Village or Village Committee (elected local government representatives) was heavily involved in HFH's programme. Local government officials at a municipal or district level often attended project start or completion ceremonies to show their support and sometimes provided public health training, approved material suppliers, designs or construction quality.

HFH also worked closely with other NGOs working in the same communities, participated in knowledge exchange programmes, implemented programmes through partner NGOs (India), and partnered with specialist NGOs (for example in micro-credit, provision of training or rainwater harvesting) when their skills were required (all countries). HFH's focus on working in partnership with communities, government, and other NGOs meant that frequent finding from the assessment was that the project had improved linkages between the communities' assisted and external actors.

In many cases, HFH also established positive relationships with material suppliers, labourers, and larger contractors supporting wider economic recovery during the reconstruction process. This was particularly apparent in Indonesia where HFH: sourced materials locally whenever possible (with sand, aggregates, and soil typically sourced from within the villages); ensured that all material suppliers were certified by local government (a potentially onerous requirement for small-scale suppliers, but HFH supported them through the process, which then made them eligible for other contracts once they had worked with HFH); and supported capacity building in local suppliers (for example, they developed a standard window design and then worked with local manufacturers to ensure that their products met the requirements of the specification).

Conclusions

Overall, the assessment found that HFH's housing reconstruction programmes after the Indian Ocean tsunami had made a significant contribution to the development of sustainable communities and livelihoods. HFH's housing programme had replaced houses which had been destroyed in the tsunami, often to a higher standard and (in most cases) complete with access to services and social infrastructure. The provision of high-quality core homes (physical assets) had reduced household vulnerability and increased the standard of living – with benefits to health and well-being (human assets) while HFH's participatory process had increased community cohesion (social assets). HFH's programme had also contributed to the development of positive relationships between communities and a range of external actors (institutional structures and processes) as well as supporting environmental and economic recovery (natural and financial assets) to a lesser extent.

The following sections summarize both the strengths of HFH's tsunami-response programme and suggest areas for improvement in future programmes where small changes in programme design or implementation (at limited additional cost) could increase the long-term impact of its work.

Site selection and settlement planning

HFH's focus on in-situ reconstruction meant that households had maintained their access to existing social networks, employment opportunities, and social infrastructure (social, economic, and physical assets). The physical assets of relocated communities were less vulnerable to natural hazards but households reported reduced access to education and employment opportunities as well as less community cohesion. This highlights that if relocation has to occur after a disaster it must be viewed holistically, with sufficient infrastructure provided and adequate support for community and livelihood development. A key area for improvement in HFH's future housing programmes is to more broadly incorporate community-wide hazard assessment and settlement planning into their community engagement process (preferably linked to wider government planning policies) and include disaster risk reduction infrastructure and activities at a settlement level.

House design and construction

HFH's policy to provide a simple core home that could later be extended enabled HFH rapidly to provide large numbers of permanent houses. The design of HFH's core home enabled people to easily adapt or extend their houses, but the fact that many households had made similar changes to their houses soon after completion may also indicate the limitations of the original core home design. HFH's commitment to negotiating tenure security for each household was a significant benefit of the HFH programme, as was the incorporation of household-level hazard assessment and mitigation. However, greater emphasis could have been placed on climatically appropriate design. In several instances, HFH introduced new construction materials or techniques, and while these examples show the organization striving to innovate, this assessment found that these were easiest for households and labourers to understand and replicate themselves when they were incremental improvements on existing techniques.

Access to services

Water supplies were typically reinstated by other actors but HFH provided toilets for each household. While the provision of toilets was a positive aspect of HFH's programme, many families had not previously had access to improved sanitation and did not understand the importance of using their new toilets or know how to maintain them in the future. This highlights the need for improvements in future programmes to ensure understanding at a household level and a long-term strategy for operation and maintenance of the facilities provided, taking an integrated approach to water, sanitation and hygiene. Similar challenges with household understanding, acceptance, and maintenance of new technologies were experienced where HFH introduced solar technologies to communities without access to mains grid electricity. HFH's programme also resulted in indirect benefits such as improved education levels as a result of greater disposable income, private areas for children to study with electric lighting, and increased motivation and well-being. The programme may have also contributed to decreased use of timber and charcoal as fuel; both reducing the use of local timber for fuel and improving indoor air quality, with long-term benefits to health.

Community engagement

HFH's community engagement process had significant benefits in terms of increased community cohesion (social assets). However, the limitations of the core home design and challenges experienced by HFH introducing new construction materials, seismic detailing, sanitation and solar technologies indicate that greater participation in decision-making (such as selection of construction materials and technologies) is required to ensure HFH's programmes meet the needs of the communities they intend to support. The assessment found that the more households and communities were involved during construction, the greater the benefits in terms of livelihood diversification and equipping communities with the knowledge and skills to adequately maintain, adapt, and extend their houses. It also highlighted that opportunities for employment generation during construction (in material supply or construction labour) were missed in many of HFH's programmes suggesting the need for a more holistic approach to livelihood support and diversification at household, community, and sector levels.

Relationships with other actors

HFH developed positive working relationships with a range of external actors in challenging situations–although partnerships with academic institutions were notably lacking. HFH's focus on working in partnership with communities, government, and other NGOs meant that the project had improved linkages between communities' and external actors and developed a more supportive enabling environment. In many cases, HFH also established positive relationships with material suppliers, labourers, and larger contractors; supporting wider economic recovery during the reconstruction process and enabling HFH to scale-up their programmes through cost-sharing arrangements. While many of these partnerships were successful, this assessment suggests that there is greater potential for partnerships in future reconstruction programmes to complement HFH's experience in housing construction with the specialist expertise of other actors to address some of the challenges raised in this assessment and maximize the impact of its work.

Recommendations

Every disaster response operation poses unique challenges as humanitarian organizations strive to support the unique needs of individuals, families, and communities in different geographical, climatic, cultural, and political contexts. Prescriptive recommendations for future programmes (such as 'use vernacular materials' or 'avoid relocation') are, therefore, less useful than approaches which can be adopted in any context. Based on this assessment the authors recommend that in future HFH's disaster-response operations take into account:

- the need for greater participation in decision-making throughout project design, construction, maintenance, and replication to ensure that programmes really meet the needs of the families and communities they intend to serve;
- the importance of considering the long-term use of houses, infrastructure, construction materials, techniques or technologies from the outset. Will families be able to maintain, adapt, extend or replicate any new interventions themselves?;
- the need for greater consideration of settlements in addition to houses to reduce risk and ensure that it is not just houses which are rebuilt but communities – complete with infrastructure and spaces for education, healthcare, livelihoods, and recreation;
- the importance of a holistic approach to recovery of people's lives and livelihoods – maximizing the contribution of all humanitarian interventions to social, economic, physical, environmental, cultural, and political recovery and resilience.

References

Arnstein, S.R. (1969) 'A ladder of citizen participation', *Journal of the American Institute of Planners* 35(4): 216–224. <http://www.tandfonline.com/doi/abs/10.1080/01944366908977225> [accessed 2 August 2013].

Arup (2010a) 'Habitat for Humanity's Tsunami-Response Shelter Programmes Sustainability Assessment: Country Report – India'.

Arup (2010b) 'Habitat for Humanity's Tsunami-Response Shelter Programmes Sustainability Assessment: Country Report – Indonesia'.

Arup (2010c) 'Habitat for Humanity's Tsunami-Response Shelter Programmes Sustainability Assessment: Country Report – Sri Lanka'.

Arup (2010d) 'Habitat for Humanity's Tsunami-Response Shelter Programmes Sustainability Assessment: Country Report – Thailand'.

Arup (2010e) 'Habitat for Humanity's Tsunami-Response Shelter Programmes Sustainability Assessment: Summary Report'.

Arup and Engineers against Poverty (2009a) 'A Sustainability Poverty and Infrastructure Routine for Evaluation (ASPIRE)', *Oasys* [website] <http://www.oasys-software.com/products/environmental/aspire.html> [accessed 16 May 2014].

Arup and Engineers against Poverty (2009b) 'A Sustainability Poverty and Infrastructure Routine for Evaluation (ASPIRE): Research and Development', *Oasys* [website] <http://www.oasys-software.com/products/environmental/aspire.html> [accessed 16 May 2014].

Batchelor, V. and da Silva, J. (2010) 'Indonesia: Understanding agency policy in a national context' in M. Lyons and T. Schilderman (eds) *Building Back Better*, pp. 135–161, Practical Action Publishing, Rugby. <http://practicalaction.org/building-back-better-book> [accessed 15 May 2014].

Chambers, R. and Conway, G. (1992) 'Sustainable rural livelihoods: Practical concepts for the 21st century', Institute of Development Studies, Brighton. Open Docs [website] <http://opendocs.ids.ac.uk/opendocs/handle/123456789/775> [accessed 16 May 2014].

Da Silva, J. (2010) *Lessons from Aceh?: Key Considerations in Post-Disaster Reconstruction*, Practical Action Publishing, Bourton-on-Dunsmore. <http://www.arup.com/Publications/Lessons_from_Aceh.aspx> [accessed 16 May 2014].

DFID (Department for International Development) (1999) 'Sustainable Livelihoods Guidance Sheets', Eldis [website] <http://www.eldis.org/vfile/upload/1/document/0901/section2.pdf> [accessed 12 May 2014].

Habitat for Humanity (2009) 'Emerging stronger: Five years after the Indian Ocean tsunami', Habitat for Humanity [website] <http://www.habitat.org/asiapacific/Know_more/five_years_after_the_asiatsunami.aspx> [accessed 10 May 2014].

International Recovery Platform (2011) 'Countries and disasters: Indian Ocean tsunami, 2004', IRP [website] <http://www.recoveryplatform.org/countries_and_disasters/disaster/15/indian_ocean_tsunami_2004> [accessed 17 May 2014].

Thorburn, C. (2007) 'The Acehnese Gampong three years on: Assessing local capacity and reconstruction assistance in post-tsunami Aceh', Australian Agency for International Development (AusAID), Humanitarian Library [website] <http://humanitarianlibrary.org/sites/default/files/2014/02/acarpreport.pdf> [accessed 16 May 2014].

About the authors

Victoria Maynard trained as an architect and has worked for UN-Habitat, Shelter Centre, and Arup International Development since becoming involved in post-disaster reconstruction following the Indian Ocean tsunami. She is currently completing a PhD in partnership with Habitat for Humanity at University College London. Victoria also writes and lectures on disaster recovery, resilience, and participatory approaches to design.

Dr Priti Parikh is a chartered civil engineer who received the ACE/NCE Outstanding Contribution Award. She has over 18 years of experience with expertise in urban slums and rural low-income housing with a particular focus on infrastructure and business models. She has substantial in-country experience in South Asia, Africa, and the UK and has led multi-sectoral projects at both city and community scale. She is a lecturer at University College London where she runs modules on sustainable development and international development. She is also a board member for the charity Engineers Without Borders, UK.

Dan Simpson has worked in international development for over 20 years, principally focusing on designing and managing community-based approaches in a variety of technical areas, including housing and human settlements, water and sanitation, maternal and child nutrition, and natural-resource management. He currently works in programme design, monitoring, and evaluation with Habitat for Humanity International.

Jo da Silva was the founder of Arup international Development (a non-profit part of the Arup Group). Her expertise spans buildings, infrastructure, disaster risk reduction, and programme management. She was the first woman to deliver the Institute of Civil Engineers (ICE), 9th International Brunel Lecture, titled 'Shifting Agendas: from response to resilience - the role of the engineer in disaster risk reduction' (2012). She was made an Officer of the British Empire (OBE) for services to engineering and to humanitarian relief (2011), is a Fellow of the Royal Academy of Engineering (2010) and British Expertise Individual of the Year (2006).

CHAPTER 3

Looking back at agency-driven housing reconstruction in India: Case studies from Maharashtra, Gujarat, and Tamil Nadu

Jennifer Duyne Barenstein with Akbar Nazim Modan, Katheeja Talha, Nishant Upadhyay, and Charanya Khandhadai

Abstract

This chapter analyses people's long-term adaptation to agency-driven reconstruction in India with reference to three major disasters: the 1993 earthquake in Maharashtra, the 2001 earthquake in Gujarat, and the Indian Ocean tsunami of 2004. Based on a three-year research project, it focuses on the overall physical condition of the houses several years after reconstruction, people's satisfaction with their new houses and villages, and the adaptations and transformations of the agency-built settlements and houses they have undertaken since these have been handed over to them. Our research showed that over the years some of the problems related to agency-driven reconstruction and relocation persist, but that the long-term consequences are somewhat less dramatic than anticipated. In fact, people have an extraordinary capacity to adapt and transform the houses and villages provided by external agencies to meet their needs. However, if external agencies had recognized people's capacities and needs, and encouraged their participation from the beginning, housing solutions could have been culturally more appropriate and people's adaptation process significantly less painful and costly.

Keywords: Post-disaster reconstruction; Relocation; Adaptation; Housing culture; India

Introduction

Most studies on the social impact of post-disaster reconstruction and relocation are carried out shortly after project completion. There is a paucity of knowledge on how people adapt to settlement and housing typologies, introduced by external agencies following a disaster, years after relocation. This chapter analyses people's long-term adaptation to agency-driven reconstruction in the context of three major disasters that afflicted India over the last two decades: the Maharashtra earthquake of September 1993, the Gujarat earthquake

http://dx.doi.org/10.3362/9781780448398.003

of January 2001, and the Indian Ocean Tsunami of December 2004. More specifically we aim to address the following questions:

- What is the overall physical condition of the houses several years after reconstruction was completed?
- Are people satisfied with their new houses and villages in the long term?
- To what extent did people adapt and transform their agency-built settlements and houses? What are the purposes of their transformations?
- What challenges and constraints did they face in their attempts to transform their houses?

This chapter is based on a three-year research project funded by the Swiss National Science Foundation and the Swiss Agency for Development Cooperation involving a team of architects and social scientists. During the first year, we conducted research in Maharashtra where reconstruction was completed over 15 years earlier. The second year focused on Gujarat where we had already conducted research in 2004 (see Duyne Barenstein, 2006a, 2010, 2013) and the third on Tamil Nadu, where we focused on the same villages we had studied within the framework of previous research projects (see Duyne Barenstein, 2006b, 2011; Duyne Barenstein and Pittet, 2013).

Relocation and reconstruction outcomes in Maharashtra 18 years after the earthquake

The context

Maharashtra's Marathwada region, located about 500 km east of Mumbai, was hit by a severe earthquake that killed over 8,000 people in September 1993. The earthquake affected about 190,000 houses distributed in over 2,500 villages. A total of 28,000 houses in 52 villages were completely destroyed (GoM, 2005). Only a few days after the earthquake, the government announced the "Maharashtra Emergency Earthquake Rehabilitation Programme" (MEERP), which was conceived and executed with the support of the World Bank, UNDP, several bilateral donor agencies, and NGOs. The government offered financial and technical support for reconstruction in-situ to partially damaged villages, while relocation and full agency-driven reconstruction was foreseen for the 52 most heavily damaged ones. Entitlements to housing assistance were defined by making a distinction between three categories of people who would get homestead plots and houses of a size that depended on their ownership of agricultural land. The Government of Maharashtra invited international and national NGOs, the corporate sector, and charity organizations to take over the full reconstruction of the most severely affected villages.

Maharashtra's reconstruction policy raises some critical equity issues as wealthier households received considerably larger houses and homestead plots than poorer ones. By assuming that landholding households have larger spatial requirements than landless ones, the policy neglected the fact that for many landless households the dwelling does not only fulfil residential purposes, but also productive ones, and that spatial needs ultimately depend on household size.

Nowadays it is recognized that relocation has severe consequences on affected communities' livelihoods and well-being and accordingly should be avoided (Jha et al., 2010). In Maharashtra, however, disaster-affected communities apparently did not oppose resettlement. A survey carried out by an Indian research institute shortly after the quake revealed that the majority of people had lost faith in their traditional building capacity and preferred to move to modern and seismically safe villages (Vatsa, 2001). This encouraged villages that were not originally identified for resettlement to demand relocation, and accept agencies' relocation and reconstruction offers.

The success of the Maharashtra post-earthquake reconstruction programme in terms of meeting people's needs, cultural sensitivity, and addressing people's vulnerabilities is controversial. Jigyasu (2002) and Salazar (2002a, 2002b) maintain that the reconstruction programme pursued by the Government of Maharashtra was inadequate. They recognize that due to poverty, migration, and other ongoing socio-economic changes many traditional houses had become vulnerable. But they regret that vernacular architecture was blamed for the high number of casualties and question the viability of replacing culturally and ecologically appropriate settlements with modern ones. Jigyasu (2001) maintains that people's preference for relocation and modern houses was influenced by the negative attitude towards traditional housing of the junior engineers who surveyed the earthquake-damaged villages, and by the fact that villagers were forced to take decisions when they were still deeply traumatized. Jigyasu and Salazar both expressed concern about the large size and layouts of the new villages, the inappropriate house designs and construction materials, and the poor quality of construction. They further maintained that by providing people different house sizes, the reconstruction programme not only exacerbated social inequality, but also contributed to the marginalization of the landless artisan castes, who need large homesteads to exercise their traditional occupations. Jigyasu and Salazar (2010) argue that the reconstruction approach followed in Maharashtra has made people more vulnerable. According to their observations, the incompatibility of local livelihoods and new villages led some people to abandon the new villages and move back to their old ones where repairs were undertaken without any material and technical guidance. Their observations, however, were made while reconstruction was still ongoing and accordingly did not incorporate people's adaptation to their new housing conditions in the long term.

Overall reconstruction outcomes

Our research in Maharashtra was carried out in 2011–2012. It included rapid appraisals in ten villages and in-depth case studies in a sample of five villages. It revealed that not all assumptions with regard to the impact of relocation by scholars during or shortly after the completion of reconstruction were correct. At present, all relocated villages are fully inhabited and in no case has there been a return to the ancestral villages. On the contrary, we found several examples of villages that were not relocated by any agencies after the earthquake where the communities themselves, without any external support, have taken the initiative to self-relocate, and in some cases are still trying to obtain external aid to this aim. The reconstruction entailed an abandonment of the traditional building technologies characterized by stone masonry with mud mortar and heavy earth roofs, not only by external agencies but also by the people themselves. This technological change is partly related to the loss of confidence in particular in traditional roofing (which provided thermal comfort but was considered to be the main cause of the high number of casualties) but also the shortage of good quality timber required for making this type of roof.

In most cases, the agency-built houses are still inhabited by their original owners or by their children. The relocation into grid-patterned villages did not weaken social cohesion and the traditional caste system as we had assumed. In fact, even though most agencies did not pursue a participatory approach, community leaders were intensively involved in the allocation of the agency-built houses and tried to ensure as much as possible that people belonging to the same community would continue living next to each other. The large size of the new villages (up to five times the footprint of the old villages) in the long term proved to be an advantage because it allowed people to make extensions to their houses so as to accommodate the housing needs of the new generations and hence a densification of the village.

Most people moved to the new villages over 15 years ago, only elderly people feel somewhat nostalgic about their old villages, while the younger generations appreciate the 'modern' features of their new villages and houses. Our survey further revealed higher levels of satisfaction amongst poorer households who only received the smallest houses and plots; they considered their present housing conditions better than before the earthquake. It was noted that a majority had made some extensions, the dimension and quality of which reflected their livelihood-specific needs, the evolution of their family, the availability of space, and their financial capacity.

The case of Malkondji

Malkondji is a relatively remote village, 40 km from the district capital, Latur. At the time of the earthquake, it had 1,562 inhabitants distributed over 281 households. Seven people lost their lives in the earthquake and five were injured. Before the earthquake, the vast majority of the people lived in traditional *malwad* houses characterized by stone masonry walls and heavy wooden roofs covered with a thick layer of mud.

Malkondji was 'adopted' by one of the few NGOs that employed a highly committed professional team of architects and planners. An appropriate site for building the new village was acquired by the government only 600 m from the old village. The planning process of the new village was participatory and the NGO responded to people's needs and suggestions both with regard to the new settlement and to the design of the new houses. The NGO that adopted Malkondji refused to build houses of different sizes for three categories of people depending on their ownership of agricultural land. Based on its commitment to give the same treatment to all people, they built 336 identical core houses. The Government of Maharashtra later added additional housing units in the larger plots that were given to those families who were entitled to larger houses according to its policy (see Figure 3.1). The houses are made of Concrete Block (CB) load-bearing walls, with Reinforced Concrete (RC) plinth and lintel bands and RC flat roofs. The NGO core house with its size of 34.5 m² consists of a compact single-family unit including a main block with a kitchen and a sleeping room, and a separate block with a bathroom and a toilet. The fact that the dwellings were placed at an extremity of the plot greatly facilitated future expansions in the remaining portion of the homestead plot in front of the house.

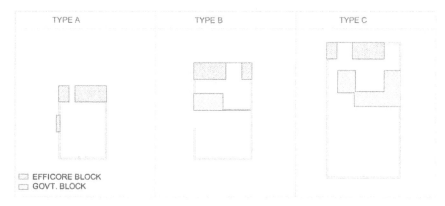

Figure 3.1 Plans of agency - (ie agency-provided) provided houses in Malkondji

What is unique about Malkondji is that the settlement plan of the new village attempts to reproduce the clustered type of neighbourhood typical of traditional villages, though on a much larger footprint. The old village had a size of only 5.81 ha, the new village had a size of 22.7 ha. Communal spaces and ten public buildings, including a primary school, temples, an office for the *Gram Panchayat* (local government), a *Mahila Kendra* (Women's community hall), an *Anganwadi* (kindergarden), a primary health care centre, a cooperative society building, a veterinary clinic, and a library were also provided. All these buildings, except the library, are currently being used as intended. Particular attention was given to the plantation of large numbers of trees, which provided the community with comfortable outdoor public spaces for social interaction and enabled them to bring their deities and other culturally meaningful elements from the old village to the new village. At the individual house level, the NGO also responded to people's request for walls around compounds. This ensures privacy and is crucial for an inward-oriented spatial organization of the house and related domestic activities.

Nearly 18 years after relocation, the vast majority of the agency-built houses in Malkondji are inhabited. The people of Malkondji are highly satisfied with their new village and houses. The construction quality is good and close to two decades later houses show no major signs of deterioration. In contrast to houses built by other contractors, they have no major cracks in the walls and the concrete roofs are not leaking. The village is more spacious and greener than the old village and most people have larger homestead plots, allowing them to plant trees and to keep their goats and cattle within their homesteads.

Comparison of the village map of 1996 with the one of 2011 (see Figures 3.2 and 3.3), shows that the vast majority of people have made some extensions to their houses, the cost and quality of which primarily depends upon the households' financial capacity.

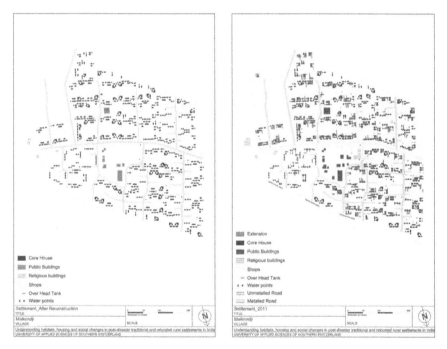

Figures 3.2 and 3.3 Village maps of Malkondji (1996 and 2011)

Shortly after moving, most families built a *tulsi vrindavan* (a small masonry enclosure for the sacred *tulsi* plant) and an external kitchen, while later on some added a cowshed and storage space for keeping fodder and utensils, and additional rooms to accommodate new family members (see Figure 4).

Better-off households often made considerable investments to shift and transform the main entrance to their homes to reproduce the main features of the traditional house. Several houses, particularly those along the main road,

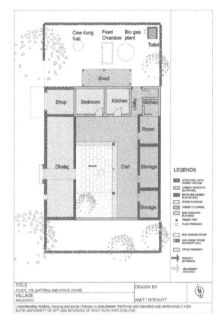

Figure 3.4 Example of extensions carried out to a core house in Malkondji

painted their entrances with two mythical door guards in order to welcome prosperity. While the quality of the contractor-built core houses is good, the current situation is somewhat less encouraging with regard to the quality of extensions. While out of fear of earthquakes people have abandoned their traditional roofing system by replacing it with tin sheets, the vast majority did not adopt any earthquake-resistant features in building new walls. Due to economic constraints and insufficient concerns about safety, these are often built with mixed building materials such as mud, stone, burned earth bricks and cement blocks (see Figures 3.5 and 3.6).

Figures 3.5 and 3.6 Transformed houses in new Malkondji

To conclude, the case of Malkondji shows the importance of providing homestead plots big enough to allow for extensions and transformations, which are part of the process of appropriation and personalization of a house but also a basic requirement to accommodate new family members. The fact that good quality compound walls were built as part of the core unit was fundamental for people to feel at home almost immediately after relocation, to enable them to transform and extend their agency-provided houses, and to adapt them to their personal needs. It is regrettable that this is the only agency we came across in Latur that responded to such deeply anchored cultural requirements. With regard to the perseverance of unsafe building practices, it would be too simple to blame the contractor-driven reconstruction approach for having missed the opportunity to enhance local building capacities. In fact, based on interviews with people it appeared that economic constraints and a somewhat fatalistic attitude towards risk, more than lack of know-how, were the main factors behind the perpetuation of unsafe building practices.

Reconstruction outcomes in Gujarat 12 years after the earthquake

The context

The earthquake that hit Gujarat in 2001 was the worst experienced by India in the last century. About 20,000 people lost their lives and over one million were rendered homeless; 344,000 houses were completely destroyed and 888,000 reported damage, while 450 villages were completely flattened (GSDMA, 2006). The reconstruction policy announced by the Government of Gujarat only two weeks after the earthquake was clearly inspired by the policy followed by the Government of Maharashtra after the earthquake of 1993. However, while in Maharashtra there appeared to be a high societal consensus to the proposed reconstruction approach, this was not the case in Gujarat, where it met with stiff public resistance (Duyne Barenstein and Iyengar, 2010). A systematic public consultation carried out by the local NGO network Abhiyan in 480 villages revealed that 93 per cent of the Gujarati villagers rejected the idea of relocation (Abhiyan, 2005). This eventually led the government to abandon its relocation plans and to opt for an 'owner-driven' reconstruction approach. This approach consisted of offering financial and technical assistance to all those who preferred to undertake reconstruction on their own and did not want relocation and full scale 'adoption' by an external agency. Given this choice, over 72 per cent of the villages opted for financial assistance and to rebuild their houses on their own. The government's owner-driven reconstruction programme included a number of enabling mechanisms: civil engineers were placed in all villages to supervise the construction; subsidized material banks were established in all villages to ensure access to good quality building materials and mitigate the risk of increased prices; building codes and guidelines were adapted to local building technologies; and large-scale training courses were offered to house owners and local masons. Despite the government's abandonment of the Maharashtra relocation and contractor-driven reconstruction approach, many agencies replicated the same contractor approach they had followed eight years earlier in Maharashtra.

Overall reconstruction outcomes in Gujarat

In 2004 we conducted a household survey aimed at comparing citizens' satisfaction with different reconstruction approaches. We found that the highest satisfaction was achieved by owner-driven reconstruction with financial and technical assistance from the government, complemented with additional material assistance from local NGOs. All families whose houses were built using this approach reported that their housing situation was better than before the earthquake. A second approach, government-supported, owner-driven reconstruction without any NGO top up, was almost as popular, with 93.3 per cent of those households reporting being fully satisfied. Relatively high levels of overall satisfaction (90.8 per cent) were also reported under a third approach: local NGOs using a community-driven approach. Satisfaction decreased when houses were built by contractors: 71.8 per cent of the people reported being satisfied with contractor-built houses built in-situ where contractors' profit imperative was held responsible for low construction quality. Only 22.8 per cent of the people who received contractor-built houses in relocated sites reported being satisfied and only 3.5 per cent considered housing quality adequate. People complained about lack of participation, discrimination in favour of local elites, and disruption of family networks. Many people refused to move to new villages, and houses remained unoccupied. The study also showed that reconstruction by contractors was more costly and required more time than owner-driven reconstruction (Duyne Barenstein 2006a).

The case of Fadsar

Fadsar is a village located in Jamnagar district, which at the time of the earthquake had 1,380 inhabitants. It was one of the villages that we included in our comparative analysis of different reconstruction approaches in 2004 as an example of contractor-driven reconstruction in relocated sites and where the levels of satisfaction were the lowest. Initially, the villagers intended to opt for government supported owner-driven reconstruction. However, a large internationally-funded NGO succeeded in convincing the village elite to accept their offer to rebuild their village at a new site close to the old village, through personal incentives and benefits. Ultimately, the whole community was left with no other option than to follow the decision of their leaders. The NGO that adopted Fadsar had previous reconstruction experience from Latur and decided to follow the same approach, i.e. to build houses of different sizes for different landholding categories of people. However, many landless families in Fadsar are cattle herders and their spatial requirements are primarily determined by the ownership of cattle. The compact old village surrounded by the farms was located on slightly elevated ground that protected them from floods; the new grid-patterned village was built on the floodplain, making it very prone to inundations during the monsoon (see Figure 3.7). The community had tried to persuade the NGO to build the village on slightly elevated ground adjacent to the old village but the NGO refused. With regard to the house design, there was no community consultation with the result that the new houses were completely incongruent with local lifestyle. The construction of the 317 houses was completed in 2003 but due to a profound sense of alienation and dissatisfaction many people had still refused to relocate by late 2004. Those who did were struggling to adjust to their new living arrangement at a site that they remember as being infested by snakes and scorpions, and which flooded during the monsoon (see Figure 3.8).

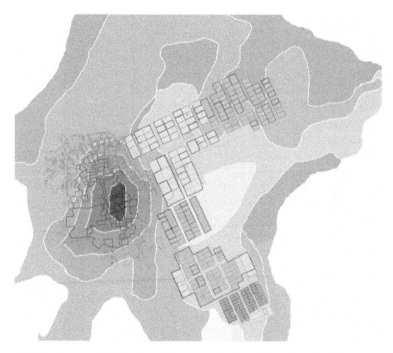

Figure 3.7 Village map of old (on the left) and new (on the right, grid pattern) Fadsar

We returned to Fadsar to study people's long-term adaptation to the new village in 2012, expecting to find it desolate and abandoned. However, we found that over the years, thanks to their own initiative, people gradually succeeded in transforming the new settlement into a vibrant village. To achieve this, four residential houses were sold or donated by their owners to the community and transformed into temples, and trees were planted in several critical communal places to create shaded areas for social interaction. Over 90 per cent of the houses were occupied, mostly by their original owners, with only those belonging to migrants being temporarily vacant. Only a few families sold their NGO houses without ever occupying them in order to build a house on their own, while a group of five families sold their small NGO houses a few years later to return to their old neighbourhood.

Over the years, 77 per cent of the dwellings were extended and transformed. The first important addition made by those who could afford to, was the construction of compound walls, important for the privacy of the family. Concurrently, families made arrangements for cooking outside. The NGO houses were equipped with a room that was supposed to serve as a kitchen, but was inappropriate for cooking with firewood in the traditional way. Adding a veranda for an outdoor shaded area was a culturally and climatically essential housing element. Several households also made significant investments to make up for the poor quality of construction by repairing leaking roofs and replacing poor quality doors, window frames, and shutters. Over the years, people also started to make additions to accommodate new family members and in particular those who received larger houses and plots have been quite successful in transforming their NGO house to reproduce the traditional housing typology (see Figure 3.9). This required not only significant financial means but also space, which poorer households who only received smaller houses and plots did not have. Indeed, both the design of the NGO house, its position within the homestead plot, as well as the size of the plot have obstructed rather than facilitated extension. Accordingly, it is not surprising that 72 per cent of the unaltered houses are the smallest ones, where spatial and economic constraints often collide.

Surprisingly, people in Fadsar have adjusted over the years to their new village much better than we had anticipated they would in 2004. However, the new village does not satisfy their spatial requirements. The village has a total population of over 800 cattle. These animals and their fodder require space that is not available in the new village. To this end, many villagers still rely on their properties in the old village. At present, the old village is far from abandoned and continues to play important socio-economic and cultural functions. A collective effort has been made to restore its temples and to create a connection between the new and the old village where all cultural and religious festivals continue to be celebrated and people anticipate that future housing requirements will be met by building new houses or repairing the old ones in the old village.

Figure 3.8 Empty agency-built houses in Fadsar in 2004

Figure 3.9 A transformed large house in Fadsar in 2012

Looking back at reconstruction outcomes in Tamil Nadu nine years after the Indian Ocean tsunami of December 2004

The context

The earthquake that hit northern Sumatra in December 2004 resulted in one of the most destructive tsunamis of recorded history. In India, it killed over 12,000 people of which the majority belonged to Tamil Nadu's fishing communities. It was estimated that over 130,000 houses had to be replaced and about 10,000 needed repairs (ADB et al., 2005). These figures, however, did not result from an accurate damage assessment. In fact, because the government intended to resettle all tsunami-affected communities at a safe distance from the coast, a detailed housing damage assessment was not considered necessary. The unprecedented availability of humanitarian aid for reconstruction meant the disaster was considered an opportunity to upgrade the housing conditions of all people. The intention was to upgrade the houses of those living in traditional houses, considered by outsiders as primitive, even if they were of good quality and had not been affected by the tsunami (see Figure 3.10). Fishing communities' resistance to relocation and difficulties in finding land at an acceptable distance from the sea forced the government to abandon its relocation policy, while nevertheless remaining firm on a no-construction zone of 200 m from the high-tide line.

Allowing communities to remain in their original villages should have compelled the government to reconsider the required number of new houses. This, however, was never done. The large amount of money that was available for reconstruction meant that agencies had an interest in building as many houses as possible. This, combined with external agencies' prejudices towards vernacular housing, and the fact that the fishing communities felt entitled to free houses, led the government and NGOs to offer new houses to all coastal families even if they had not been affected by the tsunami (TISS, 2005).

Figure 3.10 A typical self-built traditional house in coastal Tamil Nadu

Housing reconstruction in Tamil Nadu was completely taken over by national and international NGOs, private corporations, and charity organizations. The government limited its role to defining the regulatory framework, coordination, and monitoring. However, this was the task of the district administration who had no additional human resources to perform this extraordinary task, and no specific unit was set up with this aim. The government promised multi-hazard resistant houses and laid out detailed conditions with respect to minimum investments in housing, building technologies, size of houses, and homestead plots. According to the official policy, each family was entitled to a flat-roofed reinforced concrete house of 325 square feet (ca. 30 m^2), a size that is barely sufficient to accommodate a nuclear family. The assumption that fishers live in independent nuclear families with lifestyles similar to the urban middle classes is also reflected in the design of the proposed houses, which in spite of their small size were typically divided into a living room, one bedroom, a kitchen and a detached bathroom. Such a design contrasts sharply with fishing communities' traditional houses, which in most cases consist of a large veranda, one multi-purpose room, a small *puja* room (prayer room, in the case of fishermen also used for storage), and a fully detached kitchen. The new design was followed with minor variations by all agencies involved in reconstruction (Duyne Barenstein and Pittet, 2013).

The veranda, the most important space in self-built houses, was generally omitted or was too small to fulfil any function. The government policy stipulated a plot size of 60 m^2 in urban areas and 125 m^2 in rural areas. However, due to the difficulty of finding land the resulting plots were smaller in most cases. Thus, while according to the government policy the houses were conceived as extendable core units, the lack of space on the plots made them unsuitable for extensions but also for planting shade trees and for allowing people to maintain their outdoor-oriented lifestyle. In many villages, reconstruction led to a systematic demolition of undamaged vernacular houses and to the felling of all trees. The destruction of coastal habitats had multiple, dramatic consequences on the health and well-being of coastal communities. In their in-depth anthropological village studies, Naimi-Gasser (2013), Duyne Barenstein and Trachsel (2012), and Duyne Barenstein (2011) found that reconstruction, post-tsunami, led to severe social conflicts, depression, a nucleation of extended families, the marginalization of women in the housing processes, social isolation, and the deprivation of elderly people and widows from informal but effective social security systems. The above-mentioned studies were all conducted less than one year after people moved into their new houses, which raises questions about the long-term consequences of such dramatic changes to people's habitats and housing conditions.

Overall reconstruction outcome nine years after the tsunami

Research in ten villages in Tamil Nadu started in September 2013 and was completed in March 2014. We found that in general reconstruction focused exclusively on housing at the expense of the habitat as a whole. The quantity of houses built was disproportionate to the number of houses affected and their quality is generally poor. In cases where villages were rebuilt in-situ, this was done by demolishing all pre-tsunami houses and by felling all trees. Relocated settlements were often built on low-lying land subject to water logging, leading to health hazards and a rapid deterioration of the houses. In some villages, as many as 6,000 valuable trees such as mango and tamarind were felled to maximize the space for new houses and to allow contractors to build their mass housing projects more rapidly.

Nevertheless, most houses are inhabited and people are making an effort to adapt them to meet their needs by raising floors (to prevent the house being flooded), planting trees, adding external kitchens and verandas, building fences with organic material or compound walls, and adding thatched roofs on top of their houses' concrete roofs. However, their endeavours are constrained by the small size of their homestead plots and by house designs that did not anticipate people's extension needs.

The case of Seruthur

Seruthur is a village in Nagapattinam district with a population of approximately 3,000 people, all belonging to the fishing community. The old village was an organic clustered settlement facing the sea with a few narrow paths leading to the beach. It comprised approximately 550 houses. Close to 90 per cent were traditional dwellings characterized by brick walls with lime or mud mortar, and steep thatched roofs. Some 8 per cent of the traditional houses had tiled roofs while only about 3 per cent of the housing stock consisted of 'modern' houses with RC flat roofs. Old Seruthur was protected from the scorching heat by large numbers of trees that allowed for an outdoor-oriented lifestyle typical of coastal communities. The tsunami severely affected the village, killing 165 people destroying about 30 per cent of the houses. While only one local NGO offered some financial aid to repair damaged houses, shortly after the tsunami a national NGO with no previous experience in reconstruction offered to build 600 houses in a site approximately 1 km from the old village. However, after completing a row of 200 poor-quality houses they discontinued the project, apparently due to shortage of funds. Subsequently, another agency offered to build an additional 230 houses.

The houses built by this agency were of such poor quality that the people repeatedly approached the district administration to intervene. As no action was taken, they organized a rally and demolished some of the houses with their bare hands. After this incident, they organized a local committee to supervise the construction and the quality improved to some extent. Whilst at least from a quantitative point of view these 430 houses satisfied Seruthur's housing needs, three more NGOs came to Serethur to build new houses as long as five years after the tsunami, building another 154 units in another site adjacent to the old village. All 584 NGO houses were built by external contractors with no community participation at any stage of the project cycle. While their quality scores rate between moderately poor and very poor and their size varies between 30 and 42 m² (see Figure 3.11), many families repaired their pre-tsunami houses and continued to live there.

Figure 3.11 Example of house built by one of the agencies involved in the reconstruction of Seruthur

At present, 87 per cent of the new NGO houses are occupied. This rate is relatively high considering that 113 pre-tsunami houses in the old village continue to be inhabited. In fact, many new houses are occupied by young couples who married after the tsunami. With no external housing assistance, these young couples would otherwise have been living with their extended family or would only have been able to afford a very modest fully thatched dwelling. This explains why the poor quality, culturally and climatically inappropriate houses are, in most cases occupied, and that around 50 per cent of the households expressed broad satisfaction. Only a few years after occupying their new houses already 52 per cent of their owners had made some extensions or transformations, the quality of which primarily depends on the residents' economic situation (see Figure 3.12). In some cases investments were also made to make up for the poor construction quality. A common addition is a thatched roof on top of the flat RC roof. In this way, they gain a much-needed extra room where they can sleep during the hot summer nights. In about 10 per cent of the cases, no material extensions have been made but major efforts were put into improving climate comfort through tree plantation.

Figure 3.12 Example of extensions of an agency-built house in Seruthur

To conclude, nine years after the tsunami Seruthur is a village divided in three relocation sites characterized by rows of poor quality houses built in plots that are too small to allow for adequate extensions to accommodate new family members. Significant investment is required to make the agency-built houses liveable, but this is feasible for only a few households. None of the agencies that were involved in Seruthur's reconstruction had considered the need for communal spaces for social interaction and for creating habitats in harmony with local livelihoods and lifestyles.

Summary and conclusions

Looking back at agency-driven reconstruction outcomes several years after three major disasters in India has shown that success varies from case to case depending on contextual factors and on the agency's reconstruction approach.

The case of Malkondji clearly shows the long-term positive impacts of involving professional architects and planners in implementing a participatory reconstruction project. This has led to good quality of construction and to a settlement plan and house designs that greatly facilitated people's individual and collective adaptation to the new village, contributing to a less traumatic relocation experience. An important element that facilitated the extensions and transformations of the houses was the provision of relatively large plots, compound walls, and the placement of the core unit in a corner of the plot. The combination of these three elements allowed house owners to extend within the compound walls, thus recreating a spatial arrangement in harmony with local lifestyles and livelihoods. Equally commendable was the unique attention paid by the agency to the plantation of trees, which greatly contributed to the creation of healthy and comfortably shaded outdoor communal spaces whose role in communities' well-being and social cohesion cannot be overestimated.

The case of Fadsar shows that when professionals and communities do not engage, relocation tends to be much more problematic. Due to the communities' lack of involvement in project planning and implementation, settlement plan and house designs were incongruent with local lifestyles, and relocation was highly traumatic. Indeed people recall that during the first two years in the new village, they lived in what they defined as a state of shock. The construction of compound walls was the first extension undertaken by most people, before even moving to the new village, and was of pivotal importance for their well-being. However, only wealthy households could afford good materials and construction quality; the majority built them with salvaged materials and accordingly they remain highly vulnerable to seismic shocks.

The fact that people adapted reasonably well in the long term to the new village and are currently relatively satisfied is primarily the result of their individual and collective efforts to transform their houses. That they were able to retain their properties in the old village is also key. Moreover, the rapid rise of land and property prices that has taken place in Gujarat over the last decade means people are very aware of the increasing value of what they got for free. In fact, even though the NGO houses were of relatively poor quality and on hand-over were valued below construction cost, their current market value has more than doubled.

In Tamil Nadu, people are also profoundly aware of the value of land and housing. Accordingly, even though the agency-built houses are generally of poor quality and culturally inappropriate, owners expressed a higher level of overall satisfaction than we would have expected, notwithstanding the dramatic change in lifestyle that moving to the new settlements entailed.

In the case of Seruthur, many families living in the new settlement are young couples who married after the tsunami and whose alternative would have been to live with the grooms' parents. They appreciate the fact that they became owners of a house on their own, which would have been beyond their means without external aid. Those who can afford to have started improving and extending their houses, often even before moving in. Even more than in Maharashtra and Gujarat, endeavours to reproduce housing patterns and habitat in line with traditional livelihoods and lifestyles is constrained by small plot size and a settlement layout that hinders extensions and transformation processes.

Our research shows that the capacity to adapt and transform agency-built villages and houses to culturally appropriate places is strongly influenced by the settlement layout and by the house designs. Unfortunately, only a few agencies recognized the importance of planning settlements and houses in such a way as to facilitate future extensions; the majority built rows of houses without any consideration for the need for communal spaces.

The three reconstruction experiences reviewed in this chapter have in common that people demonstrate a high degree of resilience in terms of overcoming the trauma of post-disaster relocation thanks to the short distance between their old and their new villages. In all three, people immediately began to adapt and transform their agency-built houses in an attempt to reproduce an outdoor but privacy-sensitive lifestyle. Extensions were often made by mixing new and old building materials and technologies and relatively limited attention was given to safety considerations. While the quality and sophistication of extensions inevitably depends on the economic status of the house owners, it was noticed that the house design, the position of the dwelling on the plot, and the plot size strongly influenced the quality of the extensions made to the agency-provided core houses.

To conclude, the fact that even when new settlements and houses are not culturally appropriate and of average to poor quality, people have the will and, to some extent, the capacity to adapt and transform their new houses and villages to meet their needs, hence in the longer term being relatively satisfied. However, this does not justify the failure to involve professional planners, architects, and communities as has characterized too many agency-driven reconstruction projects in India. The additional time and resources that may be required for a more inclusive reconstruction approach are certainly more than justified if we consider the long-term consequences on people's well-being and safety.

References

Abhiyan, B. (2005) 'Coming together: A document on the post-earthquake rehabilitation efforts by various organisations working in Kutch', United Nations Development Programme and Abhiyan, Bhuj.

ADB, UNDP, and World Bank (2005) 'India post-tsunami recovery program: Preliminary damage and needs assessment', Government of Tamil Nadu [website] <http://www.tnrd.gov.in/externallyaidedprojects/Tsunami_rehabilation/india-assessment-full-report[1].pdf> [accessed 20 May 2014].

Duyne Barenstein, J. (2006a) 'Housing reconstruction in post-earthquake Gujarat. A comparative analysis *HPN Paper* 54, Overseas Development Institute, London.

{--} (2006b) 'Challenges and risks in post-tsunami housing reconstruction in Tamil Nadu', *Humanitarian Exchange*, No. 33: 38–39.

{--} (2011) 'Housing reconstruction in Tamil Nadu: The disaster after the tsunami in India', in: D.S Miller and J.D. Rivera, *Community Disaster Recovery and Resiliency. Exploring Global Opportunities and Challenges*, CRS Press, Boca Raton.

{--} (2013) 'Communities' perspectives on housing reconstruction in Gujarat following the earthquake of 2001', in J.Duyne Barenstein and E. Leemann (eds), *Post-Disaster Reconstruction and Change. Communities' Perspectives*, CRS Press, Boca Raton.

Duyne Barenstein, J. and Iyengar, S. (2010) 'India: From a culture of housing to a philosophy of reconstruction', in M. Lyons and T. Schilderman eds. *Building Back Better: Delivering People-centred Reconstruction to Scale*, pp. 163–188, Practical Action Publishing, Rugby.

Duyne Barenstein, J. and Leemann, E. (eds) (2013) *Post-Disaster Reconstruction and Change. Communities' Perspectives*, CRS Press, Boca Raton.

Duyne Barenstein, J. and Pittet, D. (2013) 'An environmental and social impact assessment of post disaster housing reconstruction. The case of Tamil Nadu', in J. Duyne Barenstein and E. Leemann (eds), *Post-Disaster Reconstruction and Change. Communities' Perspectives*, CRS Press, Boca Raton.

Duyne Barenstein, J. and Trachsel, S. (2012) 'The role of informal governance in post-disaster reconstruction and its impact on elderly people's social security in coastal Tamil Nadu', in J. Duyne Barenstein and E. Leemann (eds), *Post-Disaster Reconstruction and Change. Communities' Perspectives*, CRS Press, Boca Raton.

GoM (Government of Maharashtra) (2005) 'Maharashtra emergency earthquake rehabilitation programme (MEERP)', Government of Maharashtra [website] <http://mdmu.maharashtra.gov.in/pages/meerp/profile.htm> [accessed 20 May 2014].

GSDMA (Gujarat State Disaster Management Authority). 2006., Grit and grace. The Story of Reconstruction. Gandhinagar, GSDMA Press.

Jha, A., Duyne Barenstein, J., Phelps, P., Pittet, D., and Sena, S. (2010) *Safer Homes, Stronger Communities. A Handbook for Post-disaster Reconstruction*, The World Bank, Washington DC.

Jigyasu, R. (2001) 'From "natural" to "cultural" disaster. Consequences of post-earthquake rehabilitation processes on cultural heritage in Marathwada Region, India', ICOMOS [website] <http://www.icomos.org/iiwc/seismic/Jigyasu.pdf> [accessed 20 May 2014].

Jigyasu, R. (2002) 'Reducing disaster vulnerability through local knowledge and capacity', Phd Thesis, Norwegian University of Science and Technology, Dept. of Urban Design and Planning, Trondheim.

Jigyasu, R. and Salazar, A. (2010) 'A decade of lessons from Marathwada: Earthquake vulnerability, politics and participatory planning', in: A. Revi and S. Bhatt (eds), *Recovering from Earthquake: Response, Reconstruction and Impact on Mitigation in India*, Routledge, New Delhi.

Naimi-Gasser, J. (2013) 'The remembered trees. Contractor-driven reconstruction and its consequences on communities' well-being in coastal Tamil Nadu', in J. Duyne Barenstein and E. Leemann (eds), *Post-Disaster Reconstruction and Change. Communities' Perspectives*, CRS Press, Boca Raton.

Salazar, A. (2002a) 'The crisis of modernity of housing disasters in developing countries. Participatory housing and technology after the Marathwada (1993) earthquake', World Bank [website] <http://info.worldbank.org/etools/docs/library/156603/housing/pdf/HousingDisasters.pdf> [accessed 20 May 2014].

Salazar, A. (2002b) 'Normal life after disasters? 8 years of housing lessons, from Marathwada to Gujarat'. Available from http://www.radixonline.org/gujart6.htm [accessed 25 February 2014].

TISS (Tata Institute of Social Sciences) (2005) 'The state and civil society in disaster response. An analysis of the Tamil Nadu tsunami experience', TISS [website] <http://www.tiss.edu/tiss-attachements/downloads/the-state-and-civil-society-in-disaster-response-an-analysis-of-the-tamil-nadu-tsunami-experience> [accessed 20 May 2014].

Vatsa, K. (2001) 'Rhetoric and reality of post-disaster rehabilitation after the Latur earthquake of 1993: A rejoinder'. Available from http://www.radixonline.org/gujarat5.htm [accessed 15 March 2014].

About the authors

The authors are currently engaged in a joint research project on 'Understanding habitat, housing and social changes in post-disaster traditional and relocated rural settlements in India' funded by the Swiss National Science Foundation.

Jennifer Duyne Barenstein is the director of the above-mentioned project. She has a PhD in social anthropology. Her academic and professional interests focus on the socio-economic and cultural dimensions of housing, post-disaster reconstruction, and resettlement. She is the head of the World Habitat Research Centre (WHRC) of the University of Applied Sciences of Southern Switzerland and was one of the lead authors of 'Safer Homes, Stronger Communities. A Handbook for Reconstruction after Natural Disasters' published by the World Bank in 2010.

Akbar Nazim Modan has an MA in Architectural Regeneration and Development from Oxford Brookes University, where he specialized in post-disaster reconstruction. After working for several years in Gujarat, Kashmir, UK, Northern Cyprus, Turkey, Iraq, and Haiti he joined the WHRC as a senior researcher in 2012.

Katheeja Talha is an architect from MEASI Academy of Architecture, Chennai, India. Her thesis and her concurrent work focuses on gender and the political implications of space. At present, she is a researcher with the WHRC and a volunteer with the Youth Action on Climate Change Solidarity Group.

Nishant Upadhyay was trained as an architect at the University of Lucknow, India. His main interests lie in cultural sustainability and settlement conservation. He was a researcher with the WHRC from 2011 to 2012. Currently he pursues a Masters Degree in Conservation of Monuments and Sites at the Catholic University in Leuven, Belgium.

Charanya Khandhadai is an architect from MEASI Academy of Architecture, Chennai, India. Her previous and current work primarily focuses on incubation of strategies and ideas for urban and rural planning. Currently she is a researcher at WHRC.

CHAPTER 4

A market-based programme to improve housing in the mountains of northern Pakistan: Addressing seismic vulnerability

Nawab Ali Khan and Charles Parrack

Abstract

The Building and Construction Improvement Programme (BACIP) has been working with the high mountain communities of the Gilgit-Baltistan region of Pakistan since 1997. Alongside its contribution to the general built environment and housing improvement of the area, the programme is engaged in the development and promotion of solutions for making the buildings seismically resistant. Gilgit-Baltistan falls in a high seismic zone and the earthquake of 2005 caused the death of nearly 90,000 people in the neighbouring state of Azad Kashmir and the Khyber Pakhtunkhwa province of Pakistan, which share long borders with Gilgit-Baltistan. BACIP believes that investment in making communities safer will minimize the chance of loss of life and assets and reduce the cost of reconstruction. BACIP works with local communities in a participatory manner to improve the local housing by improving safety and comfort without changing the local culture and way of living. For the sustainability of its approach, it has made efforts to make its solutions part of the local market so that entrepreneurs and artisans are available to manufacture, sell or construct these solutions. A number of profitable enterprises have been established. Alongside hands-on training and demonstration, BACIP uses media such as radio for the promotion of its solutions and awareness of communities. In December 2013 with the support of the Building and Social Housing Foundation (BSHF), BACIP revisited a number of houses that were constructed using seismic-resistant technologies and it was found that the solutions applied to these houses had greatly contributed to the safety and comfort of the users. 100 per cent of the houses were in use and were occupied by the original owners.

Keywords: Seismic resistant housing; Post-disaster reconstruction; Seismic wire reinforcement

The area – Gilgit-Baltistan

Gilgit-Baltistan, formerly known as the Northern Areas of Pakistan, was formed by the collision of the Indian tectonic plate with the Eurasian plate some 40 million years ago. It is located at the junction of three of the most famous

http://dx.doi.org/10.3362/9781780448398.004

mountain ranges – the Karakoram, Himalaya, and Hindu Kush – containing 14 of the world's highest mountains, all above 7,706 m high including world K2 at 8,612 m.

The area has strategic importance for Pakistan as it borders China in the east, Afghanistan to the north, and Jammu and Kashmir in the northeast. It is connected to the Khyber Pakhtunkhwa province of Pakistan in the west. The historical Silk Route passes through this area as well as the Karakoram Highway connecting the capital of Pakistan, Islamabad, to the southern part of China in Kashghar.

Over 1.5 million people, living in an area of some 72,496 km², depend almost entirely for their energy and construction needs on scarce natural resources, predominantly the forest. The glaciers and snow-melts from the mountains are the key source of fresh water. The river Indus has its source in Gilgit-Baltistan and flows through the plains of Pakistan to the Arabian Sea, irrigating agriculture across Pakistan and contributing significantly to the water needs of the country.

Alongside the beauty of the mountains lies danger. 80 percent of the estimated 150,000 households in Gilgit-Baltistan are living in an area of high seismic activity. Over 200 people lost their lives in the Diamer District in 1981, and another 22 people died in Astore District in 2002 when earthquakes hit the area. The magnitude of the earthquake in Diamer was 5.8 and in Astore was 5.5. About 90,000 people lost their lives as a result of the Kashmir earthquake of 2005 and 5,700 people died as a result of the Pattan earthquake of 1974 in the adjacent state of Azad Kashmir and Khyber Pakhtunkhwa province and the resultant damage has cost many millions of dollars. In these earthquakes, most people lost their lives due to the collapse of poorly constructed buildings with no seismic protection. These non-engineered buildings pose a great threat to the life of the local communities living in this high seismic area. Buildings which can stand up to earth tremors are important to protect human lives and minimize economic loss.

Local housing construction

The vulnerability of the local population is made more acute by the construction of their houses. There are an estimated 120,000 houses in the area and each year approximately 3,000 new houses are built (Ahmad and Abbassi, 2001). Over 90 per cent of the houses are non-engineered, built by the owners or local masons and have little or no seismic resistance measures.

The majority of the houses in this area are built with dry stone walls, made using mud and smaller stones to stabilize the larger stones. Wooden posts are often set into the walls to support a heavy roof, constructed from layers of grass, and birch bark on a layer of branches and topped with compacted clay soil. The branches lie on large wooden beams, which are supported by a number of heavy wooden columns in the centre of the house (see Figures 4.1 and 4.2). Large stones that span the widths of the wall provide some structural stability. Other construction types include cement blocks, adobe blocks, and stone construction stabilized with cement mortar (Sedky and Hussain, 2001). Even when cement mortar is used, it tends to be of low strength due to sub-standard aggregates and poor quality workmanship. The massive walls offer little resistance to ground movement, and combined with a heavy roof are a significant danger to life in an earthquake.

In the event of a major earthquake, the pillared construction would remain standing, but periphery non-masoned walls would eventually fall out of their framing. If the walls of the adjacent rooms (stores) fail to withstand the earthquake, the pillars would topple sideways causing the whole massive roof to collapse, burying the inhabitants under the heavy roof and rubble (Nienhuys, 2006).

 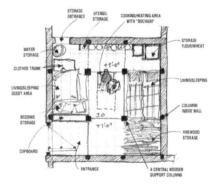

Figure 4.1 Heavy roof construction held up by wooden posts

Figure 4.2 Plan of traditional house construction

Analysis of the 2005 Kashmir earthquake showed three main reasons for the major destruction of housing and infrastructure.

1. Many of the collapsed buildings were constructed prior to the introduction of the building code in 1986, and were constructed via self-build.
2. Many of the buildings constructed after 1986 did not follow the code.
3. Elongated buildings with large openings performed poorly; in an earthquake area, square-shaped buildings are recommended. The concrete quality of nearly all constructions was substantially under the design values due to poor execution in the application of steel reinforcements, low quality of the aggregates and poor curing under hot or too cold local climate conditions (AKPBS, 2013).

In 2007, the Government of Pakistan supplemented the Pakistan Building Codes 1986 by adding the Pakistan Building Code – Seismic Provision 2007.

This provides specific codes for professional engineers and structural designers for the seismic design of buildings and building structures for the whole of Pakistan.

However, there are a number of challenges for the implementation of the Pakistan Building Codes in remote and mountainous regions like Gilgit-Baltistan, where over 90 per cent of the buildings are constructed by villagers themselves (self-help builders and artisans) themselves without involving engineers and professional designers. One of the major challenges is the absence of building control mechanisms in the form of a building control authority and legislation in Gilgit-Baltistan especially for the remote areas and villages.

Lack of education, capacities, affordability, and required infrastructure are major challenges for the endorsement of these codes in the region. For these reasons the codes should have been supplemented with simple construction guidelines in the form of manuals, books and other documents, preferably in local languages, well illustrated, and accessible to the local builders and artisans working during the construction of seismic-resistant and thermally efficient buildings and structures. The manuals do not need to explain the engineering principles behind the improvements. Besides these simple guidelines, hands-on training of artisans and demonstrations of the techniques and technologies in the field for education and awareness of the community are essential.

The Building and Construction Improvement Programme (BACIP)

The Aga Khan Planning and Building Service in Pakistan (AKPBS,P), through a social development programme, have been working on a project with the aim of creating resilient communities and building capacities to address issues of housing improvement and disaster risk reduction. It is not strictly a reconstruction project, as there is no specific disaster that triggered the programme, but has been motivated by the high seismic activity of the region, which suffers frequent medium-sized earthquakes. BACIP started in 1997 in the high mountains of northern Pakistan and is still being implemented at the time of writing.

Development of the programme

BACIP started as an action research project in 1996. The main aim of the research was to investigate the housing and living conditions in the area. Particular issues that were examined included thermal comfort in the cold climate, ventilation, and smoke pollution from cooking and heating. Seismic vulnerability was identified in the research aims as one of the issues with a significant impact on living conditions.

A participatory process was facilitated by BACIP, engaging community households using Participatory Rapid Appraisal Techniques, and 60 different issues were identified by the participants related to their living conditions such as issues of cold, damp, poor ventilation and smoke, and poor quality construction. Demonstration projects were developed from the research findings to explore and define responses and solutions to these issues. BACIP developed solutions around five thematic areas: thermal efficiency, illumination, indoor air pollution, cooking/heating, and seismic resilience.

> Wall, roof and floor insulation products as well as roof-hatch windows control leakage of warmth. Better smoke-free stoves, stabilized mud floors and wall construction techniques address the problems of dust and smoke. Lighting is addressed by the construction of windows, promoting energy efficient tube-lights and creating awareness about painting while improved wall and roof construction and water proofing techniques reduce dampness. BACIP's culturally sensitive and cost-effective toilets provide convenience to the house-dwellers while the shortage of space is addressed by in-house items such as bedding racks, kitchen cabinets, washing/cutting tables and better grain storage techniques. On a broader scale, the wall and roof construction techniques provide greater resistance to seismic shocks and create awareness about housing construction outside historical landslide and flood regions which reduce the danger to life (Sedky and Hussain, 2001).

The solutions or technical improvements were primarily developed by experts, however local community households had a chance to reflect on the performance of the solutions during their testing period. Feedback from participants in the trial period reverted to the process to further refine the solutions and improvements. The solutions were then placed in various houses to demonstrate their possible uses and to raise awareness amongst local households. The households selected as demonstration households were given the product for free but on condition that they used the products as per the BACIP guidelines, and that they allowed the neighbours to visit the house and observe the benefits of the product to inspire replication of the products in their houses. BACIP observed that on average, one demonstration project gave rise to ten replications.

As a result of this action research project, local households that had not participated in the trial started approaching the BACIP programme asking for the same solutions in their own homes. The next part of the project was to consider how to ensure wide take-up of these solutions. BACIP decided that the best approach was to figure out how to make these solutions available in the market. The rationale was that although the people in the area would not be reliant on an organization to facilitate the solutions, there would be an organic market-based take up of the ideas and products. The initial focus was on building the capacity of individuals or firms that were already doing related activities. BACIP supported the development of enterprises in the area to develop and market these solutions by funding entrepreneurs and training artisans in relevant techniques and to produce the materials as they were new and not available in the market place. Two specific criteria were applied: first, that the person must be in a similar business or trade; and second, that they are willing and have the capacity to become a BACIP entrepreneur. For example, there were already carpenters who could manufacture windows, so they were taught to make the BACIP roof-hatch windows and double-glazed windows. Similarly there were tin smiths in the market who already had some infrastructure in place and with additional skills they could manufacture the energy-efficient stoves.

As a first step, BACIP mobilized active entrepreneurs and manufacturers who were in a similar business, trained them in additional skills, and provided them with start-up finance to support the production of these new products or buy some extra tools needed for manufacturing these products. Skills training was also given in marketing and sales techniques. Loans were interest-free but required two guarantors; and in the majority of cases loans were repaid in full within the time. Repayment periods were generally 12 to 30 months depending on the size of the initial loan. The funding of entrepreneurs helped to generate a small industry in the area. BACIP developed some 60 housing solutions but there were about 10 products for which there was high demand and enterprises were established around these products. From an initial 15 grant-funded entrepreneurs in 2004, a market of over 50 enterprises has developed in the region (see Figure 4.3) (BACIP, 2013). As the market grew and the demand for BACIP products increased, people approached BACIP proactively wishing to undertake training, access start-up loans and become entrepreneurs. Those completely new to the sector received longer-term intensive support to ensure the success of their enterprise.

The final phase of the project was to move towards institutionalizing the products and lessons that had been shown to work. This involved working

Figure 4.3 A BACIP enterprise that is selling stoves, water warming facility

with local government to formalize the techniques in building guidelines. Building codes do exist in the area, but as the vast majority of the houses are owner built, the building codes are not followed. The building guidelines were more likely to be followed as they were far more user friendly than the codes, they were written in both national and local languages (building codes in Pakistan are written in English), and they had additional pictorial information. The guidelines were developed in partnership with the Pakistan Engineering Council and local universities. Still, an approach that just involved policing through codes and guidelines would not work on its own. Therefore, in parallel with technical advice, awareness-raising activities were organized, such as radio talk shows and radio drama programmes that incorporated technical themes. Radio is the most popular medium in the area and all households own one. Other awareness-raising activities included roadshows, brochures, and seminars and conferences with professional groups. The building principles were also institutionalized through partnerships with local universities to ensure the ideas and solutions are part of the curriculum for engineering students who will in the future be the planners and builders for the area.

The solutions were installed in about 40,000 houses in the area. Of these, 10,000 were directly supported by BACIP. The remaining 30,000 were installed as a direct result of the incentives and activities to institutionalize the awareness of the issues and facilitate the solutions through the market.

BACIP's comment on how this was achieved in practice:

> Once we developed a successful solution (techniques/technology/ product), we then trained a number of manufacturers and entrepreneurs around those products who will manufacture these products and sell them in the market. BACIP does the marketing through awareness and marketing programmes. People who are interested in those products and services either contact BACIP, who then connects them to these entrepreneurs, or people directly contact the entrepreneurs for services or products. The entrepreneurs / manufacturers are in turn paid by the households (personal communication with BACIP, 24 March 2014).

BACIP anticipated how demand could be assessed and met as the market grew. They assessed demands from communities through a representative, known as a 'resource person', in each village. There is at least one resource person supported by BACIP for each village with a population of 100 households. These resource people get a small percentage from the installation of products in one house. They work as a marketing force for the programme. There are over 200 resource people throughout the region.

Seismic resistance

The seismic risk mitigation solutions developed by BACIP included site planning advice to raise awareness of risky sites, techniques to make the roof construction lighter in order to reduce the risk to life of a roof collapse, and an innovative wire mesh wall reinforcement technique. The wall reinforcement is seen as the most effective seismic resistance technology in the construction of these types of houses to minimize risk to life in an earthquake. About 100 houses in the area were built by BACIP to demonstrate the wire mesh wall reinforcement techniques. However, this construction technology has been slower to replicate than the other issues due to affordability of the necessary work.

So far, the seismic resistant principles have been adopted in 253 buildings. The take-up of seismic-resistant building is expected to expand due to the raised awareness of disasters after the 2005 earthquake and 2010 floods, and the need to rebuild flood damaged houses due to the 2010 floods. AKPBS,P recently planned a reconstruction project for the flood-affected households of 2010 and some 500 households potentially will adopt these solutions in the rebuilding of their houses during 2014–2017.

There was an awareness of seismic-resistant construction in traditional construction in Gilgit-Baltistan, with historical evidence present in large ancient buildings such as the forts. Vernacular seismic resistance is evident in housing in the timber-frame structure locally known as Katore- or Daji-(Dhajji) style construction, where there is clear cross bracing offering resistance to ground movement.

> In the past, a wooden tie-beam construction was made in the length of the wall consisting of two parallel (fruit tree) wood sections connected to each other with short sleepers. In some cases, these lengthwise wooden strips have been applied in the corners of the walls only (Nienhuys, 2006) (see Figure 4.4).

This traditional construction is made out of wood which is unaffordable for construction due to over-exploitation of the available forests. Almost all of the 1.5 million people in the area directly or indirectly depend for their energy and construction needs on the forest, which covers less than 5 per cent of Gilgit-Baltistan. Wood is, therefore, too precious to use as a building material. Hence, there is a need to develop solutions which do not use timber construction.

One solution would be reinforced concrete buildings, which offer significant earthquake resistance- (better than that offered by wire mesh wall reinforcement) but they are very expensive for the majority of the local population. A traditional house in one of the villages would cost about US$100–$150 per m². A building strengthened with reinforced concrete would cost two to three times as much, at an unaffordable $300 per m². A more economical solution was needed, and one of the technological solutions developed during the BACIP programme was an innovative new construction: galvanized wire mesh to bind different layers of the building together (see Figure 4.5). It was cheap and easy to manufacture and BACIP ensured it was available in the market by developing enterprises around wire-mesh manufacture and distribution. This technique added only 10 to 15 percent to the cost of a traditional house.

Galvanized wire reinforcement is a technique that has been utilized to offer seismic resistance where wood is scarce and where good quality concrete is not achievable, either due to the difficulty of obtaining suitable materials or inadequate workmanship.

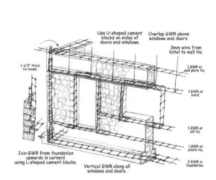

Figure 4.4 Traditional building with wooden tie beams

Figure 4.5 BACIP galvanized wire technology (GWR) for new construction

Galvanized wire reinforcement offers less seismic resistance than a reinforced concrete framing technology, however, in addition to the cost there are technical issues with reinforced concrete which can make it less desirable for use in remote areas. First, if quality control of the construction process is not carefully controlled the finished product is significantly weaker than the design expectations; Nienhuys suggests only half as strong. Second, reinforcement design is often seen to be faulty. These technical issues can only be overcome by a well-trained workforce, and quality control is difficult to implement with non-engineered and owner-built replication of the technology.

In addition, in high mountain areas such as Gilgit-Baltistan, effective curing of the concrete can only be achieved if the temperature is warm enough, and this time in the year tends to conflict with the time necessary to plant crops. Construction is, therefore, often carried out at unsuitable times.

The wire technology is primarily for non-engineered buildings which are built by poor families with very little or no engineering inputs. These are self builders and in the majority of cases the houses built are single storey. The challenge is that for the poor it is an additional cost to their budget for construction of a house. Microfinance programmes were implemented in partnership with a local bank for small-scale housing improvements and about 700 households have obtained such loans up to 2014. The repayment rate is over 95 per cent. However, for the ultra poor, who cannot even repay the loan amount, BACIP have not been able to come up with a solution except providing a high subsidy.

Looking back at the project

In 2013, the project was revisited to assess the performance of the interventions carried out by BACIP (see Figure 4). The focus of the visit was to review the aspects of the project related to reducing earthquake risk, but these initiatives also need to be seen within the context of the wider programme. Twenty out of the original 100 seismically resilient houses were revisited, selected through simple random sampling from the data available with BACIP. The households were evaluated on the five impact indicators: user satisfaction, beneficiary targeting, replication, technical performance, and livelihood impact.

Qualitative research methods were followed to gather information on how projects have changed since they were completed, and how that has impacted the life of the inhabitants and the wider community. Data was gathered from beneficiaries through in-depth interviews and focus group discussions. Findings of previous internal and external programmatic studies were used to corroborate the findings of field research study. Findings have also been substantiated with physical observation by the researchers, pictures, and other evidence where possible.

User satisfaction

In terms of user satisfaction, the results were very encouraging. Almost 100 per cent of the households said that the house has increased their safety and comfort and decreased the maintenance needed. The users also expressed the belief that they had a reduced chance of subsequent damage due to earthquakes.

> Retrofitting has been done in our house with the application of different earthquake resistant construction techniques such as BACIP wire. Other energy efficient and housing improvement products have also been installed. We know that these techniques have enhanced the resilience of our house and also it is energy efficient, therefore it is now more comfortable, safe, durable and secure. Now we feel that we will be safe in any earthquake (BACIP, 2013).

Beneficiary targeting

Out of the 20 houses visited, inhabited by some 180 people, 100 per cent were still occupied by the original owners, with no renting or letting (see Figures 4.6 and 4.7).

Replication

The uptake and replication of the seismically resilient wire-mesh building techniques has been slower to replicate than other BACIP initiatives such as

Figure 4.6 Shahbaz Khan, a disabled person and the original owner of the house, with his wife outside their improved house

thermal insulation. In private homes, this is mostly due to the affordability of the necessary building work. BACIP comment that households would like to build the new seismic-resistant technology into their houses but cannot afford to do it [BACIP reference]. As a result of the 100 houses built in the area demonstrating seismic-resilient building practice, 253 buildings have subsequently been constructed by communities and organizations replicating the use of these techniques.

Figure 4.7 External view of Shah Raise's house which was reconstructed using seismic-resistant technology, thermal insulation, and illumination techniques

BACIP has been working on making communities aware of the seismic risk in the area since 1996. However, after the Kashmir Earthquake of 2005, communities observed the destruction caused by the earthquake. BACIP also started radio programmes on creating awareness of the use of the BACIP wire technology in making their new houses safer. As a result of the awareness from the radio programmes and the experiences of the 2005 earthquake, many households have decided to build seismic-resistant houses. When the floods of 2010 destroyed and damaged about 3,000 houses in Gilgit-Baltistan area, some 500 households [BACIP reference] potentially will be facilitated in the construction of seismic-resistant houses under a reconstruction programme of AKPBS,P in 2015–2017.

BACIP also report much interest in seismic-resistant building techniques from public and community organizations who are building schools and health facilities and other communal buildings (see Figure 4.8).

Figure 4.8 Principles of seismic resistance and thermal efficiency have been adopted in Faizabad School

Technical performance

Since the time the seismically resilient wire-mesh building techniques have been used, no major earthquake has occurred. There have been medium-sized earthquakes, which have left the 20 houses surveyed unscathed. No cracking was visible when they were inspected.

There is additional evidence to support the strength of the BACIP house technology from a different type of disaster. A landslide in Attabad caused a blockage of the Hunza River and created a 20-kilometre long lake, inundating several villages, and causing the collapse of all houses with the exception of one house built using the BACIP wire-mesh technology.

There have been some concerns raised about the durability of the galvanized wire (Nienhuys, 2010) due to corrosion of the welded junctions in the wire. When galvanized wire is welded, the welding process removes the galvanization protecting the steel, and corrosion can occur. For gabions made out of this material, and exposed to the environment, the wire mesh is expected to last some 20–30 years. But inside the dry construction of a building, the mesh will corrode much more slowly, with a life expectancy of 40–60 years. A better solution is to use a wire mesh which is galvanized after welding, or a knitted wire where the manufacturing process does not remove the galvanic protection. These types of wire are estimated to last 100 years.

BACIP continues to advocate the wire mesh technology and has been working in collaboration with partners to achieve wider acceptance of the technique. The technical designs have been vetted and endorsed by university partners and the Pakistan Engineering Council which gives further confidence in technical performance. However, the technology has still not been declared an official engineering option and, therefore, will not be used by local authorities and so is unlikely to be widely used in urban areas. However, BACIP is continuing to advocate for its formal endorsement and approval of the building guidelines.

With increasing road access, it is likely that the use of reinforced concrete ringbeams bands as seismic resistance will increase, however the wire mesh technology was designed for the self-builders and those with the most limited resources: 'The GWR technology is not a cheaper substitute for good quality and slender reinforced concrete wall framing, but an option for people in remote villages having no access to finance or good quality reinforced concrete. New reinforcement methods are under development with flexible polypropylene and glass fibre mesh (netting) to overcome the possible doubts about the durability of the galvanized wire-mesh.' (Nienhuys, 2010: 3).

Livelihoods

The 20 households surveyed described financial savings in maintenance and said that the house was now an asset, not a liability. Better insulation and reduced indoor air pollution had resulted in savings on medical bills due to less frequent cold-related and respiratory diseases, as well as up to 60 per cent savings from reduced fuel consumption.

BACIP facilitated the development of 50 entrepreneurs for the manufacturing and sale of BACIP products. Many of these entrepreneurs have increased their income multiple times which has supported the education, health, and other living costs of their family.

Figure 4.9 Internal view of Noor Shah's house, where the family is using the energy-efficient stove to cook food

Initially, I was reluctant to become an entrepreneur and take any risk. But the professionals at BACIP encouraged me and gave me the necessary training that raised my confidence. BACIP also provided me financial support in the shape of start-up capital with orders for manufacturing of the products. Today, because of my business, I am able to send my children to English medium schools and give them quality education. Moreover, I am able to provide my family with good food, clothes and shelter. Today, my own parents are proud of me and are living with us a happy life. All my family members are glad that our standard of living is improving.

Respondent in BACIP survey (BACIP, 2013)

Lessons learned

This is a successful project with good results, albeit from a small sample, showing satisfied users, replication of the lessons outside the project, strong technical performance, and positive impacts on livelihoods. What was done in this project which made it work well? The Aga Khan Planning and Building Service in Pakistan have been working in Gilgit-Baltistan for over three decades. The organization has built on its learning of over three decades of continuous participatory projects carried out jointly with the local communities. They did not bring in ready-made technical solutions from outside but rather engaged the local community in the issue, mapping and developing local solutions with strong technical support. To minimize the loss to life and property, the project believes in pre-disaster preparation as compared to a major post-disaster response. It has, therefore, come up with solutions which will help to reduce damage in case of an earthquake. Buildings will be safer, technology and skills will be available locally for responding to a disaster.

The main thing that stands out when looking back at this project, is the ongoing work necessary to create the effective conditions which encourage people and organizations to see the sense in taking up the solutions for themselves, and particularly to pay the additional costs necessary to implement a resilient technology. Concurrently, there must be engagement with local authorities on building codes and the introduction of locally appropriate building guidelines; and finally, engagement with the next generation of planners and builders through embedding knowledge in the curriculum of relevant local training and higher education courses. This, if it gathers enough momentum, will create a whole culture of locally embedded safer building practice, and make the seismic resistance sustainable, not just for the life of the project but for many generations to come.

It was not enough to utilize participatory methodology to create and test and demonstrate workable solutions, in this case for the seismic resistance, the wire-mesh technology. For them to be replicated, it needed an understanding of where to intervene in the market to ensure the products were locally available and affordable, it needed both technical assistance and trained artisans to be locally available, and equally important, a recognition that market-based financial mechanisms needed to be available for people to access even the modest increase in cost necessary to implement the technology.

Design locally

When a reconstruction project or community building project is proposed, it is often the case that engineering solutions will lead the design. BACIP has learned that this direction is not the right way. Local, indigenous knowledge needs to be integrated in the design and planning process. The key learning is that external agencies or technical specialists can make improvements but should not change the way of living in the area.

Integrated design has a high impact

The seismic-resistant wire mesh technology was not the only improvement made to the houses by BACIP. Thermal efficiency, lighting, and indoor air pollution were also addressed, which gave a more significant impact to the whole standard of living of households and the cumulative impact was enormous. The design did not only concentrate on making houses seismic resistant but also made them thermally efficient by using insulation techniques. Other simple techniques and technologies were used to reduce indoor air pollution and illuminate the house. The impact was a reduction of up to 60 per cent in fuelwood consumption, a reduction in indoor air pollution, increased light inside the house, reduced labour of women and children for fuelwood collection, reduced labour of women for cleaning the house, and reduction in respiratory ARI diseases.

Make the technology accessible in the market

For replication to succeed this is crucial. There are three components to making technology accessible in the market. The first is that technical assistance is available in the region to ensure knowledge of resilient and sustainable technology is transferred through trained engineers and technical guidance. Second, appropriate building materials must be readily available to buy, in this case the local market was monitored, supply was increased and manufacture supported and increased in high-demand areas via capacity-building local enterprise. Third, knowledge is transferred to skilled artisans who can implement the technology to ensure safe homes are constructed.

Access to finance

The issue of access to finance is key to replication and BACIP has worked with local financial institutions to achieve this. According to a BACIP PEECH report (Janjua, 2013), some 700 households have already benefited from such loan financing and the repayment rate is over 95 per cent.

> One of the most successful and impressive partnership arrangements under the project was undertaken with the First Micro Finance Bank [FMFB]. The role of FMFB in providing financing for households to purchase the [BACIP] products was considered one of the most important aspects of ensuring the sustainability of the market chain. In spite of the pre-existing relationship between AKPBS and FMFB, as members of the Aga Khan Development Network (AKDN), FMFB was reluctant to participate in the project when the time came for their entry in 2010. Largely due to the massive defaults on loans that were occurring in the wake of the floods and large scale displacement of beneficiaries at the time, FMFB was averse to taking on any risky new interventions. Microfinance had not previously been offered for non-performing [i.e. financially unproductive], home improvement assets. They realized, however, that the [BACIP] products could be considered 'indirectly productive', as they saved the beneficiaries valuable cash, and that this freed up more of a beneficiary household's cash to make the repayments (Janjua, 2013).

Conclusion

BACIP started as a small-scale action research project in the Gilgit-Baltistan region of Pakistan aimed at identification of housing improvement issues and development of solutions, and has proved to be a highly successful development programme for improving the living standards of communities, building assets and creating livelihoods through the promotion of a safer built environment. The housing improvement solutions range from indoor air pollution to making buildings thermally efficient, illuminated, and safer from seismic hazard. The products and approaches have been replicated in Tajikistan which also shares a similar context. For the long-term sustainability and replication of its solutions, the project has made its solutions part of the mainstream market where skilled entrepreneurs manufacture and sell these products. It has not only contributed to making the existing buildings safer but also to job creation and improving the overall quality of life.

Through long-term engagement, support, technical advice and training, BACIP have begun a cultural shift in the manufacturing and construction sector in the region in favour of resilient and appropriate technologies ensuring safe homes for local people. The unique approach of the project is investing in making communities safer which will minimize the chance of loss of life and property and reduce the cost of reconstruction.

References

Ahmad, S. F. and Abbassi, I.K. (2001) *Fuel wood consumption practices, Interventions for fuel wood conservation at the household level and relative impact on conservation of forests and wood resources in the Northern Areas of Pakistan*, A joint study of World Wide Fund for Nature, Pakistan and Aga Khan Planning and Building Service, Pakistan.

AKPBS (2013) Proposed Seismic Resistant Construction Guidelines for Non-Engineered Buildings in Gilgit Baltistan and Chitral Region of Pakistan. Aga Khan Planning and Building Service, Pakistan.

BACIP (2013) Building and Social Housing Foundation (BSHF) sponsored study on the Building and Construction Improvement Programme in Pakistan. BACIP, Pakistan.

Janjua, K., (2013) *Promotion of Energy Efficient Cooking, Heating and Housing Technologies (PEECH) Final External Evaluation*, UNDP [website] <erc.undp.org/evaluationadmin/downloaddocument.html?docid=7454> [accessed 6 June 2014].

Nienhuys, S. (2006) *Galvanised Wire Reinforcement (GWR) Technology Earthquake Reinforcement for Non-Engineered Stone and Earth Constructions*, Huys Advies, Jaffna, Sri Lanka.

Nienhuys, S., (2010) *Galvanized Wire Reinforcement (GWR) Technology: Earthquake Reinforcement for Non-Engineered Stone and Earth Constructions When Good Quality Reinforced Concrete is NOT an Option*, Huys Advies Hilversum, The Netherlands. Available from <http://www.nienhuys.info/> [accessed 4 July 2014].

Sedky, N. and Hussain, A. (2001) *The Impact of BACIP Interventions on Health and Housing in the Northern Areas*, Pakistan Aga Khan Health Service, Pakistan (AKHS,P) and Aga Khan Planning and Building Service, Pakistan (AKPBS,P).

About the authors

Nawab Ali Khan is the General Manager of the Aga Khan Planning and Building Service in Pakistan (AKPBS,P) and has been associated with the BACIP programme for over 11 years. He has implemented large reconstruction projects in Pakistan in response to the Kashmir Earthquake of 2005 and the floods of 2010. He is a development professional with over 15 years of practical engagement in community development initiatives specifically in the sector of built environment.

Charles Parrack trained and worked as an environmental engineer, focusing on sustainability and community development. He leads the Postgraduate course in Shelter after Disaster at the Centre for Development and Emergency Practice (CENDEP), Oxford Brookes University. His research interests are based around the shelter and disaster areas. Charles is co-chair of Architecture Sans Frontieres – UK and has taught sustainable design studios in Architecture Schools in the UK. He is a Senior Lecturer at Brookes and teaches design and technology on the Architecture courses.

CHAPTER 5

India: Gandhi Nu Gam, an example of holistic and integrated reconstruction

Yatin Pandya with Priyanka Bista, Abhijeet Singh Chandel, and Narendra Mangwani

Abstract

Following the earthquake of 2001 in Kutchch, Vastu Shilpa Foundation and Manav Sadhna, non-profit organizations working in Gujarat adopted a Participatory Housing Approach (PHA) to reconstruction. The agencies took a leading role in housing reconstruction, while involving home-owners in the planning, design, and reconstruction of their settlement. A challenge in this was to retain the distinct identity and culture of the region, whilst providing shelter and regenerating livelihoods. The answer was a holistic rehabilitation project that focused not only on housing, but also on infrastructure such as water and sanitation, amenities including a school and shrine, and the support of small enterprises. The sustainable use of local resources and revival of local crafts were a key component of this.

A post-occupancy survey in 2013, discussed in this chapter, reveals the largely positive impact on the socio-economic and cultural fabric of the community. The village economy has grown, largely thanks to the stimulation of traditional crafts, and the vernacular built form is accepted and continued by a trained new generation. Critical to the success of the project was its understanding of housing as part of a larger, integrated community with unique social, cultural, historical, and economic relations, rather than a mass commodity.

Keywords: Post-disaster reconstruction; Participatory housing approach; Self-help housing; Holistic development; Cultural regeneration; Vernacular architecture

Introduction

On 26 January 2001, a 6.9 Richter scale earthquake struck Gujarat causing devastating destruction including the death of 13,800 people and the injury of 167,000. Approximately 1.2 million homes suffered damage and 344,000 were completely destroyed along with the complete razing of hospitals, healthcare facilities, schools, and water supply systems. Three hundred villages were flattened and 7,600 villages experienced some form of damage. Over 90 per cent of the casualties and physical damage in the state of Gujarat occurred in Kutchch.

http://dx.doi.org/10.3362/9781780448398.005

The post-disaster reconstruction effort in Gujarat has garnered praise worldwide for adopting a 'people-centred' approach to reconstruction and, therefore, generating high user satisfaction rates. Implemented in partnership between the government, the private sector, NGOs, and the beneficiaries themselves, a range of approaches were employed by the 75 agencies operating within 272 villages in Gujarat. In Ludiya village located in Kutchch, Manav Sadhna, a non-profit organization led the reconstruction effort with technical support from Vastu Shilpa Foundation for Studies and Research in Environmental Design (VSF), also a non-profit research organization. Closely working with the community, VSF and Manav Sadhna adopted a participatory housing approach (PHA) to reconstruction, where the agencies took a leading role in housing reconstruction, while involving home-owners in the planning, design and reconstruction of the house.

The overall plan involved the rebuilding of 455 dwellings in close partnership with the affected communities. The total project cost was US$630,000 of which the community contributed 20 per cent through the contribution of land, local materials, and labour. A range of partners including Manav Sadhna, GMDC, and the Council for Advancement of People's Action and Rural Technology (CAPART) financed the project. The Rejuvenate India Movement was involved in providing training for workers in the affected villages. Of the 455 dwellings, 20 were built in a newly relocated village named *Gandhi Nu Gam*, which will be the focus of this chapter.

Longitudinal study of reconstruction: Methodology

In partnership with the community, Footprints E.A.R.T.H (Environment Architecture Research Technology Housing) conducted a longitudinal impact study in 2013, 12 years post-implementation of the built fabric. This involved measured drawings, photo documentation, and informal key informant interviews and consultations. The study documented changes in the built fabric particularly with respect to materiality, technology, and usage. Structured and semi-structured interviews were conducted to measure the larger social, economic, and cultural benefits of the project to the community and region.

This chapter will illustrate the findings of the research, beginning with an overview of the post-earthquake context. The second section presents a post-occupancy analysis of the socio-spatial changes categorized into five themes: user satisfaction, beneficiary targeting, replication, technical performance, and livelihood. The conclusion distils the critical lessons and based on this, offers suggestions to inform future post-disaster reconstruction projects.

A contextual overview

Prior to the earthquake, a total of 1,800 people (350 Harijans (lower caste Hindus) and 1,450 Muslims) lived in Ludiya village, 70 km north of Bhuj, 500 km from Ahmadabad and 3 kilometres from Khavda. The settlement was divided into clusters based on religion. Due to a shortage of land, the Harijan community was further divided into two clusters. The economic livelihood of the region was generated from carpentry, agriculture, animal husbandry, and crafts-based occupations. The region is characterized by its prevalent cultural traditions, rich textile and wood craft, unique earthen architecture, colourful attire and desert ecology.

The settlement is organized in clusters consisting of varying sizes of dwelling units depending on the size of the family. As shown in Figure 5.1, each unit consisted of two key components: the *bhungas* as the primary living space and the *chowki* as the rectangular building used for cooking. Semi-open space existed in between the primary structures to cater for multiple usages. The various components were built within an elevated plinth and surrounded by a twig fence. The *bhunga*, a traditional circular dwelling typology of the region, attests to the rich crafts-based culture and intricate woodworking found in the local communities (see Figure 5.1).

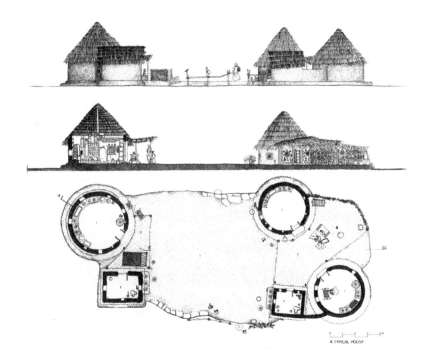

Figure 5.1 The traditional settlement layout of the region with *bhungas*, *chowki*, and a plinth

Post-earthquake context (2001)

The post-disaster situation

In the aftermath of the earthquake, VSF and Manav Sadhna conducted surveys to assess the socio-economic and physical damage in Ludiya village

Figure 5.2 After the earthquake, Ludiya, 2001

(see Figure 5.2). The physical damage included key public amenities, such as schools, religious centres, community buildings, the electric grid, and the water supply system. Prior to the earthquake, no secondary schools or health facilities existed in the region. After the earthquake and prior to the intervention, members of the community of Gandhi Nu Gam were migrating to nearby cities due to the collapse of their income source, which had been heavily reliant on the building industry.

Before the earthquake, communities throughout the region were mostly building *pucca* (permanent) houses using modern building techniques of stone masonry, crudely bonded with cement mortar. Due to adoption of these unfamiliar construction techniques, the *pucca* homes were not properly designed and were vulnerable to major damage. A baseline survey conducted by VSF documented that 36 out of 84 (42 per cent) of *pucca* buildings were razed to the ground and many suffered irreparable damage whereas only 5 out of 31 traditional *bhungas* were destroyed.

A holistic reconstruction process

Since the infrastructure in the region collapsed overnight, in order to create new development sympathetic to lifestyle, environment, and culture, certain guiding principles were agreed to achieve socio-culturally appropriate, environmentally sustainable, and functionally efficient plans:

- To develop a holistic plan informed by the social and economic needs of the community along with the needs for physical rehabilitation.
- To engage and empower the affected community by providing skills, training, and support through the reconstruction process.

- To revive the socio-cultural traditions of the local region by drawing inferences from the traditional settlement patterns and indigenous dwelling typology.
- To achieve environmental sustainability through adoption of appropriate, local, and sustainable technologies for construction.

The reconstruction process followed a series of steps to arrive at the final plan specific to each community of the affected region as listed below.

1. Establishing community trust and rapport
Due to the devastation wrought by the earthquake and the sudden trauma faced by the community, the issue of trust was paramount in the reconstruction process. A good social rapport needed to be established from inception to ensure the vigorous participation of the stakeholders in the long rebuilding process. Thus, an on-site office was set up in the village to achieve this goal, which also helped gain a closer understanding of the village and to begin the ongoing community consultation process (see Figure 5.3).

2. Site relocation
As the Harijan community had reached the physical limits of its land and was fragmented in two separate clusters prior to the earthquake, an opportunity to bring the two communities closer together was identified. The Muslim community bartered their land to the Harijan community for relocation into a new settlement. The new site was selected collaboratively, on a central location near the main road of the village. The topography of the site also possessed a depression in the landscape for the creation of a pond.

3. Participatory settlement planning
A tool in the form of a 'simulation kit' designed by architects allowed villagers to visualize and participate in the site planning process (see Figure 5.4). A Styrofoam base model with site features and roads along with colour-coded papers of different plot sizes was used. The villagers were allowed to freely move and tag the plot clustering of their preference. Through continuous consultation, a site layout was generated with plots based on kinship, clans, and social relations. The architects, then, incorporated the climatic, topographic, and spatial logic into the plan. An on-site consultation followed, pegging the plots and the *bhunga* locations, until an agreed site plan was generated. After the layout was finalized, the information was translated into a scaled plan to begin the process of physical reconstruction.

4. Designing the individual house
As noted in the housing assessment survey, the traditionally built circular *bhungas* had survived the earthquake with minimal damage. Due to their socio-cultural appropriateness, thermal properties, low cost, and familiarity of construction technology, the typology was chosen as the building strategy for the project. As a result, VSF was able to implement the project on a wider scale with a limited budget of approximately $300 per *bhunga*. Some changes were introduced in the traditional *bhunga* design, including the overhang sizes and introduction of stabilized soil blocks instead of soil for wall construction.

Figure 5.3 Consultation with the community   **Figure 5.4** Simulation kit showing the layout of plots as described by the inhabitants

5. Self-help construction

The rebuilding process was perceived as an opportunity to provide training and tools to the local community to revive the local economy (previously reliant on the built industry). A fixed amount was provided to each household to set out the plots and excavate the foundations. A soil-block-making machine was bought in India to produce stabilized soil blocks with local soil. The *bhungas* were built using stabilized soil blocks, mortar, wooden windows and doors with local manual labour. The roofs of the *bhungas* were constructed with a wooden frame covered by a thatch layer, whereas for the *chowkis,* clay tiles were used as roofing material. To define the compound and outdoor spaces, a plinth was constructed above a raised platform. The inhabitants then freely decorated the interior and exterior of their houses (see Figures 5.5 and 5.6). The total time taken for the reconstruction was four months, and prior to relocation, the community lived in their older settlement.

A holistic reconstruction plan

An integrated approach to settlement planning was adopted across the project at all sites, equally prioritizing the provision of communal and private spaces within the settlement. Public amenities for the Ludiya region were constructed including institutional, religious, and communal facilities. Educational amenities included three *anganwadis* (nurseries), three pre-primary schools, and one secondary school along with playgrounds and school amenities, costing around $35,500. The damaged religious facilities were renovated and temples and mosques were added to the community infrastructure. As no health facilities existed prior to 2001, a health sub-centre was established with medical supplies and professional health-care visits on a regular basis. Retrofitting of the *Panchayat* (Village council) building was done to restore it to working conditions. Other amenities included a grass bank, community crafts centre, and markets, costing around $8,000.

Due to the harsh desert climate and problems of water scarcity, watershed management became integral in the planning process, therefore construction of check dams, deepening of existing ponds, building of wells and underground

Figure 5.5 Painting of the façade of the *bhunga* indicating high sense of belonging

Figure 5.6 Personalized interior of a household showing its socio-cultural appropriateness

water tanks was done for around $64,600. Additionally, a water management committee for repair and reconstruction was also created. Agricultural land was provided to support farming and local food security within the region. Public infrastructure included open spaces, roads, and solar powered streetlights.

A total of 455 structures were built within Ludiya out of which 60 were relocated to Gandhi Nu Gam. Within this settlement a pond, 150 hectares of agricultural land and public amenities including schools and a temple were created in addition to the homes. The traditional settlement pattern, as shown in Figure 5.1, was followed. Latrines were introduced within the unit to promote better health practices. The sizes and shapes of the plot varied with each household to meet the family's requirements.

Analysis of post-occupancy changes (2013)

The current plan of the settlement shows additions, expansions, and adaptations on various scales. The road infrastructure has been paved, reflecting the overall transport and economic expansion of the village. Although significant land-use changes have not occurred, the communal infrastructure has grown with the addition of a public market space (*otlo* in the local language), a guesthouse and a crafts centre. The open spaces and communal spaces have continued to be maintained and utilized. Commercial spaces such as retail shops and tourist lodging have cropped up within the village (see Figures 5.7, 5.8 and 5.9).

2001

Figure 5.7 Site plan of Gandhi Nu Gam, 2001 as created in consultation with inhabitants
Legend 1. School, 2. Temple, 3. Well, 4. Lake, 5. House # 1, 6. House # 2

Figure 5.8 View of Gandhi Nu Gam, 2001 after rehabilitation

As per the changing needs of the community, the spatial typology has expanded as listed in Table 5.1. The total number of built structures has doubled since the initial construction in 2001, while 4 out of 33 *bhungas* were destroyed due to lack of maintenance or heavy rainfall and replaced. In terms of design, new ways of reconstructing the *bhungas* in hexagonal shapes using

Figure 5.9 Site plan of Gandhi Nu Gam, 2013
Legend 1. School, 2. Temple, 3. Well, 4. Lake, 5. House # 1, 6. House # 2, 7. House # 3, 8. Guesthouse, 9. Arts and Crafts Centre, 10. Agricultural land, 11. *Otlo* (public market)

new technologies are emerging, which may not be best suited for the region and earthquake resistance, but show the innovative attitude of residents.

Work sheds for carpentry or woodworking have expanded from 8 to 37 structures and are now located by the road for maximum exposure. This is an indication of the revival of home-based income generation. Simultaneously, semi-open spaces have been added to all of the homesteads to cater to multiple usages from sleeping to eating, cooking to working. The toilets that were added

Table 5.1 Changes in spatial typology

Spatial Typology	2001	2013
Bhungas	33	33 (-4 + 4)
Chowkis	12	18
Work-sheds	8	37
Semi-open spaces	1	30
Toilets	18	24
Water tanks	0	2
Total	72	144

to the dwellings as a new concept in 2001 continue to be used and maintained. The construction of attached toilets is also evident in new facilities for tourists and may indicate a rising standard of living for the residents related to the economic growth.

The data collected in the longitudinal study includes a detailed physical survey of the changes in all 21 households within the village. Out of this, three households were chosen to illustrate the changes in detail.

House #1, Acharbhai Maya Marwada

Located by the main road, this is the first visible house of Gandhi Nu Gam and also the largest. The household takes full advantage of the exposure by locating a work shed and tourist lodging by the road. The family members are mostly artisans, wood craftsmen who also work with local architects to build *bhungas* on contracts; they also keep some animals. Alongside household chores, the women do embroidery and textile work.

Figure 5.10 Exterior of the house, 2013

Two new *bhungas* replicating the original technique have been built, however, an attached toilet has been introduced. The old *bhunga* has been transformed into a retail space for exhibiting textiles and selling souvenirs. The addition of semi-open spaces, work sheds and *chowkis* is evident, even outside the plot line, to cater for the needs of the growing family and tourists. Tourism has become a major income source for the family and in turn has enabled the family to maintain a traditional lifestyle (see Figures 5.10 and 5.11). Where the original reconstruction used stabilized soil blocks, thatch, and clay tiles, now cement plaster and flooring, asbestos cement, GI and bamboo roofing have been added to the material palette.

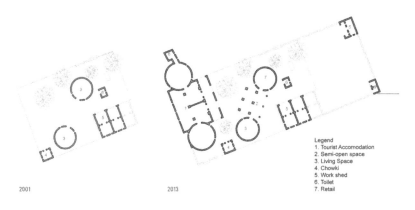

Legend
1. Tourist Accomodation
2. Semi-open space
3. Living Space
4. Chowki
5. Work shed
6. Toilet
7. Retail

2001   2013

Figure 5.11 Site plan of House # 1

House # 2: Puna Bhai

Located towards the west of site, this household is a new addition due to marriage and family expansion. The current head of the household was a teenager in 2001, and was trained in *bhunga* construction when building his own family house. He now works as a wood craftsman and *bhunga* builder, whilst his wife does textile work.

Figure 5.12 Puna Bhai's house (L-shaped form)

Although the homestead consists of the typical core units (*bhunga, chowki,* semi-open spaces), the spatial organization completely departs from the original pattern. An L-shaped plan is introduced in this typology (see Figure 5.12) with the *bhunga* located in the centre with two rectangular wings flanking both sides (see Figure 5.13). Unlike other households, the plinth is limited to the building footprint rather than surrounding the outdoor spaces. Although the *bhunga* adopts the traditional circular shape, the roof is a pentagonal structure with clay tiles. Additionally, this construction also uses modern materials such as bricks, stones, and cement.

Legend
1. Living Space
2. Semi-open space
3. Work shed
4. Toilet

2001   2013

Figure 5.13 Site plan of House #2

House #3: Rajivbhai Marwada

Located in the Southern part of the settlement, this household consists of four family members. Primary sources of income include carpentry, *bhunga* construction, and embroidery, with additional income coming from agriculture and tourism.

Figure 5.14 Women working in semi-open space

One of the circular *bhungas* was demolished owing to damage by heavy rain and reconstructed in a hexagonal shape covered with clay tiles. The construction techniques replicate the previous methods by using stabilized soil blocks, as the owner is a skilled *bhunga* builder. Semi-covered spaces and work sheds have been added to meet the needs for carpentry workshop and embroidery working areas (see Figures 5.14 and 5.15). Where the original reconstruction was covered by thatch and tiles, asbestos cement and GI sheets have been added as roofing, as well as IPS (Indian Patent Stone) flooring and RC (reinforced concrete) columns. The male inhabitant expressed his satisfaction with the homestead: 'We are happy with our house. The good part is the *chowki* that provides us with an area to work. My wife does embroidery and weaving there with other females of the family.'

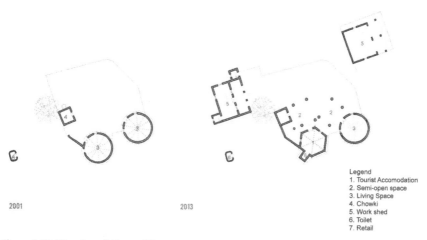

Legend
1. Tourist Accomodation
2. Semi-open space
3. Living Space
4. Chowki
5. Work shed
6. Toilet
7. Retail

2001   2013

Figure 5.15 Site plan of House #3

Impact analysis: five key themes

User satisfaction

As revealed by the survey, the highest level of satisfaction of the project was related to the location and neighbourhood planning of the settlement with close proximity to the pond, road, and other amenities. The location by the road also provided economic opportunities and access to nearby facilities. The provision of health sub-centres and ease of transport access to the health centre has enhanced access to medical care for previously prevalent diseases such as tuberculosis.

Second, the beneficiaries were satisfied with the layout of the plot and the freedom it provided for them to expand. The provision of a large open space with the core-housing unit allowed for flexible expansion and adaptation; familiarity with the building technology and the settlement pattern has allowed this. The functions of the spaces have continued to change with relocation of the kitchen, living, and commercial spaces. The introduction of latrines was widely accepted and replicated in new constructions. The need for maintenance of the initial construction and the easy accessibility of modern materials has led to an infiltration of new construction methods, which are unfortunately prone to damage if another earthquake strikes.

Beneficiary targeting

At the time of the earthquake, the current community of Gandhi Nu Gam was completely destroyed and as the beneficiaries lived in harsh conditions with no agricultural base or roots in land or location, they had considered moving closer to clusters of their relatives and communities at large in the region, while many were ready to migrate to nearby cities for possible economic opportunities. This not only meant that they had to leave their ancestral place but also, since the village is located near the border, it would have had an impact on security issues like infiltration.

The whole cluster of the Harijan community of Ludiya was re-organized on a new site while Muslim homes were upgraded in-situ in the existing village, which was by the community's mutual agreement. Right from the beginning, holistic rehabilitation was planned and, therefore, rather than emergency shelters, final homes along with collective amenities and infrastructure facilities were included in the development vision.

The reconstruction plan needed to revive the economy of the region so that people could continue staying at the same place. Thus making investments in further training of builders, supporting local artisans, and establishing connections to markets resulted in economic diversification and empowerment, as anticipated. Today, all of the original beneficiaries are still living in the village with the exception of one family that migrated to Bhujodi.

Replication

The popularity of *bhungas* as tourist accommodation has resulted in replication of this traditional typology into tourist-related facilities within Kutchch. Within Gandhi Nu Gam, a few new constructions including the guesthouse, a school, and household dwellings have adopted the circular building typology, with some changes. Translation of the vernacular typology has also occurred with the building of hexagonal *bhungas* or hexagonal roof structures. Training the youth in traditional building construction has provided them with skills for replication of the technology. The interiors of the new buildings, even when rectangular in form, continue to be adorned with customary artefacts and accessories. The community has appropriated the outdoor spaces as well with spaces for worship. The basic layout of the spaces and plot size provided during the initial reconstruction phase is flexible enough to grow and expand.

As a result, 90 per cent of the households show expansion and adaptations within and even outside the plot lines as per their specific requirements and needs. Notably, the flexible site layout has facilitated expansion of not just the residential infrastructure but also the communal infrastructure. And there is clear ownership of the housing process, as one inhabitant states: 'We have added this semi open space, as per our budget. We were given these two *bhungas,* which we are using, and this *chowki.* We have also added a workshop for my carpentry work in front. We were given a big plot, so I add as per my need and budget.'

Even in new construction that completely departs from the circular form (such as House #2), the spatial layout consists of the basic unit of core structures: two living spaces, a latrine and semi-open spaces within an elevated plinth. The relationship between indoor and outdoor spaces reflects a similar traditional clustered strategy. Continued usage of the stabilized block press is seen, because it enables cheap production.

Due to the success of the project in Gandhi Nu Gam, the same participatory design strategy was used by VSF in 14 other villages in the region for rehabilitation. With each settlement, the appropriate architecture and pattern was chosen and adapted with the community resulting in different site plans, unit plans, and material choices (see Table 5.2). The addition of different elements, including smokeless stoves, was also adapted in many settlements.

Table 5.2 List of materials used in extensions, 2013

Type of materials used	# of times used
Sandstone walls with cement	6
Brick and stone	1
Stabilized mud-brick	9
Cement wall plaster	1
Asbestos cement roofing	4
Clay tiles	14
Bamboo roofing	3
GI sheets	6
Cement floor	8
IPS flooring	4
RC columns	5

Technical performance

In the 12 years which have elapsed since the initial construction, four *bhungas* have collapsed due to heavy rains and poor maintenance. Similarly, the residents have expressed problems with continuously maintaining the thatch roof covering, which needs to be replaced once every three years for Rs. 4,000 (roughly $75). The soil walls also need to be lined every year and as a result have been changed to cement plaster. Therefore, modern materials are incrementally replacing the traditional building material range. Significantly though, the range of buildings and layout caters to the changing thermal and occupational needs of the community for different times of the day, different seasons, and different years, as expressed by one respondent: 'The construction of the *bhunga* keeps the inside cool during the days. We use the *bhunga* during afternoons and sleep outdoors in the summer and during winters we sleep in the *bhunga* and work outdoors in [the] afternoon.'

Livelihoods

Today, a typical household of Gandhi Nu Gam has greater economic leverage. The flexibility of the plan enabled adaptation to new economic pursuits, shifts in transport, and the expansion of tourism and cottage industries. The use of the *bhunga* has expanded beyond serving as a household dwelling. For example, some *bhungas*, initially meant for living, have been transformed into tourist lodges, retail shops for handicrafts, or storage spaces. The shift in use suggests a versatility and adaptability of the design. It also reflects the comfort of the local people with the technology and building method. The distinctively decorated *bhunga* enabled cultural tourism in the Kutchch region and deepened identity and branding of communities like Gandhi Nu Gam. During festivals the nightly tariff can be as high as 1,200 rupees ($20) with the average off-season price being 500 rupees ($8). This is a major supplementary source of income that is catalysing more diversified skills and a service-based economy. In fact, providing skills training was a major element of the reconstruction process. Prior to reconstruction, women were only responsible for household chores. Today, they also earn income through embroidery and textile work. It has had important after-effects in terms of creating a new cadre of specialized builders confident enough to adapt the design. As one respondent states, 'We have a great opportunity for earning as these *bhunga* forms attract a lot of tourists visiting this region. We have even added toilets for their use. We get a good income from this home-stay facility. As I was involved in construction in 2001, and I know the construction technique now, I even go to nearby places to build *bhungas* as this has become a preferred room type for home-stay facilities in Kutchch.'

Villagers currently engage in diverse economic activities including tourism, crafts, textiles, carpentry, agriculture, and building (see Figures 5.16, 5.17 and 5.18). Women have been trained in embroidery and given a platform to exhibit and display their work to potential buyers.

The location of the water source close to the settlement has significantly reduced the workload of women in house hold chores. The participatory design approach used during reconstruction provided the community, and especially women, with the ability to negotiate their interests and improve

Figure 5.17 Woodworking

Figure 5.16 Textile work

Figure 5.18 Carpentry

attributes of their lives. Even after the reconstruction, they have expanded the settlement and continued to negotiate and dialogue with NGOs accordingly to get new stages of support.

Conclusions

In post-disaster housing, the focus is usually on 'short-term', 'instant', 'rapidly deployable' shelter solutions. The case study of Gandhi Nu Gam offers an alternative argument for a holistic, long-term, and participatory housing strategy which does not limit itself to the construction of houses, but also extends towards future socio-economic sustenance of beneficiaries. Deeply embedded in a 'people-centred' approach, the project has successfully enabled the community to regain their strength and confidence to recover through the process of reconstruction. The provision of an integrated plan ensuring diverse opportunities for income generation has halted rural out-migration of youth in the region. The support of the government in boosting cultural tourism in the region has further revived the cultural heritage of Gandhi Nu Gam. As a result of the efforts, today the community has almost doubled in size and is much stronger than it was even prior to the earthquake.

In contrast to other housing approaches adopted in Gujarat, the PHA adopted in Gandhi Nu Gam has received a high satisfaction rate. A study conducted by Samaddar and Okada (2006) illustrates the subtle differences between PHA and 'owner-driven' (ODR) or 'cash-based' models, where the owners are fully responsible for the design and construction of their homes. Although the ODR model has received a higher satisfaction rate for the design of the individual dwellings, the communal infrastructure was found in a dilapidated condition, unlike the state of the communal infrastructure in Gandhi Nu Gam. It is evident that the PHA strategy was constructed with equal emphasis on public and private amenities. The process of choosing the site, bartering with the Muslim community for an appropriate location, planning the neighbourhood layout, and collaboratively working on the communal infrastructure has instilled ownership of both public and private spaces. Locational elements such as proximity to the road, water resources, agricultural land, and public amenities became important to ensure the holistic development of the village. Today, the community has continued to add to the public amenities including the construction of a market, guesthouse, arts and crafts centre, and a new school.

The rehabilitation process was also taken as an opportunity to deepen existing socio-cultural values and revive the traditional built heritage of the community. The construction and personalization of dwellings done by users themselves has instilled a sense of belonging and identity to a common heritage. As a result, the community has continued to appropriate space and make innovations such as the introduction of hexagonal *bhungas* or roofing assembly, attached bathrooms, and L-shaped plans. In doing so, the traditional and modern architectural languages are mixing together in hybrid ways. The success of this conservation effort also relies on the proliferation of cultural tourism, which has in turn helped conserve not just the built heritage but also the crafts-based culture. Thus, this study makes a strong case for continued research of appropriate architecture in general and not only for post-disaster reconstruction.

The innovations introduced during the reconstruction process have been widely accepted and adopted by the beneficiaries. The introduction of latrines, health-care facilities, and water sources has ameliorated the state of public health in the community. The food security of the region has been bolstered due to the provision of agricultural land and water harvesting strategies to support it. Similarly, to catalyse environmental sustainability, solar panels were installed and local materials were used for construction. Even in the new rectilinear constructions, the use of the soil block technology is still evident today.

Fundamental to the success of the project is the economic regeneration of the Gandhi Nu Gam community post-earthquake. Its location along the main road was critical in ensuring the economic linkages of the community to the larger region. The reconstruction process was also understood as an opportunity to strengthen the economic activity of the region by providing training and building skills, which could lead to new means of income generation. Similarly, the understanding of a house as a centre for economic activity is embedded in the reconstruction design and approach. The flexibility provided by the plan where spatial typologies have expanded to incorporate carpentry, woodworking, embroidery, tourism, and retail opportunities, was a critical element of the project from which to learn.

Finally, certain key lessons can be attained from this longitudinal study for future rural and urban reconstruction projects. Rather than viewing post-disaster shelter only through the lens of physical protection, housing should be understood as a part of a larger, integrated community with unique social, cultural, historical, and economic relationships. Critical to this process is valuing the agency of the community to lead the project through planning of the site, choosing neighbours and putting their own stamp on their personal dwellings. In doing so, the community as a whole is able to recover and gain self-confidence after experiencing loss and trauma, which necessarily accompanies the post-disaster situation.

> A town is made of buildings, but a community is made of people; a house is a structure but a home is much more. The distinctions are not trivial, nor are they sentimental or romantic: they are fundamental to the understanding of the difference between the provision of shelter which serves to protect and the creation of domestic environments that express the deep structures of society.
> (Oliver, 1981: 39-42)

References

Footprints E.A.R.T.H (Environment Architecture Research Technology Housing) (2013) *Post-Earthquake Rehabilitation – Post Occupancy Evaluation 2013, Gandhi nu Gam – Ludiya: Partnering with People, Rebuilding Rural Kutchch with Community Participation,* Footprints E.A.R.T.H, Ahmedabad.

Oliver, P. (1981) 'The cultural context of shelter provision', in I. Davis (ed.), *Disasters and the Small Dwelling,* Pergamon Press, Oxford.

Samaddar, S. and Okada, N. (2006) 'Participatory approach for post-earthquake reconstruction in the villages of Kutchch, India', *Annuals of Disasters* 49: 197–205.

About the authors

Yatin Pandya is an author, campaigner, researcher as well as practising architect with his firm Footprints E.A.R.T.H., a graduate of CEPT University in India with a Masters from McGill University in Canada. He has written articles and books on architecture, particularly on the use of space.

Priyanka Bista has over five years of experience in the fields of architecture, rural development, and community planning. Currently working for CMAP, a non-profit in the informal settlements in Port Harcourt, Nigeria, she is overseeing the construction of a community centre and developing strategies for participatory upgrading of informal waterfront settlements. Her research and design experiences have included projects in Nepal, India, Nigeria, Toronto, and Haiti.

Abhijeet Singh Chandel is involved in research in Architecture and Urbanism, with a primary interest in spontaneous housing and informal settlements.

Narendra Mangwani is an urban designer and architect also involved in urbanism and housing research.

CHAPTER 6

Challenges for sustainability: Introducing new construction technologies in post-tsunami Sri Lanka

Eleanor Parker, Asoka Ajantha, Vasant Pullenayegem, and S.Kamalaraj

Abstract

This chapter evaluates the impacts of Practical Action's owner-driven reconstruction project after the 2004 Indian Ocean tsunami. After an initial participatory housing needs assessment 175 houses were built. In addition, training was provided to over 1,000 people to develop capacity in rat-trap bond, a new technology to the area which was often partnered with a concrete filler slab roof, also a new technology. Revisiting a small selection of beneficiaries five years later showed that all houses were generally structurally sound and still assets to their original owners, but there were quality issues with some; internal heat linked to flat concrete roofs and poor application of ventilation indicated a need for improved quality monitoring during construction. The extent of replication was disappointing given that a third of the budget was for capacity building in the new methods; there was little evidence of either extensions or new builds. If agencies aim to use a resilient technology that is easily replicable by local people after the agency leaves, then an evaluation of technology options in the local context and involvement of the community in the choice of technology is required – which will likely result in the rejection of entirely 'new' technologies. The original programme focused narrowly on the provision of houses; greater benefit would have been gained if infrastructure, services, and livelihood support had been fully integrated.

Keywords: Reconstruction; tsunami; Sri Lanka; owner driven; construction technology

Outline of the disaster and its impacts

The Indian Ocean Tsunami of 24 December 2004 brought a previously unseen scale of damage to property, infrastructure and the environment, and loss of life concentrated in the 12 coastal districts in the south-east and west of Sri Lanka. The tsunami most affected the poorer regions of the country, hitting hard the vulnerable fishing communities living close to the shore in simple

http://dx.doi.org/10.3362/9781780448398.006

houses and those engaging in informal tourism related activities. The tsunami is estimated to have caused 35,322 fatalities and over 21,000 injured. Seventy-five percent of the fishing fleet was lost and around 25,000 acres of arable land affected; overall 150,000 lost their main source of livelihood. People made more vulnerable (widows, orphans, and affected elderly) were estimated in the region of 40,000.

Massive losses were experienced in infrastructure and the built environment. Figures vary but some 100,000 homes were estimated to have been damaged or destroyed (ADB et al., 2005). The scale of the disaster and media coverage of the subsequent impacts resulted in large funds being donated and made available to aid agencies for permanent housing reconstruction. This brought with it layered challenges for NGOs: targeting and coordinating reconstruction plans and quickly demonstrating fulfilment of promises made to donors.

Post-disaster reconstruction context and Practical Action's project

From November 2005, all post-tsunami rebuilding organizations, institutions, and projects were placed under a single government umbrella agency, with a centralized approach to decision-making which allowed little room for consultation, particularly with beneficiaries and local government (Lyons and Amarasingh, 2006). Rice (2005) argued at the time that there was little possibility of representation at the local level.

Government and large NGOs focused on donor-driven programmes (DDP) which initially intended to supply more than half of the new housing on land allocated and planned by central government, the remainder were to be developed via owner-driven reconstruction. House plans and construction followed government guidelines. Relocation of many Sri Lankans to new sites was necessitated by the enforcement of a coastal exclusion zone; a 100 m buffer zone in the west and south and a 200 m buffer zone in the east and north. However, between 2005 and 2006 the extent of the buffer zone was reduced by the government as a result of the reluctance of fishing communities to relocate, pressure from tourists and commercial sectors, the scarcity of land for resettlement, and scrutiny of the scientific basis for selecting the limits of the zone (Ratnasooriya et al., 2007). This significantly impacted the planned reconstruction, resulting in delays and shifting the balance of DDP and owner-driven programme (ODP) housing since fewer people were now forced to move. The number of ODP houses could now increase significantly to 80,000, as people were now able to reconstruct on their own land (Lyons and Amarasingh, 2006). Delays were also experienced in the reconstruction of housing for 'squatters' without legal land rights. Pre-tsunami, many local authorities had not ejected 'squatters' because they contributed to the informal economy locally. Practical Action reported anecdotally that nearly all who did not legally own property before were eventually provided with reconstructed houses.

Large-scale DDP housing reconstruction at such new sites did not always integrate provision of essential services and links to local infrastructure. Beneficiaries were often identified after completion so the scope for adaption to beneficiaries' needs was limited. Twenty months after the tsunami, only a fraction of the expected DDP houses had been constructed; 12,000 of the 33,000 promised, fewer still were connected to essential services and occupied (approximately 9,000) (Lyons and Amarasingh, 2006).

Lyons and Amarasingh (2006) reported that many large NGOs were unable to meet housing reconstruction targets via the DDP. In their report, they detailed that the underlying reasons for the slow progress were many fold. For reconstruction at such an unprecedented scale, complexities were not well understood at a national or agency level. There were also problems associated with the national strategic development approach, the identification of and securing of rights to suitable land, lack of experience in NGOs of constructing permanent shelter in a post-disaster context, shortage of materials and cost inflation, limited skills in resilient design and skilled trades locally, related issues with quality and standards (Practical Action, no date). Suffice to say, by mid-2005 it was becoming clear that DDP reconstruction did not appear to provide the 'quick fix' expected.

Where householders had access to land in areas permitted for reconstruction and development, NGOs were able to enter into partnership with local beneficiaries to undertake owner-driven programmes (ODP). Such an approach was the focus of Practical Action's (then ITDG) activities. ODP are often by their very nature undertaken on a much smaller scale than DDP; emphasizing co-produced design through participatory needs and capability assessments with local communities and specifically direct beneficiaries. Since Practical Action is not an implementing organization, it relies on partnering with capable community-based organizations (CBOs) and NGOs to undertake projects in line with Practical Action's principles.

Practical Action is a development agency that has 40 years of extensive experience in promoting the use of cost-effective and environmentally and people-friendly technologies that contribute to sustainable development. Since 1998, the agency has also been actively engaged in advocacy, action research, and methodological development to promote a more holistic approach to disaster risk management and development, particularly in South Asia. Out of their regional office in Colombo, Practical Action Sri Lanka had previously focused on livelihoods and income generation, mini and micro-hydro initiatives, small wind and solar power systems to serve villages off the national grid, rural road construction, and rainwater harvesting.

Practical Action's post-tsunami strategy evolved during the early stages of their intervention work as a result of their preliminary research on the effectiveness of DDP and ODP housing projects, leading them to focus on advocacy for participatory resilient and sustainable reconstruction approaches or developmental reconstruction, as Lyons and Amarasingh (2006) refer to it, through partner organizations.

The specific objectives of the project were stated as:

1. The promotion of the use of cost-effective, environmentally friendly technologies and adopting participatory and inclusive planning and design to post-tsunami housing reconstruction.
2. The strengthening of capacity, skills and knowledge that are essential for high-quality reconstruction.

In terms of housing reconstruction, the intention was that Practical Action's integrated housing services would facilitate the construction of around 150 houses using a participatory approach and appropriate technologies as a demonstration of good practice principles in ODP. The intention was that beneficiaries would be responsible for making most decisions and make a contribution toward their implementation. Such an approach would form a platform for capacity building and knowledge transfer at several levels, for example, skills development in construction in the local community and in developmental reconstruction for other NGOs via training courses and briefing documents, etc.

Practical Action wanted to ensure that their housing projects met the lifestyle needs of the beneficiaries but could also mitigate common natural disasters and reduce future vulnerability of occupying families. Their houses also needed to be environmentally sustainable and readily replicable. How could this be achieved effectively?

Community engagement and participatory design

Based on existing post-tsunami impact assessment data, initially Hambantota in the south and Ampara in the east were identified as locations suffering significant impacts and so were the focus of Practical Action's efforts. However, it soon became clear that Hambantota was receiving an oversupply of assistance so Practical Action shifted its focus to other areas in the south. Having developed its outline strategy, Practical Action proceeded to develop partnership agreements with, and the support capacity building of, local organizations, facilitate workshops with potential beneficiary communities, and construct demonstration houses using the chosen technologies.

Practical Action implemented many small-scale projects across the affected area. The case of the follow-up site is typical. This project began with the demonstration of technologies and approaches with an affected community in Matara in the south. The houses built as a result earned the acceptance of the beneficiaries and community. The Matara Trust, a local implementing agency had undertaken to fund the reconstruction of the damaged houses of this community. The first few houses in any location served as a training ground for a crew of masons who then went on to construct the rest of the site with ongoing quality assurance and monitoring. Practical Action built more houses together with the Matara Trust, while training their technical cadre and engaging the local community in construction to build their skills on specific masonry techniques. Eventually, the Matara Trust took over the rebuilding and built over 100 houses in affected communities, while Practical Action played only a technical backstopping role. The experience was expanded to other districts subsequently; mainly to Ampara, Batticoloa in the east, and Hambantota and Galle in the south with positive community response, capacity building of agencies and local individuals in construction. A number of manuals and guidance and training documents were developed during and after the reconstruction process covering topics such as rat-trap technology (Practical Action, n.d.b), designing for access for those with disabilities (Practical Action, n.d.c), and quality assurance in housing (IHSP, 2006).

Practical Action developed a rapid housing need assessment methodology. They endeavoured to ensure sessions were facilitated by experienced and multidisciplinary staff with a balance of technical, social, and development skills that would support the project going forward. A requirement was that workshops were attended by roughly equal numbers of men and women and women were given equal voice in their contribution. Careful consideration was given to timing meetings, given that many had to balance work and caring for children. Practical Action proactively sought to engage with tsunami-widowed and tsunami-displaced women marginalized by economic, ethnic, and gender factors, running bespoke activities for these groups. Members of affected communities were asked to sketch their pre-disaster homes and evaluate current housing needs and desires in terms of layout, orientation, cultural and religious requirements, and options for personalization and adaptation. Where participants needed additional support conceptualizing their needs and drawing their sketches, help was provided.

Constraints of the reconstruction project were made clear to participants in terms of building and plot size and details of the rat-trap and filler construction technologies that were to be used to ensure expectations were managed fairly. Participants were also briefed on potential improvements that could be incorporated into their new homes; chimneys associated with kitchen hearths to improve interior air quality, benefits of solid waste management and composting toilets. In other projects, small-scale interventions which provide direct benefit to only a proportion of the affected community can result in conflict and resentment. Significantly, Practical Action made clear their rationale for targeting specific households within a community so as to minimize negative consequences.

In comparison with the DDP programmes where externally designed and imposed standardization dominated, government regulation stipulated a living room, two bedrooms, a kitchen, and a toilet. Practical Action's participatory workshops were able to incorporate into the design a range of local needs and preferences in terms of housing with provision made for the privacy and safety of children. Gender perspectives were found to be important for siting kitchens and toilets; in one community, men expressing a preference for a removed detached toilet block but preferring a unit close to or attached to the house (UN, 2007). In some rural locations pre-disaster, outside kitchens and detached toilets were the norm and whilst some people were happy to have a reconstructed home that incorporated a kitchen with associated chimney and an attached toilet unit, others maintained a desire for the more traditional layout. Muslim communities requested separate bedrooms and halls for men and women and those with a disability expressed a need for facilitated access.

Workshops were not generally found to be overly onerous or time consuming. Nor did they result in an impractical range of design requirements. The project manager and team members arranged for meetings with a cross section of communities before designing type plans. Interestingly, synthesis of community input often resulted in two or three designs being drawn up by Practical Action that met the NHDA standards, remained within budget, and were found to be acceptable to all. These basic designs could be modified to meet individual needs by the use on-site of computer-aided design (CAD); allowing designers to sit with households, discuss any smaller changes (e.g. changing positions of openings, modifications of room uses), and record changes very quickly. Each household was given a copy of the plan most appropriate for them for approval before construction began. That, together with the small range of technology options, meant that costs were kept down. Prudent use of funds meant that by 31 March 2007, 163 houses had been constructed rather than the predicted number of 150.

Lyons and Amarasingh (2006) identified that relatively few beneficiaries were willing to volunteer a contribution in terms of time and money to reconstruct their own houses. They cited example cases of householders' unwillingness to monitor and manage the setting of concrete foundations and supervise labourers working on their house. Only where staff were very experienced in community mobilization did community participation in the building phase peak. They suggest that the rapid influx of aid and people and competition amongst NGOs for beneficiaries resulted in a challenging level of passivity amongst the community and Practical Action's long-term presence and developmental approach assured higher than average levels of participation compared to many other ODP projects.

Appropriate technologies?

The rat-trap bond approach which came to dominate Practical Action's post-tsunami housing projects had become an established method over two decades in India (see Figure 6.1). In 2003, Practical Action had initiated a small pilot project adopting the technique combined with filler slab RCC roofs in Nikaweratiya in northwestern Sri Lanka; the approach was not previously known in the post-tsunami project area, although traditional masonry construction was used. The pilot in the northwest demonstrated potential cost effectiveness and possibilities for replication elsewhere in Sri Lanka. The system requires standard 8" or 9" fired clay bricks. As a result of the 'rat-trap' arrangement of the bricks, construction using this method required approximately 20 per cent less bricks and cement and associated cost savings when compared with the usual approach. Where walls were greater than 15' in length, brick columns were integrated to support the roof span. Generally, an additional single story could be supported on the flat roof without the use of reinforced concrete columns and beams. There were clear benefits to the use of one type of masonry technology for the reconstruction project – sourcing, quality control, and training in the use of the materials was simplified.

Figure 6.1 Rat-trap technology, used in India and introduced by Practical Action post-tsunami after an earlier trial in north-western Sri Lanka

However, quality control of materials presented a potential problem; ensuring that the clay-fired bricks met the minimum strength requirements, that the mortar maintained the required ratio of cement:sand (1:6) and comprised clean good-quality sand. Also key to structural integrity was to ensure that the corners and junctions of the walls were properly constructed and vertically reinforced. Sound foundations were also crucial, particularly if an upper story was to be added and/or ground conditions were soft or likely to be wet. Practical Action recommended compacted dry rubble foundations.

Practical Action recommended 'filler slab' roofs as they were less heavy than conventional reinforced concrete (RC) slabs and more economical in terms of materials and cost, they also allowed vertical extension and a potential place to escape flood water. A grid of steel reinforced bars was filled with low cost filler material such as rejected Calicut tiles, clay pots or broken cement blocks and covered with concrete. Reinforcement spacing was specified and limited the maximum unsupported span which could safely support its own weight and an additional storey. This reduced the use of timber to support clay tiled roofs and allowed for vertical extension. Cost savings for roofing was quoted by Practical Action as approximately 40 per cent. GTZ reported in December 2006 that the Practical Action approach was taking somewhat longer (approximately 75 per cent of housing complete by 2006) than those projects utilizing traditional masonry houses largely due to the need to build the capacity of local masons in the new technology. Practical Action also noted that in practice filler slab concrete roofs took longer to build than tiled roofed houses as time had to be allowed for the casting and curing of the concrete. Some beneficiaries opted for tiled roofs from the start and later a decision was made to build the final houses with tiled roofs in order to keep within the allotted time frame (see Figures 6.2 and 6.3).

Figure 6.2 and 6.3 Rat-trap technology topped with a tile roof (house on the left) and a flat roof showing ventilation holes in white below (house on the right)

Each house was provided with energy-efficient stoves and a proper sewerage system, pipe-borne water supply, and basic electrical fittings. Practical Action had not explicitly set about integrating services into the housing reconstruction project; however, since completion all householders have access to potable water, with most plots having wells on site. Power was available from the local power supplier; householders who could afford it obtained power at the time they occupied the houses. Others did subsequently as and when they could afford to do so. Parallel projects developed services and facilities such as unpaved gravel roads and rainwater harvesting systems (Practical Action, n.d.a). Vehicular access was available to all resettlement sites but analysis of access to transportation and links required for livelihood activities was lacking for the follow-up.

End of project situation

Lyons and Amarasingh (2006) interviewed stakeholders and beneficiaries of the projects across southern and eastern districts as part of the end-of-project report. They identified that whilst the process had been slow to start the number of houses constructed increased rapidly. It was also identified that beneficiary engagement in decision-making and design was genuinely active rather than the tokenistic participation observed with some NGOs. Where homes had been reconstructed by beneficiaries in partnership with Practical Action, householders were pleased with the quality of workmanship and building performance in terms of insulation, potential for extension, and standards of solidity.

Existing or aspiring masons and carpenters had benefited from training and increased opportunity in the booming post-tsunami construction sector. As of November 2006, some 740 people had participated in education programmes and on-site training for skilled masons, carpenters, and labourers and awareness programmes in safe design principles and brick production, and quality monitoring.

At the end of the reconstruction period (2006), many householders were reportedly aware of livelihood strategies specific to their location, local resources and the help available. Many were engaged in supplementary income generation, for example a village largely dependent on fishing was supported by another Practical Action project to establish a boat repair facility. In another, productivity of small-scale farming was improved via a rainwater harvesting project. The local NGO network, of which Practical Action was just one member, had other members who were supporting livelihood development and diversification via micro-loans, for example.

In terms of Practical Action's wider advocacy remit, Lyons and Amarasingh (2006) found that Practical Action struggled to influence the tokenistic participatory approaches of some larger NGOs; whilst some other agencies chose to adopt the rat-trap technology after knowledge transfer, relatively few chose to integrate the participatory approaches. However with local implementation partners, levels of application of participatory process were much higher.

The end-of-project review detailed the influence of Practical Action's technical expertise. Numerous third and private sector organizations sought advice on sustainable and cost-effective technologies promoted by Practical Action but evidence of replication was lacking. Most successful projects were those where Practical Action was the primary technical partner with responsibility for supervision. Practical Action also promoted sound construction management and appropriate technologies at a national level to NHDA and RADA with GTZ (German government development agency) as an intermediary. By the end of the project, a range of appropriate technologies were to be included in Sri Lanka's Chamber of Construction Industry approved syllabus. However, by end of 2013 adoption was still to happen.

Follow-up study methods

Two of the previous Practical Action project sites were selected for the follow-up study representing both Tamil and Sinhalese speaking communities; Madihe village in Galle district from the southern province and Maradamunnai village in Batticaloa district in the eastern province. More respondents were sought from Batticaloa district since a larger component of the housing project of Practical Action was carried out there.

Respondent groups at the two locations were: (i) direct beneficiaries – householders; (ii) state bodies (local authorities); (iii) local builders (contractors and CBOs); and (iv) local masons (not necessarily those trained by Practical Action). A structured survey questionnaire was administered face to face by the follow-up team to beneficiaries in the village. Focus groups (single gender groups and mixed, adults and teenagers) were also undertaken with beneficiaries; this was supplemented with key informant discussions with community members to provide more in-depth information from householders. Interviews were also undertaken with local authorities, local builders, and masons.

Follow-up study findings by theme

User satisfaction

Analysis of the householder survey shows that the majority of the sample population were happy with their reconstructed homes. Whilst not detailed in the survey or focus-group responses, the project team reported that the majority of the residents felt that their houses were safe and the consensus was that many were happy that their houses withstood recent cyclones and floods. However, it is not clear what magnitude those recent events were relative to possible extremes that may be experienced in the region. Practical Action's housing needs assessment meant residents were satisfied with the layout and function of their homes.

Residents acknowledged that improvements could be made to the appearance of their house; most agreed that they would have preferred to have the walls of their houses plastered in order to be compatible with other types of houses in the vicinity. Rat-trap bond technology with unplastered walls has become viewed as a poor people's technology for housing particularly as the majority of beneficiaries were from vulnerable groups.

Plot size and building design was such that extension of houses was feasible and householders noted it with appreciation. Those who could afford to do so extended vertically (if they had a flat roof) or horizontally. Those who had not extended either could not afford to do so or had no need as reconstruction had given them a bigger and better house than they had before. Most commonly, the kitchen was extended or additional storage space was added. None utilized rat-trap but rather wood or concrete block to build (see Figures 6.4 and 6.5).

The beneficial presence of project managers and technical officers during reconstruction was recognized by nearly all householders. Unfortunately the system of funding adopted by funding agencies did not anticipate post-reconstruction needs such as maintenance and associated continued engagement after reconstruction. Within the available budget, Practical Action prepared an illustrated handbook (in English, Sinhala, and Tamil languages)

Figure 6.4 Galle house extension constructed with concrete blocks

Figure 6.5 Galle house with boarded extension

that was given to beneficiary households. It detailed basic maintenance procedures but residents had rarely followed the advice. The project team reported that generally the standard of maintenance was low, but this was not specific to their reconstructed houses. Some houses had been repainted and many had planted gardens. Ironically, all but one householder felt there had been money-saving benefits as a result of reduced maintenance requirements. It appears the householders and the project team may have differing views of appropriate and affordable maintenance requirements.

In both locations, green space and vegetation was present but its value to the community was unclear. There was no evidence of the development of any social spaces or community amenities by the beneficiaries directly or by trained masons using rat-trap technology. Many of the shared community buildings were constructed by local authorities through government tender procedures. Therefore, local authorities are bound to use the masonry technologies which are in government manuals; rat-trap bond is not included.

Beneficiary targeting

Beneficiaries of the project were those landowners most badly affected in areas receiving little attention from other NGOs. Practical Action proactively sought to engage with the disabled, tsunami-widowed and tsunami-displaced women marginalized by economic, ethnic, and gender factors. Five years on, the majority of the original householders still live in their reconstructed house. Several families who benefited gave their houses to their daughters as dowry when they married. These houses remained in the extended family and were not sold. One beneficiary sold his house a year or so later to invest in a textile business, he was now residing at his parental home. All had been paying local authority taxes that facilitated the provision of electricity and water supply.

Technical performance

Walk-through surveys by the follow-up team demonstrated that all houses were structurally sound. Failure to repaint walls with a recommended low-cost sanding sealer/thinner mix has resulted in deterioration of exposed brick wall surfaces. The degree to which failure to adhere to the prescribed maintenance regime may impact structural integrity long term is unclear – the consequences of long-term poor maintenance of this recently introduced technology, which may act as an incentive with commonly used technologies, are not evident yet to householders.

Houses with the necessary ventilation benefited from noticeably cooler interiors than houses constructed using popular masonry cement blocks. However, a significant minority of beneficiaries living in houses with flat concrete roofs commented on high interior heat caused by the omission of vents which allow hot air trapped in the upper reaches of rooms to escape. Several residents also commented that smoke re-entered the kitchen from the fire in the hearth. Quality control of materials and construction was clearly a problem that had long-term negative impacts for householders. The follow-up team commented that the partner organization in Madihe had not sufficiently engaged skilled masons and carpenters, so not all houses met the expected quality of construction. This is clearly a key challenge for the introduction of a new technology where new skills need to be developed rapidly and applied consistently.

Awareness about safer building had been created by technical personnel at the time of construction, but the interviewees could now not recall specifics. Knowledge of good quality, safe construction (not specific to rat-trap) appears not to have been widely retained. There was a consensus that houses have withstood subsequent cyclones and floods. It is worth noting that mechanical strength and behaviour testing (De Silva and Sooriyarachchi, 2008) undertaken post construction, revealed that rat-trap bond had less than half the strength of two brick English bond masonry. Whether these characteristics are sufficient to resist the range of hazards in the area is unclear.

Standard toilet systems were generally adequately maintained as residents were used to their operation and maintenance requirements. However, there were many instances where those who were provided with dry compost toilets (where water table levels were high) and were unaccustomed to their operation, did not use them as specified, and as a result many toilets were converted to storerooms – again ensuring effective use and providing additional ongoing support is something that agencies introducing new technologies must address if sustainability is to be achieved.

Replication of the technology

None of the interviewees could recall examples of rat-trap technology being used locally post-project, nor had they used it themselves even in an extension.

Nearly all the beneficiaries had limited incomes – occupants of houses were daily wage earners (often seasonal) – whose incomes were quickly spent as they were earned without the capacity to set aside funds for extending their houses. In a few instances, where the occupants had more stable and higher incomes, such as painters or carpenters, and were also familiar with house construction, houses were repaired, repainted or extended. Extensions were always carried out using less expensive masonry and roofing than was used by Practical Action. Concrete blocks were preferred to 9" fired clay rat-trap bond masonry, and corrugated asbestos cement or galvanized metal roofing were preferred to clay tiled roofing. Affordability was the underlying factor for extending/maintaining or not extending/maintaining houses. Cement block masonry for walls and corrugated roofing sheets are popularly viewed to be cheaper and construction workers are very conversant with working with these materials. Funding agencies had no provision to assist beneficiaries after the houses were handed over to occupants.

Respondents did comment that the current local masons were not sufficiently skilled in rat-trap bond masonry. Experienced masons trained after the tsunami were either not residing in the vicinity or had reverted to using conventional technologies. This was disappointing as approximately one-third of the budget had been used for training. Initial cost, i.e the cost for the skeleton structure of the house wherein a family can reside (rather than total cost), is the primary determining factor in people's choice of construction technology. Whilst the cost of materials for rat-trap technology might be 20 per cent less it is reported to be labour intensive, and labour costs in Sri Lanka are high and tend to increase exponentially in post-crisis reconstruction. Rat-trap methods are therefore not viewed as a cost-effective technology.

Subsequent replication by local authorities or their agents is impossible since rat-trap technology was never successfully integrated into government specifications or covered by the 'district pricing committee', and therefore, rat-trap bond technology cannot be included in tender documents. Rat-trap technology was also not included in the Vocational Training Authority and Technical Colleges curriculum.

Livelihoods, empowerment, and resilience

Home enterprise requirements were taken into account at the house design phase where possible, with some householders willing to sacrifice a bedroom to be able to run small grocery outlets, tailors, and barber shops from home. Such sacrifices should be placed in the context that the single-storey house designs developed by Practical Action deliberately allowed for future vertical and horizontal extension where plot size allowed. A consensus amongst respondents was that living in a Practical Action reconstructed house also meant reduced maintenance requirements which enabled them to devote time to earn from their livelihoods outside the home. Those with improved kitchen ventilation also commented on reduced incidence of illness and healthcare costs.

A small but significant number of beneficiaries in Maradamunnai (Batticaloa) sold their houses. All were from the Muslim community who are traditionally business oriented. They lived in their houses for about 18 months, after which they decided to sell their houses so that they could invest in business. Had Practical Action adopted a more integrated approach where all the needs of the community were addressed, more beneficiaries may have stayed long term.

Lessons learned: Were appropriate technologies implemented?

The participatory housing needs assessment approach was effective and meant that ODP housing reconstruction could provide suitably designed homes for those that owned land in an appropriate timeframe and did not result in unnecessary complication, delay or proliferation of design options. Skilled facilitation and articulation of project constraints are crucial to ensure satisfaction.

The technical expertise of Practical Action meant improvements to the interior conditions of houses were integrated into the house designs. Redesigned hearth and chimneys meant improved air quality over pre-tsunami houses and rat-trap walls and filler slab roofs, where correctly constructed, improved interior thermal comfort.

Whilst there is little doubt that well constructed rat-trap technology houses are strong and durable, there is an element of uncertainty as to the performance of the technology in the full range of hazards to which coastal Sri Lanka is exposed. Strength tests were not undertaken in Sri Lanka until after the reconstruction project, although behaviour had been assessed during its use in India. Rat-trap technology was found to have a significantly lower compressive and flexural strength than traditional masonry methods. No attempt was made to evaluate the behaviour of the rat-trap technology in the context of cyclone wind, storm surge, tsunami or regional flood loading. So householders' perception of safety has not been confirmed for extreme events.

However, when implementing a new technology, the need to up skill trained craftsmen is a considerable challenge and links to the rate of construction and quality control and monitoring during and post construction–essential to ensure durability, interior comfort, and user satisfaction. A process must be in place that quickly identifies lapses in quality, identifies causes, and finds appropriate solutions such as additional job training. It is important that those who supervise construction, particularly of new methods, are thoroughly conversant with architectural detailing and have an in-depth understanding of resultant impacts of failure so as to ensure that quality control encourages attention to detail. More effective quality control and monitoring were required here to ensure the new technology was consistently implemented to an appropriate standard.

Whilst rat-trap technology uses approximately 20 per cent less material, labour costs and the limited number of skilled builders means that local people view the actual cost as higher than that of the commonly used cement block technologies so they are unlikely to invest. In the original design, a flat roof which took longer to construct was chosen to facilitate vertical extension but some seven years later very few householders had extended. They did not need to extend or could not afford to, particularly to replicate the rat-trap method and secure skilled builders to implement it. An assessment of 'appropriateness' must surely take a holistic view of the socio-cultural, economic, and environmental context. Had workshops been held to scope views on a range of building technologies, many of these issues might have been foreseen and avoided. An analysis of householders' economic conditions means the more commonly used building approaches may have been deemed the preferred option, perhaps with some adaptation for improved performance. A more thorough participatory assessment of the proposed technology may also have identified other issues such as beneficiaries' perception that unplastered houses are for the poor. If replication of resilient and sustainable technologies is a priority, tradeoffs may have to be made between resilience and sustainability.

In this case, an ongoing presence of the implementing agency or a representative (and ongoing funds) to ensure maintenance and replication of rat-trap in houses and composting toilets is clear. It may also have supported rendering of brickwork as suggested by beneficiaries and remediation of houses with low levels of maintenance which would not only remove stigma but also provide effective protection of exposed brickwork from the elements. The benefits and challenges of introducing a new technology (short-term and long-term) should be assessed alongside those of adapting existing technologies before committing to a new technology. If the benefits of the new outweigh the alternatives, then an ongoing presence of the implementing agency is more likely to ensure it becomes a technology of choice locally and that the quality of materials and construction is consistently good.

Conclusion

The project undoubtedly provided appropriately designed houses to the majority of beneficiaries more quickly than many other reconstruction projects did. Key to this was targeting those with access to land and the effective participatory housing needs assessment and flexible design which allowed families to 'tweak' the standard design houses to meet their needs and preferences. If Practical Action had taken a more holistic approach, couching housing needs more explicitly in the broader context of sustainable livelihoods and disaster resilience, then the participatory design, aligned service provision, and livelihood projects could have better served those who benefited from a Practical Action house. However, the case for rat-trap technology as an appropriate and locally replicable technology of choice is not proven. If a range of technological approaches had been reviewed in a participatory way and consideration given to adapting popular construction methods for improved performance, durability, and sustainability, a technology that is more likely to be replicated without agency intervention may have been defined. In terms of rat-trap technology, further evaluation of strength and durability in the context of local risk assessment is needed. In addition, an integrated and comparative assessment of social, economic, and environmental sustainability in terms of material production, supply and construction, and lifestyle is required. If rat-trap technology is to become a technology of choice, its adoption into building codes and Vocational Training Authority and Technical Colleges' curriculum is essential. Only then, with ongoing support from agencies and the state, will it be a successful locally appropriate technology.

References

Asian Development Bank (ADB), Japan Bank for International Cooperation (JICA), and World Bank (2005) 'Sri Lanka - 2005 post-tsunami recovery program: Draft preliminary damage and needs assessment', JICA [website] <http://www.jica.go.jp/english/news/jbic_archive/japanese/base/topics/050131/pdf/srilanka.pdf> [accessed 23 May 2014].

De Silva, S. and Sooriyarachchi, H.P. (2008) 'Strength assessment of "rat-trap-bond" masonry panels and "calicut-tiled" filler slab system', prepared by Faculty of Engineering, Ruhuna University for Practical Action.

Lyons, M. and Amarasingh, S. (2006) 'Building back better: from aspiration to reality. housing advocacy report for Practical Action South Asia office', Practical Action [website] <http://www.library.practicalanswers.lk/all-categories?task=view&id=313&catid=72> [accessed 23 May 2014].

IHSP (Integrated Housing Service Practical Action) (2006) 'Quality Assurance Method for Post-Tsunami Housing. Training Module', IHS in partnership with German Development Cooperation (GTZ)

Practical Action (no date a) 'Walls using the "rat-trap bond" technology. Technical brief', Practical Action <http://practicalanswers.lk/PDFs/tb4.pdf> [accessed 23 May 2014].

Practical Action (no date b) 'Construction of houses with accessibility facilities for persons with disabilities', Humanitarian Library [website] <http://www.humanitarianlibrary.org/resource/construction-houses-accessibility-facilities-people-disabilities-0> [accessed 22 May 2014].

Practical Action (no date c) 'Recovering with dignity', Practical Action Regional Office, Colombo.

Ratnasooriya, H., Samarawickrama, S.P., and Mamura, F. I. (2007) 'Post-tsunami recovery process in Sri Lanka', *Journal of Natural Disaster Science*, 29(1):21–28.

Rice, A. (2005) 'Tourism and tsunami recovery process: A second disaster?' Report by Tourism Concern.

UN (2007) 'Gender perspective: Working together for disaster risk reduction. Good practices and lessons learned', UN International Strategy for Disaster Reduction [website] <http://www.unisdr.org/we/inform/publications/547> [accessed 21 May 2014].

About the authors

El Parker is Principal Lecturer in Natural Disasters at the Centre for Disaster Management and Hazards Research and Associate Head for the Department of Geography, Environment, and Disaster Management at Coventry University. She is an engineering geologist by background with a PhD in the impacts of climate change; her research covers multi-hazard and risk assessment, community-based early warning, and community preparedness for resilience and adaption to chronic and acute risks. She has been a lecturer for 15 years and course director for the undergraduate programmes in disaster management at Coventry for 10 years and has also undertaken numerous research and consultancy projects in that field.

Asoka Ajantha is a civil engineer with more than 10 years experience in owner-driven housing construction projects in northern and eastern provinces in Sri Lanka. Asoka has also worked in Pakistan and India in post-disaster contexts.

Vasant Pullenayegem has over 50 years of experience in architecture and construction, 35 of which as an independent architectural design consultant. Since January 2005 he has been working as a housing consultant on post-tsunami housing and a senior trainer with Practical Action. He is currently engaged in researching design and construction methodologies to mitigate natural disasters in the South Asian region as well as in energy- and cost-saving techniques in the design and construction of tropical houses.

S. Kamalaraj is a technical officer having nearly eight years of experience in owner-driven housing construction projects at grassroots level in the eastern province in Sri Lanka.

CHAPTER 7

Reconstruction in Vietnam: Less to lose! Examples of the experience of Development Workshop France in Vietnam

Marion MacLellan, Matthew Blackett, Guillaume Chantry, and John Norton

Abstract

Vietnam is very susceptible to natural hazards. Development Workshop France (DWF) has been working in Vietnam since 1989 following a massive typhoon which hit central Vietnam four years earlier, integrating efforts on post-disaster reconstruction programmes to promote safe construction. Since then DWF has endeavoured to ensure that these programmes are locally informed, using locally adapted technology to support sustainability within the affected communities. This chapter evaluates several of these reconstruction programmes and identifies a number of recommendations for the implementation of such schemes in the future.

Keywords*: Disaster risk reduction; Cyclone resistant construction; Safe housing; Community development*

Introduction

Vietnam is a long coastal country bordered by the South China Sea, with the majority of its population living in a narrow coastal strip of land and within the river deltas of the Red and Mekong rivers. Rice cultivation and water management are central to Vietnamese society, bringing prosperity but also sometimes ruin. Around 70 per cent of its 89 million people live in rural areas. The Vietnamese economy is growing but great inequalities remain between rich and poor. The susceptibility of the country to natural disasters has hampered the development process and it is estimated that the country's vulnerability to natural hazards is rising as a result of climate change, with these impacts costing 5 per cent of its GDP in net terms in 2010, and an estimated 11 per cent in 2030 (total GDP in 2012: US$141.7 billion) (DARA, 2012; WHO, 2013). Consequently, the Vietnamese population are accustomed to living with disasters, such as floods and storms. The central region of Vietnam experiences five to seven extreme disasters annually, particularly typhoons and associated floods, the frequencies of which have been increasing in recent years (CDRH, 2012). In this environment, poor communities face life-threatening risks; the

http://dx.doi.org/10.3362/9781780448398.007

increased frequency and intensity of storms, floods, and other climate-related disasters will exacerbate these risks. These hazards bring the threat of damage to houses, as well as a loss of assets, livelihoods, environmental quality, and future prosperity.

Development Workshop France

Development Workshop France (DWF) is a French non-profit organization, originally founded in London in 1973 as a development agency: 'Development Workshop'. DWF has been working on rural development issues in Vietnam since 1989, gaining a great deal of in-country knowledge. Following a series of severe typhoons, their local knowledge was put to use in promoting storm-resistant building techniques and the policy of 'safe housing': working to strengthen houses to reduce the damage caused by floods and storms. The current programme promoting disaster-resistant construction methods began in 1999 in central Vietnam and is ongoing. Their model of working on risk reduction at household level, and of developing guidelines for good practice, has been transferred to other countries in South-east Asia, including Burma and Indonesia. Within this programme, DWF has also implemented reconstruction initiatives after major disasters, in particular following Typhoon Ketsana in 2009, on behalf of other organizations. Several of the reconstruction programmes conducted by DWF are evaluated in this chapter.

Figure 7.1 Map of Vietnam with provinces discussed herein highlighted

Disaster context

This coastal area of the country is affected annually by natural disasters such as typhoons and floods. Generally, locals have experience of such events and a coping strategy to manage when the impact of such events is moderate – for example, by putting sand bags on the roof and by trying to store important items and food in the roof frame space. However, as in the case of many previous typhoons, the typhoons of 2009 were so devastating that such strategies were ineffective, leading to roofs being blown off and structures being damaged or destroyed. The DWF programme which began in 1999 developed prevention measures against future storms by reinforcing existing houses and by ensuring that safe construction methods were applied in new houses. In doing so, this enabled families to reduce repair and reconstruction costs and save money when the next violent storm arrived by avoiding the subsequent damage repairs costs, allowing families to fund other family priorities such as health costs, education, and income generation.

Typhoon Ketsana struck central Vietnam on 29 September 2009 affecting 13 provinces and causing widespread destruction particularly in the provinces of Quang Nam and Quang Ngai, requiring approximately 357,000 people to be evacuated (see Figure 7.1). This was followed by Typhoon Mirinae on 2 November 2009 which affected nine provinces, seven of which had already suffered in the previous typhoon. This served to worsen the situation and posed a significant setback to gains made in relief and recovery in response to Ketsana. Though many of the most vulnerable were moved to safer sheltered areas in the hope that the number of direct victims could be reduced, 180 people were still killed. The rainfall which followed caused major flooding over a wide area – including in five provinces affecting a population totalling six million.

The impact was significant on individuals and their livelihoods, causing loss of property and agricultural land when fields flooded and poultry animals–valuable economic sources for families–were killed. In addition, the consequent damage to the land prevented farmers from being able to plant rice for the next season. The economy and many community buildings also suffered significant damage. Overall, the cost of damage was estimated at €510 million (approximately 1.2 per cent of Vietnam's GDP). In Thua Thien Hue province, the focus of this review, damage was estimated at €13 million with three deaths, 375 destroyed houses, 11,350 damaged houses, 109,000 flooded homes, and 201 public buildings damaged, in addition to many roads and irrigation canals being destroyed.

During the emergency situation immediately after the typhoon, despite road and power networks having been destroyed by the floods, the Vietnamese authorities, army and the Vietnam Red Cross, along with other national organizations such as the Women's Union, were able to meet the immediate needs for food, clean water, and emergency shelter. Prior to 1999, there had been little non-governmental or international organization input after disasters in central Vietnam. Families whose homes were most damaged ended up staying with neighbours or relatives and rebuilding as they could manage with scarce resources. To put the housing situation into context, rural housing in central Vietnam prior to 1985 was very fragile, mainly built with a timber or bamboo frame, bamboo mat walls and thatched roofs. Easily destroyed, these shelters were also quickly rebuilt at almost no cost. Paradoxically, the disaster impact was quickly resolved. However, economic reforms for financial renewal (*doi-moi*), declared by the Vietnam Government in 1986, had the effect of increasing family revenues. This, in turn, spurred a gradual change in building practice: the use of very cheap and very local materials was progressively replaced by the use of more durable materials and techniques: concrete frames, fired bricks or cement blocks for walls, fired clay roof tiles or corrugated roof sheets for roofing. But there were two serious catches: first, for both technical and economic reasons, these new houses built slowly by unskilled families were badly constructed and as a result very unsafe and easily damaged; second, the rebuilding process had become monetized since materials or the ingredients – sacks of cement and steel, for example – now had to be paid for. When a flood or typhoon hit, there was still major damage and destruction, but unlike the previous cheap thatch and bamboo houses, post-disaster recovery had acquired a serious monetary consequence. There was, in effect, more to lose.

By 2009, emergency financial support provided by the Vietnamese government for each damaged house amounted to up to 5 million Dong (€175) depending on the level of damage, and was often less – disconcertingly, the sums varied according to commune level decisions – but in all cases, the relief sum was inadequate to rebuild a home, let alone to make it more resistant in future similar events. The roof frame alone would cost €100 thus making a complete rebuild impossible. Sometimes some material support was given, such as a hand-out of fibre cement corrugated sheets which are inherently fragile and break easily. A little support for livelihoods was available: for example, nets for fishing, grants to buy poultry, and some seeds were given for cultivation, but were often of very low quality. Consequently, people were obliged to borrow money to replace what they could of their losses, typically to help cover the costs of rebuilding, buying pigs and poultry, and getting good seed for crops. Borrowing was often from relatives and usurious money lenders and could be expensive and indeed push the nearly poor into real poverty. Worse, families tell of losing their homes four or five times in succession.

Background to DWF's work in Vietnam

Following the commencement of DWF's work in Vietnam in 1989, a great deal of work has been undertaken in relation to the DWF programme 'Prevent Typhoon Damage to Housing'. This experience has contributed directly to the reconstruction programmes. The 2010 impact assessment of DWF work on preventive strengthening in Vietnam, a study supported by the Building and Social Housing Foundation, concluded that DWF principles of safer construction have achieved social and official appropriation based on their effective mitigation of the impact of typhoons and this has led to widespread adoption (Phong, 2010; Norton et al., 2011). A note in passing, Vietnam has construction regulations developed some 30 years ago, but such regulations never applied in the informal sector on construction by local builders in rural areas. In 2013, the Vietnamese Ministry of Construction recognized that such regulations need both updating and adaptation to suit local realities, and asked for DWF's assistance in this task, in a programme that should start being implemented in 2014 with European Union support.

The programmes and approach

In the aftermath of the devastation caused by Cyclone Ketsana in September 2009, for example, intense reconstruction efforts were conducted. Between December 2009 and April 2010, the DWF programme in Vietnam helped to reconstruct homes respecting the ten key principles of cyclone-resistant construction devised and promoted by DWF (see Figure 7.2) and to repair and strengthen houses. DWF supervised construction by beneficiaries and local builders so as to ensure quality and develop skills. In all cases, the method of selecting beneficiaries was community driven and aimed at the poorest families, with particular attention paid to women-headed families. Communities were targeted after examining the worst affected areas and where reconstruction, livelihood establishment, and maintenance were most challenging.

The typhoon devastation, and hence the reconstruction process, was most intensive in the Thua Thien Hue Province. Once funding was obtained by DWF, they actively liaised with the Provincial People's Committee in order to get the programme initially approved in February 2010. DWF then set up monitoring committees in target communes. Recipient families were chosen by community members based on several criteria: the level of vulnerability of the home, the inability to rebuild on their own due to lack of money or no access to loans, limitations within the family – for example, disabilities or absence of an adult male (dead or departed), and a lack of skills – and as a final criteria, that female-headed households would be prioritized. Selection was made via community consensus and/or community voting. The selection took account of the financial

Một là lợi dụng địa hình
Cản luồng gió đến công trình của ta.

Hai là hình dáng ngôi nhà
Giản đơn hạn chế nhô ra lõm vào .

Mái nghiêng 30° - 45°
để giảm bớt tốc mái do áp lực âm

Ba là độ dốc mái cao
Khi gió thổi vào mái đỡ tốc lên.

Tránh làm mái đua rộng tách rời
khung sườn và mặt mái hiên khỏi mái chính

Bốn là chú ý mái viền
Tránh đua quá rộng ,mái hiên tách rời

Đảm bảo các liên kết và neo giữ chắc giữa
các bộ phận: móng- tường- kết cấu bao che
tường - kết cấu mái - tấm lợp

Năm là neo chặt các nơi
Cột, tường, kèo, mái chẳng rời nhau ra.

Gia cường hệ tam giác ngang và đứng
(thang chống chéo)

Sáu là muốn vững ngôi nhà
Thêm giằng tam giác ,thêm đà chống xiên

Bảo đảm các tấm lợp mái không bị tốc gió

Bảy là tấm lợp bên trên
Phải buộc thật chặt cho bền chắc lâu

Kích thước các lỗ cửa ở các tường
đối diện xấp xỉ bằng nhau.

Tám là cửa trước ,cửa sau.
Kích thước xấp xỉ, bằng nhau không thừa.

Figure 7.2 The ten key principles of cyclone-resistant construction:

1. Choose the location carefully to avoid the full force of the wind or flood.
2. Use a building layout with a simple regular shape, to avoid concentration of pressure.
3. Build the roof at an angle of 30° to 45° to prevent it being lifted off by the wind.
4. Avoid wide roof overhangs; separate the veranda structure from the house.
5. Make sure the foundations, walls, and roof structure are all firmly fixed together.
6. Reinforce the bracing in the structure; strengthen walls and joints/junctions to increase stiffness.
7. Make sure the roof covering is firmly attached to the roof structure to prevent it from lifting.
8. If doors and shutters cannot be shut, make sure there are opposing openings to reduce pressure build up.
9 Use doors and shutters that can be closed.
10 Plant trees around the house as wind breaks and reduce the flow of water, but not too close.

status of the beneficiaries. Costs and the works undertaken were estimated with help from DWF staff. Agreements about the work to be done and final approvals at completion were signed off by the family, DWF representatives, and local officials. Housing reconstruction was done by families and by local builders trained by DWF to use safe construction techniques. In the case of public works in these and similar projects such as the construction of a sea wall, tenders were requested from local construction companies and the best offers chosen.

On average, the reconstructed houses had a floor area of 35 m² (5 m deep and 7 m wide), using the same floor plan that is typical of the most common house size and form in the region. Most of these homes have a simple floor plan composed of three bays – the two 2.2 metres wide side 'bays' into which a double bed will fit, and the central bay reserved for the ancestral altar and ashes. Given that some plots had a narrow street frontage, this format could be turned round and if need be the room arrangement changed. These are decisions made by the family.

Most houses were built on a low plinth, but in Loc Tri houses (Location 1 below), given the exposed high flood risk location on the shore, the houses were built up on high platforms above flood level. This rectangular 1.5 to 2.0

metre plinth was built with a reinforced concrete frame and cement block retaining wall, with the interior filled with sand up to the raised floor level (see Figure 7.3) (in this coastal region, no houses are built on stilts). In all cases, the structure is made of a reinforced concrete frame (vertical columns and ring beam), and with a masonry (brick or cement block) infill wall. The roof frame (trusses) is made of timber (the family preferred choice), but in recent years as the cost of wood has risen it has become cheaper to make the roof trusses using reinforced concrete (sometimes painted to look like wood), over which timber battens are fixed and onto which the roof covering is attached. The roof is covered by fired clay or cement roof tiles, or by corrugated iron roof sheets. The roof covering is then secured either by thin horizontal metal restraining bars over the corrugated sheets or with narrow thin reinforced concrete ribs that run at one metre intervals from the ridge down to the eaves to hold down the roof tiles. The latter is a technique used in good quality traditional roof construction, such as the houses of the wealthy or in pagodas, and encouraged by DWF in its house strengthening programme. DWF discourages the use of fibre clement roof sheets as these are brittle and break when subjected to high winds. All connections between components and columns are strengthened with metal brackets or, as an option in houses very close to the sea where corrosion is an issue, tied together with heavy duty fishing line.

Revisiting DWF's reconstruction and preventive strengthening projects

To evaluate the success of the programmes applied by the DWF in Vietnam, not just related to Cyclone Ketsana but to all work conducted there since

Figure 7.3 Dwelling under concrete plinth, reinforced concrete frame and cement block retaining wall, with the interior filled with sand up to the raised floor level

1989, surveys of between 15 and 19 respondents were conducted in four locations (Locations 1–3 in relation to reconstruction efforts and 4 in relation to preventive strengthening of buildings) and categorized into the recurrent themes of beneficiary targeting, user satisfaction, technical performance, replication, and livelihoods.

Location 1: Loc Tri Commune, Thua Thien Hue Province

This commune consists of a community of fishermen located in southern Thua Thien Hue province in a hamlet beside a small creek off the lagoon not very far from the centre of the commune. The project was funded by the French Ministry of Foreign Affairs.

- *Beneficiary targeting:* Beneficiary families were both those who had houses damaged or destroyed and those who also moored their boats next door (the boats were used as part-time floating homes – a fragile existence but part of their lifestyle). These families were offered two types of support: to have their fishing boat harbours reinforced and to have a safe solid house. For social and economic reasons made clear by the inhabitants, the proposed rehabilitation programme was to rebuild or strengthen houses in the existing village beside the lagoon and to construct a strong sea wall along the narrow estuary for the protection of each family's fishing boat, key to their livelihood. The project used a system of cash grants (not loans which would have had to be repaid), family contributions when possible (such as unskilled labour), and technical support from DWF with training and guidelines for local builders. Work was supervised by DWF. The families participating in the project also contributed financially within the limits of what they could afford based on a capacity assessment. Houses were built on the spot that their previous home had occupied. It should be noted that where resettlement has been proposed by the government, most families return to their original home for livelihood reasons.
- *User satisfaction:* After several years, all families are still living in their rebuilt houses. No damage has occurred in subsequent typhoons. They stated that they were happy with their houses, finding them to be spacious enough to live in, more comfortable than living in a boat and feeling them to be safe due to secure raised platform foundations. Residents feel that the dwellings could withstand a small typhoon but were unsure about the impact of a major typhoon.
- *Technical performance:* In practice, the experience of major storms since reconstruction shows that the houses resist typhoons extremely well. Half of respondents had improved their dwellings either by tiling floors or extending the building (the latter completed with an awareness of typhoon damage reduction techniques). The residents said that they could not have built such accommodation without assistance from the project, or that it would have taken many years to do so without

help. The beneficiaries report that if improvements are needed, financial assistance (in the form of loans) is available. Loans for house strengthening were put in place by DWF in 2008 with support from the Ford Foundation and managed by (and with their own 33 per cent seed fund contribution) the Vietnamese Bank of Social Policy. DWF had set up this loan package specifically to make affordable loans available for the strengthening of houses or to cover the extra cost of making new/rebuilt houses storm resistant. The loan programme is ongoing, without more DWF input. Repayment rates are above 85 per cent.

- *Replication:* In this community, non-beneficiaries have applied some of the safe construction techniques, including putting restraining bars on the roofs to protect them from high winds, making sure that there are four reinforcing bars in the columns instead of only three (which is insufficient), and making sure that doors and windows can be securely closed. These families are very poor and they do not build public amenities themselves. Although poverty is also a constraint that stops people making their home safer, having a safer home both saves money and improves the quality of life. Fifty per cent of beneficiary families have expanded their homes and applied the same safe construction techniques. This extension is usually for income-generating activities.

- *Livelihoods:* The project has brought jobs as local builders have been used and continue to be used, and overall the residents claim to be more stable, both physically and financially.

Location 2: Binh Dong Commune, Quang Ngai Province

Typhoon Ketsana destroyed houses in this coastal village in central Vietnam and the ensuing reconstruction programme was funded by the International Federation of the Red Cross/Crescent (IFRC) with the aim of rebuilding safe houses on the same land.

- *Beneficiary targeting:* The Vietnamese Red Cross and commune leaders identified the beneficiary families. In each case, the People's Committee makes a preliminary list amongst poor families with damaged or destroyed homes. Before, these families lived in temporary shelter. The houses are owned by the beneficiary. DWF designed several example house types for reconstruction, based on local house types and layout. Cash grants for reconstruction were provided to beneficiaries who were shown different types of example houses by DWF so that the family could then discuss the adaptation of the house designs to meet the needs of their household, for example, making layout changes (changing room sizes and layout on their plot of land, and deciding how much they could contribute and thus potentially add to the total rebuild). The houses were built by local builders who received training from DWF, with family support in most cases.

- *User satisfaction:* Those questioned were happy with their homes and felt them to be resistant to typhoons, and cited particularly that they like the solid foundations and the use of restraining bars on the roof, making it much less likely to be blown off during a typhoon. Losing the roof is the most common damage in unsafe houses. The new houses need few repairs and this saved money and labour. The residents say they plan to remain living in them until they die. Because residents are no longer 'scared at night', they suggest that they sleep better and that this makes them more economically productive. It is reported that although the high plinth is ideal from a flood resistance point of view, they do to some extent hinder access for people with mobility difficulties, but that the general real opinion was that disabled people can manage with help from other family members and the safety of being above flooding was of paramount importance. Plot sizes (with very narrow alleyways) did not allow for ramps and this was a constraint in this location. The houses are not intended as core houses, but are of a size that is generally considered a standard family home in central Vietnam. The beneficiaries report that if improvements are needed, such as tiling the floor, financial assistance, in the form of loans, is available.
- *Technical performance:* Construction was supervised by local builders who received training and supervision from DWF. Following the reconstruction of dwellings, those surveyed considered the new constructions to be safe, experiencing less leakage from roofs and requiring less maintenance.
- *Replication:* Non-beneficiaries appear to have replicated some of the techniques used in the reconstruction efforts. Materials are available locally to enable replication but trained builders are required to undertake or advise on these tasks.
- *Livelihoods:* The women feel more relaxed and local builders have been given employment, particularly by those wanting to expand their houses. As the beneficiaries sleep more peacefully they are more economically productive and have more funds as they spend less on maintenance and/or repairs. The high foundations however, do pose a challenge to disabled people.

Location 3: Dak Tram Commune, Kontum Province

Dak Tram is an impoverished minority community in the central highlands of Vietnam which originally stood on a hill but was resettled nearer to the river when a school was constructed on their land. After the destruction of their homes by Typhoon Ketsana's resulting river flooding in 2009, they were relocated by the government to a safer area within the commune. For reconstruction, cash grants were provided by the IFRC and the design discussed with families with various options proposed by DWF technicians and social workers, and the final design agreed with the families. Due to the lack of local builders, a construction company was used.

- *Beneficiary targeting*: The choice of beneficiaries was made initially by the People's Committee of the Commune, then democratically by the local community and checked by the Red Cross. All funding was provided by the IFRC. House strengthening loans have not yet extended to this highland province and residents have to use their own savings to make added improvements.
- *User satisfaction*: Respondents to the survey questionnaire said they were satisfied with their newly constructed dwellings, even commenting that they are beautiful with good design and quality of construction (an important issue in Vietnam). It was commented on that DWF staff were always friendly. In the highlands traditionally many houses are built on stilts, but this was not the case in this area (in another area in the highlands, Gia Lai, DWF proposed houses on stilts to families). Residents remarked that access to water can be problematic in the dry season and to this end collective wells were also provided.
- *Technical performance*: In this highland minority community area, due to the lack of local builders a construction company was used. With these buildings, damp and draught problems have been improved and damage from insect attacks has been reduced. Houses had integrated storm resistance and respected local building layouts.
- *Replication*: There is no evidence of replication of the safe construction techniques in these very poor highland areas. No extensions are reported and if residents feel they need more space, they simply build a new annexe construction as opposed to extending their home.
- This, then, correlates with a more secure and sustainable livelihood, as individuals are stronger and are less prone to sickness, allowing them to work more regularly to earn a regular income. Whole families will have improved health, which also resonates in fewer absences from school for children who previously would have suffered from the unhealthy conditions in the home.

Location 4: Preventive strengthening in Quang Tho Commune, Thua Thien Hue

This location differs from the others in that it focused on a project to prevent the impact of typhoons and floods, the historical focus of DWF since 1989 until the present day (2014). The project component in a high typhoon risk environment on the coastal plain involved the preventive strengthening of fragile houses owned by the poor in a rural coastal commune with work carried out by local builders. This intervention, along with many other DWF project actions, formed part of the long-term DWF programme of promoting the preventive strengthening of existing houses, and included training of local builders in safe construction techniques and raising public awareness, and was funded by the European Community Humanitarian Office (ECHO), and previously by Canadian International Development Aid (CIDA).

- *Beneficiary targeting*: Poor families and, as a priority, women-headed families where the husband was no longer present. Selection was by community and hamlet decision, with a vote on who to select.
- *User satisfaction*: Respondents felt their houses were beautiful and were secure given the concrete beams fitted. Prior to the project, locals thought their houses were safe but since the project they understand their vulnerabilities and that they are now much safer, and indeed are healthier (they do not worry now about possible damage and losses from future typhoons), and feel secure in their new safer homes.
- *Technical performance*: When maintenance is required, local masons or carpenters are called upon. A concern reported is the possibility of damage by ants, and people felt this should be regularly monitored. One suggestion as to a potential improvement to their new dwellings was that a ramp might be useful to enter the dwellings for those with a disability – something that they can easily do as the houses are not on platforms and there are ramps already for bringing in motor bikes at night for safety.
- *Replication*: People copy the techniques of the project as they find them useful in making a building more resistant to disasters. However, the costs are high in implementing these techniques and often the people do not know how to implement them.
- *Livelihoods*: The project has meant that respondents, previously living in temporary fragile homes, have been able to acquire their own safer homes much earlier than they would have been able to do without such assistance. The beneficiaries report that if further improvements are needed, financial assistance (in the form of loans) for house strengthening is available from the Vietnamese Bank for Social Policy – an innovative preventive strengthening loan programme initiated with DWF financial support and technical guidance in partnership with the Vietnam Bank for Social Policy was started in 2008. These loans are not to be confused with emergency relief support mentioned earlier in this chapter and provided by the government and other national agencies.

Overview

Over and above these specifics, there are a number of commonalities which can be seen from the results of these surveys. For example, the new homes constructed have remained in the hands of the original beneficiaries who also state that the new dwellings are clean and solid and have reduced the family workload on repairs and maintaining weak structures. This has helped both men and women and, so families say, have facilitated husbands and wives working together rather than being drawn away to work on repairs caused by storms and floods. In all cases, respondents claim to have saved money due to a reduction in the number of repairs required as their new dwellings are more resistant to the elements. The knowledge of all respondents with regards to disaster prevention has also improved thanks to builder training and awareness-raising programmes using public events, posters about the ten key principles of cyclone-resistant construction, plays, TV shows, radio reports, and the press. As a result, locals now possess the knowledge to build cyclone-resistant constructions, thanks to the safer construction programmes run in all partner communes by DWF to train commune builders and leaders in safe construction principles and practice (a day and a half long hands-on and theory training programme for all concerned commune builders and community leaders). The main limitation on replication is money and, in the highlands, it was also claimed, by a lack of skills. An additional common observation made is that DWF staff are regularly described as friendly, helpful, and available.

Taking a more general view, DWF strategies used in reconstruction processes and in all their Vietnam programmes include:

- Focusing on communication: Through participative animation and/or advertising (e.g. Figure 7.4) – anything to reinforce the prevention idea in the long-term memory of the community. For example, using popular media, theatre, concerts, inter-commune boat races, mobile displays, school events, and plays by children. Children are actively encouraged in school and in the community to promote the message 'Vaccinate your home against storms!' using school plays, posters, competitions, and parades (see Figure 7.5).

Figure 7.4 A risk-reduction slogan on a chin strap

Figure 7.5 Schoolchild's painting of a house blowing away during a storm

- Credit availability: Initially supported by the Ford Foundation, in 2008 DWF introduced a new loan package, in collaboration with the Vietnam Bank for Social Policy, to provide credit for house strengthening, to be repaid by recipients over five years. DWF put up two-thirds of the capital to start this programme, the Vietnam Bank one-third. The loans are still operating. Repayments options are flexible if negotiated with the Bank and depend on circumstances – for example if a disaster occurs repayments can be deferred. The pilot phase is complete and the Vietnam Bank is continuing the programme, which is also being adopted by the Government. Repayment rates are over 85 per cent. Loans are sanctioned by the Women's Union and the People's Committee at commune level, and lending targets poor families. The amount per family has been pegged at €500, and the Vietnam Bank is thinking of raising this amount in 2014.
- Facilitating safer infrastructure: DWF has worked with the communes of Thua Thien Hue to strengthen public infrastructure including safer schools, markets, and health facilities. These public buildings also serve as refuges.
- Developing skills: DWF provides training on resistant construction techniques in order to improve the quality of constructions. All builders, and community leaders in a commune are invited to participate in short training programmes. Many thousands of builders have been trained since 2000 and over the following 14 years. Training takes place in a partner commune in the context of a support programme to assist families living in fragile homes where their homes have been damaged. Trained builders both earn an income and act as building advisers to the community. Families trust these local advisors and these trained builders apply the safer construction techniques in their work. Training of builders and community leaders in safe construction takes one and half days per session including theory and hands-on practice.
- Facilitating production opportunities: DWF works with local producers who produce components such as the metal brackets used for connections between structural components, which make the structure safer. Roof tiles that can be tied to the roof frame have been reintroduced.

Recommendations

Based on the evidence of many studies (Cocchiglia, 2007) carried out on the DWF programme in Vietnam over the past 25 years, including the Building and Social Housing Foundation funded impact study (Phong, 2010) following the attribution of the World Habitat Award, the promotion of preventive strengthening in existing and new building (including reconstruction undertaken in these locations throughout Vietnam) has been shown to have had a positive influence on the lives of the beneficiaries and on their resilience to future events. The knowledge gained from these efforts is diverse and DWF have extracted six generic recommendations for the implementation of such schemes in the future:

1. Housing as a process, not only a product

After a disaster, reconstruction is still too often considered as a question of delivering shelter in the form of a number of complete (or core) houses to a number of 'victim' families with the associated major constraints of logistics, the supply of building materials, and project planning. Housing is too often seen only as a product, akin to water filters or bags of rice; a quantity to be transferred to a population by international (or national) organizations, 'shelter consultants', and projects managers, most of whom know very little about community-driven construction processes. Within this, developing skills in communities that integrate safer construction processes and techniques is often neglected.

Housing has to be considered as a process, although it can be seen as a complicated process and one that in all cases includes many actors and many components. It remains that in reconstruction and indeed in preventive strengthening, concerned families and local builders must be at the centre of the construction process that is adopted. A process that needs to consider how the family lived before the disaster, how they would like to live in the future, the importance of different spaces in the home, the social position of the house in local society, and the working relations between families and local builders, local authorities and lending agencies, all of whom are part of the building process.

The house design phase has to be done with local 'technicians' who may be architects or, even more often, local builders who can be easily trained about safety and who are able to converse with the concerned families, to ensure that designs will be fully appropriated by, and appropriate for, the family. Flexibility in design, adaptation to local architectural styles, and a capacity to work with families are all essential for the appropriation of the techniques that make for a safe house. 'Participatory design' may take time and can appear to make it difficult to achieve a synthesis of different needs – safety, adaptation to family needs, proximity to work, the availability of resources that can not only be used immediately but can then go on being used in the future, should be a key principle if one wishes to achieve housing that is durable, safe, and adapted to each family's needs and capacity. This has consistently been the case in the DWF safer housing process in Vietnam over the last 15 years. In addition, in housing implementation, construction should be supervised not only by projects but also by families who invariably do this strictly. It implies that post-disaster reconstruction should be accompanied by training and public campaigns on safer house designed to resist identified hazards and this has been the case in DWF's actions in Vietnam.

2. Disaster risk reduction in reconstruction: 'Building safer and better'

Integrating disaster risk reduction (DRR) in reconstruction is, surprisingly, not always considered a priority, because response is too often based on the rapid delivery of transition shelter to re-house people in as short a time as possible and without considering the specific broader context in which a disaster has taken place or is likely to re-occur. For example, after the recent series of typhoons in Vietnam in October and November 2013, limited state financial support to help families was provided, it varied in amount from one commune to another and was, in all instances, largely insufficient to cover the costs of repairs for damaged houses, and was never accompanied by any form of information on measures to ensure that repairs to the roof would be sufficient to survive the arrival of the next typhoon. An oversight which left these same families as, or even more, exposed to subsequent damage caused by the next typhoon which arrived several days later. In 2014, DWF with European support is addressing this problem in central Vietnam. This is not just a problem in Vietnam – in 2013, a DWF survey after Typhoon Pablo (Mindanao Island, December 2012, Philippines) showed that reconstruction work was not integrating basic typhoon-resistant features in reconstruction (Norton, 2013).

DRR in construction needs to develop and apply key principles of safe construction which reflect local practice, materials, and build on local know-how as a starting point and link to appropriate material for training and disseminating safer construction techniques amongst the local community of builders and technicians. This implies that whilst principles of safety can be transferred from one place to another, actual technical and practical solutions have to be developed locally and not brought from other places and countries.

3. Funding and transparency

Most programmes implemented by DWF have been made with 'cash grants', because in the case of Vietnam, after a disaster, the local market for construction (materials, builders, etc.) is not totally disrupted and families have been encouraged to manage their own reconstruction whenever possible, engaging them in understanding and monitoring their rebuilding process. Grant allocation depends of the local situation (what hazards) and technical constraints (an example in flooding areas is the need for high foundations), and the composition and capacity of each affected family (number of persons, possible family contribution) to achieve safer housing. In the DWF Vietnam experience families have been shown to be conscientious about managing the purchase of materials and construction labour. This has generated transparency within the local community and an acceptance of different levels of support amongst different beneficiary families. This has been achieved by working with an overall affected community, and gathering enough information from families on their needs, capacities, and social differences.

4. Support by specialist social workers?

Frequently in the immediate aftermath of a disaster, organizations prepare programmes and plans to rebuild affected or destroyed communities based on a sectoral approach, each with its own sectoral specialists for health, water, food, cleaning, education, shelter, logistics (often from abroad), and each evaluating the way to cover the immediate and long-term needs of the communities in a specific sector and each working in a degree of isolation. Neither families nor communities see vulnerability in a sectorial manner, nor do they consider achieving safety as being a sectoral issue. They link all their issues, and decide what to do or what can be done on a broad base and based on capacity and a range of priorities. The house is not considered as the first priority, but the survey leading to this chapter confirms that the safer house leads to savings (and thus to many other things), to better health and more; thus decision-making about reconstruction and priorities is also not purely a financial or technical issue.

For Vietnam, DWF made another choice to mix all these 'specialities' into one team developing a holistic view of family and community capacity, the risk and needs, and the construction solutions and communication methods that would suit this context, bringing together and complementing different skills to create a good capacity to communicate with families, evaluate works to be done and to supervise, animate training, or public campaign for safe housing and calculate the costs of actions.

5. Long-term memory

DWF Vietnam team has worked as a group over many years and considered that this is important for the strength of their institutional long-term memory, which is in turn reflected in the working relations that the team has with the beneficiary families. In turn, despite the fact that the team is made up of social workers, people with communication skills, as well as architects and engineers, the staff are encouraged to operate as a team and through this to develop individually more holistic skills that improve their ability to interact with families and communities along with community and more senior leaders. The team have worked to avoid developing a sectoral view of families, their built environment, and the issues they face after disaster.

6. Post-reconstruction evaluation

The origin of this study was an evaluation that housing programmes are considered as 'finished' when the house key is given to the family and the report to the donor completed and sent, with little subsequent assessment to see how well the product worked. Long-term post-disaster reconstruction evaluations are quite rare. Generally they are only made in case of extreme events with long-term reconstruction (such as after the Tsunami 2004 in Asia) where there have been a lot of learning opportunities, which provide various reports on the necessity for a 'better approach'. This current publication provides an attempt to address this issue and is to be hailed.

In many cases of reconstruction globally, housing is still seen too often as a product made during reconstruction efforts; something then to be transferred and given to the recipients but with little knowledge of how it was achieved nor any transfer of knowledge of what makes it a safer built environment. In these cases, families deciding to extend at a later date have learned no lessons. In seeing housing as a process, however, families must be at the centre of the (re)construction process. For example, consideration must be made with regard to how the family lived before the disaster to ensure this will not change significantly, and also how it will live after it. Beneficiaries must input what different spaces and functions within the dwelling should be provided. Communities need to be engaged in selecting beneficiary families and in the consideration of local perceptions about styles of building. Local participation in planning and implementation phases is essential. Individual families must be consulted on the designs being proposed to ensure that they are appropriate to their needs as well as to risk reduction. In DWF programmes, with support provided to several thousand families, very few houses are identical but all integrate safe construction principles. This element of 'participatory design' is essential if durable housing, which meets the needs of recipients (and their future needs, for example in terms of expanding their home) is the aim.

Conclusions

The findings from post-reconstruction evaluations are shown to be significant and useful in informing future plans and policies. The work of DWF has been commended internationally, receiving the World Habitat Award in 2008 and the Sasakawa Award Certificate of Distinction from the United Nations International Strategy for Disaster Reduction organization (UNISDR) in 2009. However, despite successes, too many inhabitants of central Vietnam remain highly vulnerable and the indications are that climate change will increase the impact of storms and thus vulnerability. DWF has been working to ensure that the lessons highlighted here are exported to other provinces in central and southern Vietnam and there is activity in South-east Asia in Myanmar (post cyclone Nargis) and in Indonesia (long-term strategy for safe construction after the tsunami and earthquake in Aceh in 2004). DWF also provided advice in the Philippines after major typhoons in 2012 to reduce the impact of regular environmental calamities.

Changing national and local strategies for safer construction, particularly for the poor, is not achieved quickly, and yet most projects have a life of two to five years. DWF in Vietnam and in the South-east Asian region has worked for 25 years to develop a change in attitudes about the methods and the possibilities of making shelter and local public buildings safer using ideas that marry local knowledge with technical requirements. In 1999, local authorities in Vietnam did not acknowledge that the houses of the poor could be made typhoon resistant. It has taken the long-term presence of the agency, numerous demonstrations of safe construction and the publication of a national and 12 associated provincial, atlases of "Housing Vulnerability and Strengthening" in collaboration with the Vietnamese Ministry of Construction. The aim going forward is to develop a closer link between safe technical requirements in construction and local realities achieving safe housing and reducing vulnerability. As a result, in December 2013, the Ministry of Construction in Vietnam asked DWF to collaborate in redefining the construction guidelines for safe construction in all flood and storm-prone parts of coastal Vietnam. Building on DWF's 25-year experience in Vietnam has gone from demonstrating – and proving – safe construction methods and community development at community and household level, through to influencing national thinking on safe construction. Such a process cannot take place in two or five years; it takes a long-term commitment for true innovation and transitional change to happen: for DWF to form a partnership with government and actually be able to influence central government has taken many years.

Overall, the aim of DWF is the development of a culture and practice of prevention. "This is achieved through a variety of methods: partnership between local government and vulnerable communities, training of locals as advisors in safe building design, developing communication and education initiatives to change attitudes to mainstreaming DRR in construction, and the provision of a dedicated credit to enable safe rebuilding and/or building strengthening as a priority which is now implemented by the Vietnamese government." In addition to this, participation of beneficiaries has been shown to be vital – incorporating their ideas, practices, culture, and plans at all stages of the reconstruction process.

References

CDRH (2012) *Country Disaster Response Handbook – Vietnam*, Center for Excellence in Disaster Management and Humanitarian Assistance. Available from: http://www.coe-dmha.org/shared/pdf/disaster-mgmt-ref-hbks/Vietnam_DisasterResponse_Handbook2012.pdf [accessed 3 June 2014].

Cocchiglia, M. (2007) 'Building disaster resilient communities. Good practices and lessons learned. A Publication of the "Global Network of NGOs" for Disaster Risk Reduction', UNDP and UN-ISDR, Geneva. Available from: http://www.unisdr.org/files/596_10307.pdf [accessed 1 June 2014].

DARA (2012) *Vietnam Country Studies* [website] <http://daraint.org/wp-content/uploads/2012/09/CVM2ndEd-CountryStudy-Vietnam.pdf> [accessed 28 May 2014].

Norton, J. (2013). Development Workshop mission to assess damage, needs and action after Typhoon Pablo, Compostela Valley, Mindanao, Philippines, 22–29 March 2013.

Norton, J., Chantry,G., and Phong, T. (2011) 'Impact study on developing local capacity to reduce vulnerability and poverty', Building and Social Housing Foundation, UK.

Phong, T (2010) Impact Study on Developing Local Capacity to Reduce Vulnerability and Poverty in Central Vietnam, Hue, DWF.

WHO (2013) 'Research Summary. Priority Setting for Health Policy and Systems Research in Access to Medicines in Viet Nam', Alliance for Health Policy and Systems Research, World Health Organization. Available from: http://www.who.int/alliance-hpsr/projects/alliancehpsr_vietnamatmresummary.pdf.pdf [accessed 20 May 2014].

About the authors

Marion MacLellan is a Senior Lecturer in Development Studies for the Department of Geography, Environment, and Disaster Management at Coventry University. Her research interests lie predominantly in Sub-Saharan Africa, and in particular in human development issues – livelihoods, education in emergencies, children and orphans, AIDS, and disaster management. She is working with practitioners in the Democratic Republic of the Congo on the development of a network of disaster managers based in the global South and is external examiner for the postgraduate sustainable development programme at the University of Makeni, Sierra Leone.

Matthew Blackett is a Senior Lecturer in Natural Hazards and Physical Geography for the Department of Geography, Environment, and Disaster Management at Coventry University. He completed his PhD and post-doctoral position at King's College, London working in the remote sensing of earthquakes and volcanoes. He is now co-director of Coventry University's Centre for Disaster Management and Hazards Research.

Guillaume Chantry is a civil engineer who worked for 35 years in the field of human settlements and housing, with a focus on disaster-prone areas. He has been the programme coordinator of DWF's disaster risk reduction activities in Vietnam and South-east Asia since 1999.

John Norton is a founder member of Development Workshop (1973) and has been President of Development Workshop France since 1998. He has an MA in Architecture from Architectural Association in the UK and has done numerous research and activities in the field of human settlements and disaster risk reduction as well as published a number of articles on these topics.

CHAPTER 8
Integrated people-driven reconstruction in Indonesia

Annye Meilani, Wardah Hafidz, and Ashleigh King

Abstract

After the Indian Ocean tsunami of 26 December 2004, an enormous surge of international aid poured into Aceh province and Nias Island, the worst affected areas in Indonesia. Immediately after the event, Urban Poor Linkage (Uplink) Indonesia arrived in Aceh and started to work with the survivors in 23 of the worst affected villages.

Using donor aid estimated at US$25 million, more than 10,000 people benefited from the Uplink programme in the longer-term recovery and rehabilitation of their homes and communities. At all stages of the recovery process, the community were involved in planning, building, and monitoring as much as possible. This was later called a people-driven participatory approach by the Hunnarshale team from Gujarat.

This chapter aims to describe both the successes of Uplink's work in these areas as well as to reflect on the lessons that could be applied to similar situations in the future in five key areas: user satisfaction, beneficiary targeting, replication, technical performance, and livelihoods.

Keywords: Tsunami; Indonesia; Aceh; People driven; Long-term recovery

Introduction

On 26 December 2004 at 07:59 local time, an earthquake measuring 9.3 on the Richter scale struck the Indian Ocean, its epicentre located 155 kilometres west of the Indonesian island of Sumatra. The quake caused a 15–30-metre high tsunami (UNEP, 2005) to strike the country's coastline, devastating thousands of people's lives, homes, and livelihoods. The northernmost province of Aceh was worst affected by the disaster, with a final report by the Multi Donor Fund in December 2012 stating, '220,000 people dead or missing and over half a million left homeless in the region' (MDF-JRF Secretariat, 2012: 10).

Aceh province and Nias Island were the two worst affected areas of Indonesia, with fishing communities along the west coast of Aceh Besar and Banda Aceh suffering greatly from a huge loss of both life and infrastructure. Furthermore, the latter has been described as 'the story of two tsunamis' due to the enormous surge of unregulated, mismanaged international aid that poured

http://dx.doi.org/10.3362/9781780448398.008

into the area in the immediate aftermath of the event (Syukrizal et al., 2009). This study looks into the work of Urban Poor Linkage (Uplink) Indonesia, who worked with 23 of these worst affected villages that had lost 47 per cent of their population to the natural disaster (World Habitat Awards, 2007). Uplink aimed to provide not only immediate relief for survivors, but also longer-term recovery and rehabilitation for their homes and communities.

The research used to produce this study was carried out in the sub-district of Peukan Bada in the district of Aceh Besar and Uleuleu in Banda Aceh City in September 2013. Using focus-group discussions and in-depth interviews, researchers were able to highlight both the successes of Uplink's work in these areas as well as reflect on the lessons that could be applied to similar situations in the future.

Project intentions and design

Uplink Indonesia is a coalition of grassroots and community-based organizations and NGOs focused on tackling the problems of urban poverty through three key strategies of organization, advocacy, and networking. In the context of the Indian Ocean tsunami, their focus was to rebuild houses and infrastructure as well as working towards economic renewal, reinforced social and cultural relations, and environmental regeneration in the 23 targeted coastal villages.

After the devastation of the tsunami, the Indonesian government proposed a relocation strategy for people to move from affected coastal villages to safer areas further inland. Disregarding their wish to return home to rebuild their lives and livelihoods, the government had not consulted victims themselves, instead asserting a scheme that uprooted people, rather than restoring and improving their quality of life. Uplink worked in collaboration with communities and like-minded individuals to oppose this government initiative, proposing a far more participatory approach to re-establishing communities at both a grassroots and policy level.

Using donor aid provided in response to the disaster, Uplink assisted survivors in the initial stages of recovery between January and March 2005, helping beneficiaries move back to their villages, building temporary houses, and developing a longer-term rehabilitation programme. In February 2005, the government issued a policy to relocate houses from a two-kilometre zone along the coast that was considered inappropriate for living and polluted, etc. Together with the survivors, Uplink developed an alternative concept that allowed people to decide about the settlement and rebuild their lives in the same place. The network used safety as a basis for their counter proposal in which people would make their communities safe by creating a protective ecological buffer between sea and village. They presented and gained approval for the redevelopment alternative to the government's relocation strategy in March 2005, ensuring they had coverage and support from international media throughout the process.

With an estimated cost of US$25 million, Uplink's people-driven participatory approach was to ensure the safety of villagers through a series of ecological barriers which would separate the sea from inhabited areas, as well as new permanent housing for every family that lost their home as a result of the tsunami. At all stages of the recovery process, the community were to be involved in planning, building, and monitoring as much as possible. Very early on in the project Uplink worked with the community to carry out land surveys. Given that in many cases the tsunami had washed away both physical borders and tenure documents, this process proved essential as it allowed Uplink to clarify and subsequently certify land rights for the affected communities. These boundaries could then be worked within during the production of new homes.

Survivors were also involved in land mapping, design options for the new houses, material purchases, and data collection. Aside from these more practical tasks, survivors were trained to act as inspectors and trainers themselves during the building process, allowing them to develop more technical skills and take ownership of their houses during the construction stages. Each village selected a project management team to oversee the building process. These representatives were chosen, trusted and monitored by the community, thus re-establishing a sense of social cohesion. Strengthening villagers' confidence, skills and expertise proved to be a crucial part of not only their physical recovery but also of their psychological rehabilitation.

Uplink wanted to ensure their approach dealt with both the immediate and long-term recovery of the targeted villages, striving for social, economic, and cultural recovery as well as preparedness and protection for the future. A combination of training and village-based loan funds was intended to give survivors the opportunity to re-establish both their own livelihoods and communities. As a thick layer of sand had been deposited on the top soil (preventing farming) and many men were too traumatized to return to fishing, a particularly significant step in this was the creation of stabilized soil block-making plants, which provided survivors with both employment and new skills during the period of recovery. An emphasis was placed on sourcing building materials locally, so as to stimulate local economies, with nearby settlements only being approached if necessary labour or material needs could not be sourced within the village itself. By re-establishing opportunities for people to work and earn a living, Uplink's holistic approach to recovery dealt with matters beyond that of an immediate need for just shelter.

One of the key ambitions for Uplink's project was the creation of the Jaringan Udeep Beusaree, meaning 'Village Solidarity Network' (JUB) which was a coalition of all 23 villages, creating an integrated economic zone to manage their natural resources (Campagnoli, n.d.). It was through JUB that communities were able successfully to oppose the government's relocation policy, and it was hoped that the group could continue its work once Uplink completed its programme and left the area.

Achievements and outputs

Uplink's project resulted in 640 temporary houses between February and May 2005, followed by a further 3,256 permanent houses being built after this. This result contributed around 2.5 per cent of the estimated needs of 130,000 new houses set by the Agency for the Rehabilitation and Reconstruction (BRR) of Aceh and Nias (da Silva, 2010). One hundred of these permanent dwellings were for members of the Free Aceh Movement (GAM), who had returned in August 2005 after signing the peace agreement in Helsinki. A series of infrastructure works were also completed, including natural barriers between villages and the sea, dykes and ditches to reduce the likelihood and severity of future flooding, and well-signposted wide escape routes to evacuation centres located on high ground. Another key output of the work carried out by Uplink was the implementation of ecological measures, devised to improve both the environmental performance of villages and people's understanding of their responsibilities as individuals. These measures included training and implementation of organic farming techniques, using renewable energy to power public lighting, organic wastewater treatment facilities, and the introduction of community-level recycling.

Uplink's cohesion with JUB was crucial during the time of recovery and rehabilitation in Banda Aceh. By developing both the advocacy and mobilization skills of the organization, it was able to grow stronger and more skilled in its ability to represent the villagers in talks with government and other official bodies. In 2007, when Uplink left the area in question, two community organizers remained in the area to continue supporting the work of JUB until the end of 2010.

In order to assess both the positive and negative impacts of Uplink's work, five key categories have been established, each looking at a different aspect of the project. By highlighting the key outcomes and challenges within each category, an overall judgement can be made as to the main successes of the project as well as any lessons learnt.

User satisfaction

Uplink's technical team worked with local people to produce five different house designs that people could choose based on their individual needs and ambitions. The houses were 36 m^2 in size, and although this complied with government regulations, it was significantly smaller than the inhabitants' original homes. The project assumed this was reasonable, as the tsunami had reduced family sizes considerably – villages on the coast counted only 10 to 20 per cent survivors – and that people would be able to extend their houses later if they were able to benefit from additional livelihood activities and a strengthening economy. This, however, proved to be a major concern to the beneficiaries, who said that if houses had been made bigger originally, they would not have had to spend so much money extending their properties after the project ended. Given that local economies have suffered greatly since international aid ceased, families have found it difficult to afford the additions that they felt were necessary to provide a suitably sized home. This highlights a slight discrepancy between the ambitions of the agency and those of the owners but it should be considered that people's priorities are very much influenced by contextual factors. During the post-disaster recovery period an emphasis on safety and security was probably the greatest concern for those moving back to affected areas, whereas during times of economic hardship, monetary concerns are more likely to be at the forefront of people's minds. This aside, there was an overall sense of satisfaction amongst beneficiaries, regarding their feeling of safety within the home.

Many also expressed concern over the style of the Uplink homes given their rural context. It is apparent that given the more stable environmental situation, inhabitants' aesthetic ambitions have gradually become more prominent. However, with the constraints of limited funds and time, it would have been difficult for Uplink to provide larger houses. In addition to size concerns, many also expressed a desire for traditional Acehnese ornament to have been included in the design so as to produce a less 'urban' architecture. Many have responded to this by personalizing the simplistic design of their dwellings with individual decorative styles.

Another key point raised regarding user satisfaction is that of the house layout. In Acehnese life, the kitchen plays an important role in the everyday life of families and the community. It is an informal space to socialize with relatives, neighbours, and friends – whereas the parlour is a more formal space – and should, therefore, be both spacious in size and positioned separately from the more public living room. Uplink's housing design placed a relatively small kitchen at the front of the property. Many families have since remodelled a kitchen as an extension at the back of the property so as to provide an informal and larger space. A similar criticism was seen in the placement of the bathroom which was inside the house and, therefore, visible to guests. In Acehnese culture, this was seen to be offensive and many families have, therefore, moved the bathroom to the outside of the house, at the rear.

Overall, users expressed a sense of satisfaction with their new houses. They appreciated the feeling of security that such well-built structures provided and, in comparison to other agencies' projects where beneficiaries were often not allowed to make any contribution to the design or building process, they feel a sense of belonging within their homes.

Beneficiary targeting

The majority of beneficiaries are still living in the house that was provided to them by Uplink. Indeed, in focus group discussions it was estimated that over 90 per cent of beneficiaries were still living in their homes. There are few cases of abandoned or unkempt properties in the villages that were visited during the field research, implying an overall success of the project. It would

Figure 8.1 Spacious kitchen in the back part of the house, made from materials recycled from temporary house

appear that people are generally happy with the location and standard of dwelling, which may be a result of the sense of ownership that was generated by this participatory, user-driven scheme. This may also stem from Uplink's careful consideration of both location planning and housing typology.

Since the events of 2004, a number of survivors have married and, therefore, share one of the two properties that were provided to them. In these cases, the remaining house has been rented out, providing inhabitants with extra income. However, this has not necessarily proved to be an easy process as those looking to buy or rent properties have two key concerns given the currently stable natural environment that exists in Indonesia: location and size. If a house is in a strategic area, regardless of its quality, it is worth more money. Given the time that has passed since the 2004 tsunami, it would appear that people feel less concerned about the structural integrity of properties, thus making Uplink homes less economically valuable for beneficiaries. However, they are perceived to be safer and stronger than most other agencies' houses and can certainly be seen as a huge asset in terms of communities' preparedness for potential future threats.

During the field research, a number of instances were seen whereby inhabitants had partly altered the function of houses so as to accommodate their lifestyles and needs. One of the most common examples was the conversion of the front of dwellings into small businesses and shops, allowing people to re-build their livelihoods after the catastrophic impacts of the tsunami. Another example of inhabitants maximizing the potential of the homes can be seen in many of the stilt houses which were one of the five designs originally put forward. In many instances, these have been transformed into two-story structures with inhabitants using one floor as a living space and the other as either a shop or guestroom.

Figure 8.2 House abandoned by owner since he remarried and now lives with his new spouse outside the village

Uplink's houses have given people the opportunity to adapt and extend their properties and, therefore, helped them to rebuild their livelihoods as well as their family lives. In the light of the economic and time constraints that were faced during the rehabilitation programme, the houses that have been produced are relatively flexible buildings which people can adapt to serve their needs.

Replication

In order to provide safe, structurally sound houses, many innovations and new technologies were introduced to survivors at the beginning of the reconstruction phase so as to train and educate them not only for this project but also to develop their skills for the future. Examples of such techniques include the use of blocks across the wall to ensure robustness, meaning that rather than aligning blocks only end-to-end, wall thickness is increased by also arranging blocks crosswise. Earthquake-resistant ring beams in the foundations were also used to increase the structural integrity of the houses. It was noticed in the cases visited in the field study that the technologies taught and adopted in the reconstruction phase have not been used in more recent extensions, resulting in poorer quality structures. This is largely seen to be a result of economic constraints, given the collapse of the Acehnese and indeed wider Indonesian economy since international aid came to a halt. It was unanimously stated in the focus group discussions conducted during the field research that beneficiaries wished Uplink had used more conventional building techniques which would have used only half as many blocks, allowing the remaining materials to be used to extend properties.

In cases where inhabitants have moved their kitchen and bathroom space to the back of the building, recycled materials from the temporary homes originally provided to survivors have often been used. This can be seen as a positive means of recycling since such temporary structures are often merely abandoned or discarded once the emergency phase is over. The additional space that has been created by moving these two rooms has allowed families to incorporate extra bedrooms at the front of the house, which has often been necessary in cases where children have been born after the reconstruction phase was completed.

Since 2005, a number of small earthquakes have struck this same area of the Indonesian coastline. Inhabitants say they have felt safe within their new homes which have certainly withstood the low magnitude shocks. Safety awareness is seen to be gradually rising as was anticipated and hoped for in the Uplink programme.

With regards to Uplink's approach being replicated in other situations, the organization collaborated with the Australian Red Cross to provide a similar participatory approach on Nasi Island, off the coast of Banda Aceh, following the disaster. They are also implementing similar plans in post-earthquake reconstruction in Yogyakarta. Other NGOs were also seen to transfer such a user-driven approach to their own programmes in Aceh province following the events of December 2004. The Indonesian government later put the participatory principle in the master plan published in April 2005 for the rehabilitation and reconstruction of the regions and communities of Nanggroe Aceh Darussalam province and Nias Island, North Sumatra province.

Figure 8.3 Uleelheu, 2006, immediately after reconstruction

Figure 8.4 Uleelheu, 2013, seven years after reconstruction

Technical performance

During the construction stages, technical field supervisors were provided to ensure houses were built to a sufficient standard. Inspection training was also given to house owners and members of the village who became both masons and building inspectors as part of the process. It was hoped that by training locals in such techniques, they would not only develop a sense of ownership and pride towards their house but would also be able to use these skills to rebuild their livelihoods once the programme had ended. Indeed, such longer-term benefits can be seen by one inhabitant's experience as part of the village builder team. Samwil, 32 years old, from Lam Keumok village in Aceh Besar said,

> We were trained in the technical aspects of housing and infrastructure construction. I was in charge of building drainage and a public facility. I now work as contractor and together with some village builder team members, we got a project from the government to build a road in Aceh Jaya district.

One of the key technical failures of the project that became apparent in conversation with community members was that of the biological filter septic tanks. Unfortunately, the extra attention that these 'biofil' systems required became too much of a burden for beneficiaries to cope with and so most have now been replaced with more traditional systems. A similar problem occurred with many of the solar panels installed to power streetlights and community centres in certain villages. Once aid workers finished their programme and left the area, inhabitants had to call the Jakarta office to ask for assistance in solving technical difficulties that were occurring with the lamps. Eventually the systems were abandoned as it was felt that the hindrance of their maintenance outweighed their economic and environmental benefits.

With regards to the houses themselves, eight years after the project was carried out they are still standing strong which can be considered indicative of their good structural performance. Miswar, from Lam Geueu village in Aceh Besar noted, 'The house is very strong. All the technical aspects: foundations, walls, and roof were considered and built seriously from the beginning. The nailing of the roof is very strong, suitable for areas with strong winds like ours.'

Some basic maintenance is inevitably required as walls need to be painted regularly to avoid damage from the rain. Inhabitants living in the stilt houses apply insect repellent to wooden surfaces once a month – window sills in particular – to ensure insects do not damage the wood. In keeping with traditional methods, kerosene is also applied to the floors in a number of cases to keep them clean and shiny. Other than these minor works, residents have found their homes to be easily managed and of good quality.

The only other criticism of technical aspects is the absence of a porch, resulting in front doors weathering rapidly due to the heavy rains often experienced. Most families have added a covered area at the front to create a protective entrance space (see Figure 8.5). Some residents have also used galvanized iron sheeting as a protective layer on the external faces of wooden walls to protect them from water damage (see Figure 8.6). Overall, survivors felt that the simplistic yet sturdy design of the Uplink houses provided them with a secure dwelling in which to live.

Figure 8.5 A porch has been added to the front of the house

Figure 8.6 Wooden wall covered with metal sheeting to protect it from rainwater

Livelihoods

Uplink's recovery approach across all targeted villages was to provide not just domestic shelter for survivors but also to restore and improve existing livelihoods through the re-establishment of community facilities, the reinforcement of community solidarity, and the promotion of new social equalities that were previously not in place.

Physical facilities that were built included mosques, small-scale industries, a community kitchen, and community centres, all of which played an important role in helping communities to recover. For instance, the community centres were used to undertake trauma healing activities such as patchwork with women. Uplink had observed that people, when idle, tended to look back and get trapped in the past, and so tried to keep them busy and meeting and working with others, including on construction. All this supported them in being more positive, active, and productive people.

An emphasis on using local materials and labour proved to boost local economies whilst grants allowed people to set up small-scale businesses in order to re-establish their own livelihoods. Practical measures were also implemented for dealing with potential flood threats such as improved road networks, river dykes, embankments, and sanitation provisions. This level of infrastructure went beyond the immediate needs of survivors.

By increasing the variety and level of skills that people had, it was anticipated that people could generate income. Typical training activities included acupuncture, block-making, pavement slab production, composting, mushroom cultivation, disaster management, rice farming, earthquake-resistant construction, and pedi-cab businesses. As a result, survivors were able to develop a sense of self-belief as well as strengthening their resilience to any future challenges.

By increasing people's skill sets, Uplink enabled beneficiaries to broaden their employment opportunities, as is seen in this account of one man who worked as a truck driver prior to the tsunami but now uses the skills he learnt during the recovery phase to operate as a contractor. Zaini Yahya from Lam Rukam village stated,

The housing reconstruction was done by the owner. I managed my house building process with the help of two other people so I could save the fee for the builder. I used the money to build a bigger house than the standard size. The size of my house is 7x8 m^2. Having learned a lot from the technical team, I developed my construction skills and now work as small contractor, building houses from floor to roof.

It was predicted that in the five years following the 2004 tsunami, huge development in the region would continue, requiring quality building materials. In reality though, the majority of the block-making plants have closed down. It is believed that this is a result of cultural factors in the Aceh region. Due to the area's rich supply of natural resources, the community is accustomed to a more middle class style of living, making money predominantly through trading rather than manual labour. As a result, there was an overall reluctance to continue working at the block-making factories once the rehabilitation process had ended. Indeed, even during the programme of recovery, beneficiaries often found it easier to make money through other organizations' cash-for-work programmes. It can be seen that this aspect of Uplink's strategy may have proved to be worthwhile during the early months but has largely failed in its longer-term ambitions.

Another key benefit of Uplink's livelihoods programme was the positive impact it had on women's position and power within society. Acehnese women are traditionally strong and independent, but the religious neo-conservatism that had taken hold in the province had undermined that and as a result prior to the tsunami, women had little say in community matters. The open policy of Uplink and their participatory approach included all members of society in the entire process. By increasing the engagement of women in the public sphere, Uplink addressed gender inequalities that existed long before the disaster itself. It can be seen that women were empowered within their communities and are subsequently still able to organize, participate, and negotiate with men long after the programme ended. Linda from Kampung Pi village noted,

> During reconstruction, every week we had a meeting where all partici-
> pants could speak their mind. It was a new thing for me at the time as a
> woman to speak at a public forum. I learned from the process and now I
> am confident to represent my village at the district- and sub-district-lev-
> el meetings actively offering ideas and solutions especially on women's
> issues.

Indeed, by working in such participatory ways, a sense of security and stability were established with community cohesion prevailing. An increased understanding by both government and other agencies of the importance of community participation became apparent. Although JUB is no longer in operation, villagers hope that they will continue to work together to face any future challenges.

Figure 8.7 Stilt house modified into a restaurant, 2013

Conclusion

Uplink Indonesia saw the devastation of the Boxing Day tsunami as both a disaster and an opportunity. Instead of focusing on rebuilding homes and communities as they were prior to the event, they wanted to establish greater resilience and preparedness than had previously existed. One of the most crucial examples of this is the increased role of women within society. A participatory approach in all aspects of rehabilitation was seen by survivors to aid their personal recovery as they were absorbed in the process of rebuilding their homes. Syaiful from Lamte village in Aceh Besar affirmed, 'Witnessing the process of the house building was like a symbol of building our new life.' An awareness of safety and people-driven reconstruction was developed through this holistic and integrated scheme, dealing with both the physical and non-physical aspects of recovery.

From the observations made during the post-completion focus-group discussions and interviews, four key lessons can be drawn from the experiences of the survivors themselves.

Involving survivors in every stage of reconstruction

One of the most successful aspects of Uplink's approach was their emphasis on community participation. Unlike other agencies, they ensured that everyone became part of the planning, construction, and monitoring processes, which resulted in inhabitants taking control of both the quality and design of their new homes. Residents highlighted that their involvement not only aided them in their psychological recovery but also benefited the quality of their homes. When comparing Uplink's approach with building processes by others, they can see better choices of building materials and quality of construction in their own dwellings. The feeling of ownership that resulted helps to ensure sustainability.

Sensitivity to local culture

Certain aspects of the homes did not comply with cultural issues that are specific to Acehnese life. Despite Uplink's participatory approach, the importance of the kitchen was overlooked, resulting in spaces that were too small and inappropriately placed within the home. Families believed that if this matter had been considered earlier on in the design process, they would not have had to spend significant amounts of money remodelling their kitchens after building work was completed. However, it should be considered that during the reconstruction phase major constraints were put on both funding and time, making it a huge challenge to provide affordable and appropriate housing designs for such a vast number of people.

Post-disaster livelihoods programme

Whilst the empowerment of women and a grants scheme implemented by Uplink successfully reduced social and gender inequalities and allowed small businesses to grow (see Figure 8.7) aspects such as the block-making plants were less successful. The size of the blocks, copied from India, was much larger than those commonly used in Indonesia, thus making the material less marketable. In any reconstruction project, it is essential that survivors can re-establish and improve their livelihoods once aid agencies have left. In the case of the Aceh province, it was relatively easy for people to earn a living through cash-for-work programmes during the immediate recovery phase, but it has become more difficult due to an international and local economic demise. Uplink made a substantial effort to implement a strong livelihoods programme but recent contextual factors have reduced its impact for survivors.

Post-reconstruction phase assistance

During the reconstruction phase, a number of new technologies and innovations were introduced to survivors, not just for carrying out the immediate building work but also to increase their skillsets for longer-term recovery. A programme of this nature requires assistance over time in accordance with beneficiaries' learning capacities. Examples of this being less successful can be seen in both the solar panel initiative, as implemented in coordination with Greenpeace, and the 'biofil' tanks that were installed in some villages. In these cases, training proved to be insufficient to allow residents to continue using such technologies without the help of aid agencies.

A similar issue can be seen in the failure of JUB to continue after Uplink's departure from the area. Despite attempts to support the growth of this community organization, it lacked the necessary managerial and organizational structure to remain active. It can be seen that a rehabilitation programme of this scale and nature needs to account for post-completion assistance to ensure communities have mastered the skills that are necessary to maintain and develop both non-physical and physical aspects that are built during the construction phase in order to allow long-term recovery.

In conclusion, the participatory and all-inclusive approach of Uplink in Aceh is seen to have been an overall success. A number of agencies have adopted such a strategy in similar situations to provide communities with the skills and knowledge to rebuild both their homes and livelihoods. Although certain weaknesses are apparent in the longevity and continued impact of the scheme, residents have expressed a feeling of security and belonging in their homes, with many of the beneficiaries using the skills that were learnt during the reconstruction process to improve their livelihoods.

References

Campagnoli, F. (n.d.) 'JUB/Uplink in post-tsunami Aceh: Achievements, potentials, limitations', N-AERUS [website] <http://www.n-aerus.net/web/sat/workshops/2007/papers/Final_Campagnoli_paper.pdf> [accessed 30th Nov 2013].

Da Silva, J. (2010) *Lessons from Aceh*, Practical Action Publishing, Rugby. Available from: http://publications.arup.com/Publications/L/Lessons_from_Aceh.aspx [accessed 12 March 2014].

Multi Donor Fund – Java Reconstruction Fund Secretariat (2012) 'MDF-JRF Working Paper Series: Lessons Learned from Post-Disaster Reconstruction in Indonesia. The Multi Donor Fund for Aceh and Nias: A Framework for Reconstruction through Effective Partnerships', Multi Donor Fund [website] <http://www.multidonorfund.org/doc/pdf/WP_Ops_ENG.pdf> [accessed 15 May 2014].

Syukrizal, A., Hafidz, W., and Sauter, G. (2009) 'Reconstructing life after the Tsunami: the work of Uplink Banda Aceh in Indonesia', International Institute for Environment and Development [website] <http://pubs.iied.org/14582IIED.html> [accessed 10 April 2014].

UNEP (2005) 'After the Tsunami: Rapid Environmental Assessment Indonesia', United Nations Environment Programme [website], <http://www.unep.org/tsunami/reports/TSUNAMI_INDONESIA_LAYOUT.pdf> [accessed 12 May 2014].

World Habitat Awards (2007) 'Integrated People-Driven Reconstruction', <http://www.worldhabitatawards.org/winners-and-finalists/project-details.cfm?lang=00&theProjectID=742064F6-15C5-F4C0-9966E4B4F5449223> [accessed 30th Nov 2013].

About the authors

Annye Meilani joined the Urban Poor Consortium in 2007. Since then, she has been actively involved in organization and advocacy activities with the urban poor in order to achieve urban poor rights fulfilment in Indonesia.

Wardah Hafidz is an Indonesian activist who works closely with and for the rights of the nation's urban poor. She currently serves as coordinator of the education and capacity building programme at the Urban Poor Consortium, a leading NGO in Indonesia that focuses its work on urban poverty issues. She is the main protagonist of 'Jakarta Disorder', a 2013 documentary film about gentrification and democratization in Jakarta.

Ashleigh King is an Architecture Masters student at Oxford Brookes University. Having specialized in Development and Emergency Practice during her fifth year of study, she has a keen interest in Shelter after Disaster projects and hopes to pursue this once she has completed her degree.

CHAPTER 9
Guatemala: Knowledge in the hands of the people

Kurt Rhyner

Abstract

This project sets an example of culturally and technically appropriate reconstruction, taking reconstruction into development. Its placement within Catholic parishes ascribed to liberation theology, searching for social change and empowerment of the poor masses, was an ideal setup. The hands-on management at all levels and decentralized process contributed to the dedication and trust the beneficiaries had in the project and its management. The project developed a strong grassroots movement and the construction of 150 houses with self-help in 24 different villages of Baja Verapaz was only the visible part of a larger development. The educational component was the centre of activities and served as a base for other projects in Guatemala and neighbouring El Salvador. The houses were built with improved adobe structures. Publications produced by the project influenced similar technologies in at least half a dozen countries of Latin America. An integrated evaluation conducted 23 years after the project completion shows an extremely high rate of acceptance, with all houses inhabited and with good maintenance. This was also confirmed in a visit a further 12 years later.

Keywords: Guatemala earthquake; Adobe; Grassroots movement; Assisted self-help; Dual education

Introduction

It all began on the night of 4 February 1976, as a devastating earthquake struck Guatemala, killed more than 20,000 people, and left 250,000 homeless. An unprecedented wave of humanitarian aid helped to rebuild the country, but also contributed to changing its housing culture. Two months after the disaster, Caritas Switzerland and Swiss Solidarity approved funds for reconstruction and contracted a young Swiss architect, Kurt Rhyner, to assist Caritas Guatemala in the implementation of the 'Baja Verapaz' project, in the district with the same name in the centre of the country. The project started in June 1976 and came to an end in 1978.

Guatemala is the most northerly of the five Central American countries. Its area is 108,890 km² with a population of 13 million, mostly of Mayan

http://dx.doi.org/10.3362/9781780448398.009

origin. Two-thirds of the country is hilly and mountainous and thanks to its year-round temperate climate, Guatemala is sometimes referred to as 'the country of eternal spring'. Located on the crossing of three continental plates, the country is periodically devastated by earthquakes. Thus, finding disaster-resistant solutions for housing that are affordable to the general population are extremely important.

For centuries, people have built with adobe, using the earth beneath their feet to make sun-dried clay bricks. It only costs time and physical energy. However, adobe and fired clay tiles were blamed for much of the damage suffered. Architects and engineers had never really considered adobe a viable material and the commercial sector was actively promoting 'modern' materials like cement, concrete blocks, steel, galvanized corrugated iron sheets, and asbestos-cement as they were eager to sell their materials. The cement industry as well as the distributors of galvanized iron sheets moved in, all too often with the financial support of international aid organizations who found those materials to be more appropriate. The general public wanted something as solid as possible.

There was a general fear of earth construction and a feeling it should be banned altogether. Most houses in the affected areas were built of adobe, and also most damaged houses were of adobe. Many new cement-based structures had behaved better in the earthquake. Nonetheless, Caritas Switzerland decided to dedicate part of its aid to support reconstruction using local materials in an effort to propagate sustainable solutions but Caritas Guatemala received the project with suspicion. During this time of 'liberation theology', much of the Guatemalan Catholic church was actively promoting social change. The influential local church did not oppose the plans and some of the priests and nuns actually liked the idea of working with the age-old traditions to improve people's skills.

The project sought to adapt popular knowledge of adobe construction through application of engineering principles and the findings of a UN study after the 1970 Peruvian earthquake. In addition, damage assessments around Salamá's hardest hit villages showed that the earthquake had destroyed not only adobe buildings, but also many 'cement' structures. The Peruvian Government report (Comisión de Reconstrucción y Rehabilitación de la Zona Afectada, 1970) as well as others (Morales et al., 1993) have repeatedly proven that the weak part of a wall is the layer between the adobes, and not usually the adobes themselves. Therefore, if bonding of the adobes is ensured, a well-made traditional adobe house can resist horizontal loads through its mass if the walls are thick enough–and safety in earthquakes is good. Today, a large body of serious literature on this subject exists, which was not the case in 1976.

Common errors in adobe construction were deficient foundations, poor masonry work, a lack of horizontal reinforcement, and deficient roof construction. These issues were addressed through the use of some cement and lime in the construction of foundations, through education of a team of masonry promoters, production of square adobes which allow for improved interlocking corners, a horizontal reinforced concrete ring beam on top of the walls, and a solid roof construction with the centre supported by a wall. These design features can resist the predominantly horizontal earthquake forces. The difference between a good adobe house and a deficient one was about 20 bags of cement and 25 kg of steel for the horizontal reinforcement and the foundations, at an approximate cost of US$100. The other improvements did not necessarily augment the monetary cost of the house.

It was clear that with this project, several far-reaching goals should be met:

- re-establish confidence in traditional low-cost construction;
- provide technical education for grassroots builders;
- ensure monetary input into the local economy and regeneration of local markets;
- empower the local population through different development actions.

Quick participatory response

Impoverished communities are often more susceptible to the devastating impact of earthquakes as they live in poorly built houses that collapse easily when shaken. Their residents are seldom involved in the process of designing stronger houses using techniques or materials they can afford or that local industries can provide. This project pursued their active participation. It was clear to the donor and the project management that this project should do more than just rebuild houses; it should contribute to an awareness of sound local construction techniques and solid local workmanship. The cash injected from outside should have wider results than just replacing something lost. Through activation of local technologies, it is possible to strengthen the local economy and provide jobs for small-scale producers of materials.

By early July, the architect and his family had settled in an adobe house in Salamá, the capital of Baja Verapaz. The priests of Salamá and Rabinal invited him to go along on their visits to the outlying communities and present the idea of a reconstruction project using adobe. They gathered together *delegados de la palabra* (lay pastoral agents) from remote communities and from families in the peri-urban *barrios* (neighbourhoods). During those meetings, the architect discussed ideas for new housing with the people. Without exception, they wanted cement block construction with corrugated galvanized iron roofs, although all were aware of the costs which would have been prohibitive for them. The local salary level for a day labourer was below $1 per day, while a bag of cement cost around $5. Adobe was the only walling material that most people could produce themselves.

Hesitation and, sometimes, fear of using adobe also held them back from becoming involved in the project. However, one of the priests decided to build a house for himself in the neighbouring town of San Miguel Chicaj and settled there to attend the faithful. This model house gave an opportunity for the masonry team to exercise their newly-acquired knowledge of using adobe under the direct guidance of the architect. It was also a key factor in motivating the people to decide to build using adobe.

Villages soon started organizing house-building groups to be ready for the dry season which was the time to make adobes. At the end of the rainy season,

Figure 9.1 On the day of inauguration at the priest's model house

the first group started to produce adobes and by Christmas 1976, nine groups with a total of 38 families had already begun. The adobes were then ready for construction a few months later.

Figure 9.2 Dual education for builders was ongoing over the whole project cycle

Building the capacity of the people

The main objective of the project was to show the affected population in the rural areas of the district of Baja Verapaz that it is possible to build safely with the soil under their feet. This was to be achieved through setting up an informal 'dual education programme' wherein young people would be trained and educated by building adobe houses in different communities of Baja Verapaz (see Figure 9.2). The houses were designed to respect the local architectural tradition, but with improved technology. The material cost (including timber, roofing tiles, doors, and windows) was repaid by the beneficiaries into a revolving fund of Caritas Guatemala, while the technical and infrastructural costs were assumed by the project.

Local people were taught how to produce good adobe, how to build the houses, and provided with credit to pay for the materials needed such as cement and steel for foundations and the ring beam, timber and tiles or corrugated galvanized iron sheets for roofs. Whenever possible, the materials were purchased locally. More than half of the timber was sawn by hand in the same village and all roofing tiles were produced in the district. This had the multiple benefits of purchasing from local artisans, thereby actively promoting their products as well as reinforcing local production networks.

A model house was built for the local priest in San Miguel Chicaj (see Figure 9.1) to demonstrate the improvements in relation to most of the damaged structures:

- a solid foundation with rocks and cement/lime mortar;
- good adobes and careful masonry work;
- interlocking corners with external buttresses;
- horizontal ring beam of reinforced concrete;
- a solid roof construction.

Six masons, carefully selected from different villages, pooled their knowledge and received theoretical education from the architect. Many of the masons were *delegados de la palabra* and had learned many group-related skills through their pastoral duties, often being more social workers than pastoral agents. They were literate and learned to interpret plans. The self-builders were all poor people without formal jobs, mostly day labourers, and subsistence farmers in the villages. As mentioned previously, adobe construction is a technology for the dry season which combines well with farming. Thus, it was important to begin by November, when the rains subsided, and to have a roof over the house by May when the rains would start again.

In most places, the adobes could be produced near the house, and sometimes even in the backyard. However, in Salamá, it was found that production on a river bank was more appropriate as the correct mix of sand and clay was available right on-site and as the neighbourhood had no water system. This led to the start of a very important side-project: the extension of the municipal water system to the barrio. All families contributed with labour. Caritas sponsored the water pipes, and the municipality installed an additional pump in their system (see Figure 9.3).

Figure 9.3 The project dynamics in Salamá brought improvements to the community

Decentralized organization and collective action

Salamá is far away from Guatemala city and access at the time was difficult because the only road had been cut when a bridge over a large river was destroyed by the earthquake. There were no telephone connections and all communication was personal or by telegraph from town to town. The priests communicated from parish to parish through radio. The paved road gave way, in remote areas, to bumpy and winding dirt roads that would become impassable during the rainy season.

The architect lived in Salamá ensuring a close and interactive relationship between him, the masons, and the beneficiaries. The hands-on management at all levels and decentralized process contributed to the dedication and trust the beneficiaries had in the project and its management. It enabled the people to identify with the project and view it as their own. The grassroots organization of the work groups evolved into a movement that began to seek ways to improve their lives in other ways. A poor neighbourhood of Salamá, Santa Elena, took the lead. A group of women and men started to organize the neighbourhood and soon a dynamic movement was under way, with capacity classes, digging of latrines and, of course, house construction.

Each work group consisted of three to six families which would build their own houses, under the guidance of a mason. They collected stones for the foundations and produced all the adobe. The families who involved themselves and succeeded to produce adobes were 'people who go the extra mile'. They were among the most aware of the communities, people who could understand the importance of learning how to build with their traditional material in a manner to resist earthquakes. Many were active in the church and had learned useful social skills that enabled them to organize their work groups.

Every Saturday, the masons met together with the architect and his local counterpart Guillermo Chavarria (a farmer with great skills as a social worker) on a work site and planned the activities for the following week. Each mason attended a group and, if distance permitted, two groups, staying with them through the week. The house builders provided room and board for the masons. As the project expanded, additional masons had to be trained and employed and the work load for the architect grew enormously. Each group would decide on the size and form of the house. This often created long and heated discussions, as everybody tried to squeeze the maximum possible out of the tight budget of $400 that was available for materials for each house. The discussions centred on the number of doors, the type of roofing material and timber needed and where to buy them. This often created useful new links, as they negotiated with the local producers of tiles and timber. Some groups managed to finish reconstruction within 150 days, while others took more than a year and a half, because groups worked according to their capacity, sometimes stopping to farm.

Supported by the local priest, Salamá became the centre of activity. Over time, historical social divisions opened up between the parishes of Salamá and Rabinal, a cultural centre of the indigenous population. In the second year of the project, the priest of Rabinal, who was also the head of the regional Caritas, resented the widening gap between dynamic Salamá, and not so active Rabinal. He started to use his administrative power to put a brake on Salamá's development. The ensuing tensions between priests caught the attention of the national Caritas office that had observed how a 'house-building project' had become a 'house-building movement'. With their support, the expansion of the project to other parts of the country became a reality. New project proposals were presented to European donors and several were approved, based on the experiences in Baja Verapaz. The ensuing projects would build in much the same ways, but the social movements were locally distinct.

As the programme grew so did demands on the architect. As he was required to attend new projects in other parts of the country, the masons were required to take over technical decision-making and work with a weak administration that favoured one parish over another. By that time, a total of 39 groups were working throughout Baja Verapaz. The masons demonstrated enough solid technical knowledge and organizational experience to continue, and the social skills to navigate tensions. The project slowed down, but the quality of the construction did not suffer, with regular supervision in place.

The weekly meetings of the Salamá movement grew in size and sometimes more than a hundred people would participate. The people discussed ways of improving their barrio and they even started organizing cultural activities, participating in local exhibits, and decorating their own float for the annual parade. Swiss television produced a 20-minute report focusing on the social aspects of the project.

This type of social movement aroused suspicion in government circles in those days of growing social unrest and oppression. The project came to a virtual standstill in 1978 when the political situation became more difficult and government repression made social activities impossible. The leading priest of Salamá was expelled from the country, while another priest from Salamá was found murdered in a street of the capital city. The communication between Caritas headquarters in Guatemala City and project areas became difficult. The architect had moved to another town and could not revisit the project for security concerns until decades later.

An evaluation after 24 years

In 2001, an in-depth evaluation of the project was carried out by students of architecture and engineering at the University of San Carlos, who visited 43 of the 150 houses. They discovered that all but one were in good condition, and although there was variation as to the degree of maintenance, 72 per cent of the surveyed houses were still in the hands of the original beneficiaries, and the remainder in the hands of their offspring. Many people recalled that immediately after the earthquake they were afraid of adobe, but today they feel comfortable and happy to have their adobe house. Only 7 per cent of those interviewed would have preferred another technology. Many young people living nearby spontaneously asked to be considered for a similar project in the future.

Revisiting after 36 years

Salamá has changed dramatically. It was a shock to visit the town where we lived 36 years ago; paved roads, signal lights, and a one-way traffic flow attests to the development that has taken place. People with whom we spoke all referred to this great change as having occurred in the last 10 years. After the peace agreement in 1993, people were still afraid to invest, the economy was going slow, and it wasn't until the beginning of the new century that confidence began to grow. The same is visible in most parts of the country, with the exception of the major cities where the upswing came earlier. Villagers, however, lamented that all the money flows to Salamá and that the outlying villages are neglected. Sixteen houses were visited, in Santa Elena, San Miguel, and San Francisco, and observations were made across the project area.

User satisfaction

Most houses have now been passed on to the next generation. More than half of the properties were very well maintained, none was in disrepair and all of them were inhabited. Some of the houses of elderly people needed plaster repair and a new coat of paint. Everybody appreciates the agreeable room climate and the older generation who lived through the earthquake mention that the many strong tremors of the last decades have not damaged the houses.

In the wider project area, almost all houses are lived in; often they are the core of a family compound that has been built up little by little with formal and informal dwellings. We did encounter one house that had been demolished, because the granddaughter of the deceased owner lives in the US and she had a large house built in its place, with steel bars sticking out of the concrete roof to begin a second floor, a practice known as 'architecture of hope' – it implies the hope to have funds in the future to keep building.

All people interviewed expressed their satisfaction with the house and several members of their families were interested to know if there was a possibility of another project. The fact that several houses had been sold and are inhabited by the new owners, who were all satisfied, shows the project houses are still desirable.

Beneficiary targeting

It is clear that the project reached people who had lost their homes, and were prepared to build their own houses. A large majority of the original families occupy the houses as homes and viewed them as permanent dwellings. The participants of the project were building them not only for themselves and their children, but also for their grandchildren. Over the past 36 years, a small number have been sold, in two cases by the third generation, in another case because the armed conflict obliged the owner and his family to flee into exile. The nature of this project accounts for the high level of continuing owner occupancy. It was not a resettlement project. People built the houses themselves on their own land in their own village and, consequently, had high stakes in ensuring a family home for the future. Several families had to formalize their land titles, as they had only possession of it, not ownership. This is a specific condition of laws in Central America, which differentiate between *posesión* (informal tenure) and *propiedad* (formal tenure). The legal arrangements were facilitated by the architect.

Not everyone wanted to build their own house and some of the first candidates dropped out early on. The initial task of adobe production is a hard job, as the earth had to be mixed and the watered mud trod with the feet, then lifted out of the pit and formed into wooden moulds. After a drying for a couple of days their surface is cleaned with a machete and they are stacked. While the rural families were more used to hard physical labour, it was unusual in peri-urban neighbourhoods. Several candidates dropped out as they simply did not want to do the hard work. The high physical entrance cost undoubtedly made for a tough selection – of the most active members of the socially disadvantaged – that was helpful for the success of the project.

The project had the goal of bringing confidence in local techniques; it wanted to have many successful activities in many places, and it wanted to create local leadership. Most of the families that dropped out continued in the social movement and many of them benefited from other aspects of the project such as the introduction of drinking water to the neighbourhood.

Replication

Our first stop when revisiting the project in 2013 was at a house that was sold by the sons after the owner died. They had built a second house using the same technology a few years after the project, and both are in perfect condition and inhabited.

Next to the model house of Father Carlos in San Miguel Chicaj, the immediate neighbours built a copy a few years later, engaging a local mason, Alfonso. He told us that he had learned to build such houses by helping to build Father Carlos's house. He later continued to build many adobe houses as a trade and he himself lives in one. He believes it to be the best material as it is cool when it is hot and warm when it is cold, and is strong and resistant. In Barrio Santa Elena, we encountered Celso, who was about 26 years of age at the time of reconstruction and was the youngest beneficiary (see Figure 9.4 and 9.5). Through the project, he became interested in carpentry and now has a small workshop and three employees. He remembers vividly and guides us to some of the houses that he helped build.

In four more Guatemalan municipalities, adobe projects were started in 1977 and 1978, with a total of 200 houses. Each of those projects was organized in a different way depending on the local situation. While most were in dry

Figure 9.4 Celso building his house in Salamá, 1977

Figure 9.5 Celso's house and carpentry shop, 2013

areas, there was one project site where the rainy season is long and everything had to be well organized to take advantage of the dry season. In all of those places, the activity was started with one or two masons from Baja Verapaz, who would pass on their knowledge to local tradesmen.

We saw several houses with extensions built with the same technology. Here the family of the granddaughter of the deceased builder lives and she is very proud of the house and invited us to look around (see Figure 9.6). Other than having changed some of the timber last year, they have not had anything done as the other parts are still fine.

Figure 9.6 Her grandfather built the house in 1977

Domingo, who is now more than 70 years old, also built his own house 36 years ago (see Figure 9.7). His house is in good condition; they added an extra room a few years after the project finished. He lives there with his wife and other family members. He is now disabled, his son has died, but a grandson built a house of cement blocks next to it ten years ago. The original project house became a core house for a family compound, something we encountered again and again as we visited project houses.

Figure 9.7 Domingo, now 70 years old, in front of the house he built 36 years ago

Fabian and Amalia are also over 70 years old. Their house is in good condition, although it could use a new coat of paint, and it has been enlarged using adobe technology (see Figure 9.8). Their granddaughter recently built a house in front, with walls of concrete blocks. As it turned out to be much more expensive than planned, she has not been able to finish it as she wanted. The extension into a family compound is possible because the plots of land were large enough to absorb other buildings; however, there is not enough space on which to make adobes.

Felipe was one of the group members of four families that became champions in the house-building movement. He is now 82 years old and still works to earn a living. The house is inhabited by his son's family, they have put a shade tent in front; on the next plot a three-story house was built. Felipe now lives in a small house made of cement blocks, built 10 years ago. His son

Figure 9.8 Fabian and Amalia in front of their house, 2013

built the adobe house, part of the work team of four youngsters between 15 and 19 years old.

In rural areas, people continue to build with adobe as they have land on which to build and to produce the adobes, as well as time during the non-agricultural periods in which to fabricate them. In the urban areas, several limitations emerge such as lack of space which is often intensified by not owning land. People must have land and money in order to build. Where money to build is not at hand, people must resort to either projects or loans, both of which have associated problems.

Projects struggle as too little development funding is available for housing. For most organizations, it simply is not a priority until a disaster occurs. Post-disaster reconstruction projects take place within a special situation. The emergency itself and the resulting social instability combined with relatively large sums to finance projects create circumstances that do not particularly lend themselves as a basis for replication. With regard to loans, not only do they involve high interest rates, often they are linked to the purchase of certain materials and unreasonably high standards. Forcing the use of specific technologies becomes a vicious circle that limits the possibility of replication of any non-mainstream or consumer technology introduced in a post-disaster situation.

The experience of Salamá became the starting point of decades of dedication to providing disaster-resistant and secure housing to the poorer sections of societies across South America. It led to the formation of Grupo Sofonias.

When this group began an adobe programme in the Dominican Republic, the architect of the Salamá project hired Francisco, one of the masons from Baja Verapaz, and contracted him as instructor. Francisco then spent two months teaching other masons in that programme. The manual produced for Baja Verapaz was very widely distributed and still is a standard work today. Many publications on adobe have since emerged, even copying the same drawings. Housing projects in Nicaragua, El Salvador, Honduras, the Dominican Republic, Cuba, and Ecuador have used this manual. Perhaps the national and international engagement towards establishing norms for building with soil, teaching young professionals how to build in a disaster-resistant manner with local materials, executing housing and reconstruction projects in these and other countries, can be seen as replication too. The organizational system that made the project a success has been incorporated into housing projects of Grupo Sofonias and the EcoSur network in other Latin American countries and different disaster-response situations.

Technical performance

According to the evaluation after 24 years and looking back over more than three decades, it becomes clear that the technical performance of the houses has been good. They have been able to withstand various strong earth tremors. None are in bad shape, though some could do with repairs to the plaster or a new coat of paint.

The architect lobbied for official adoption of adobe norms. Such norms, however, never materialized in Latin America, where adobe is still banned as a load-bearing material in almost all new construction regulations.

Livelihoods, friendships, and conflict

During the project period, local livelihoods were intensified through the production and purchase of materials locally, unfortunately diminishing considerably after the project due to the increasing violence in the country and more recently because modern materials are offered on credit. Nevertheless, some beneficiaries such as Alfonso the mason and Celso the carpenter continue to make an income from skills learned in the project. In a few cases, the use of houses has been changed to accommodate livelihood activities, e.g. in the case of Tomas. He has passed away and his son now owns the house which is well located for commerce, on a road which is now paved. The son runs a stationery shop. Prior to that, he used it as a bicycle shop for which he has now built a larger structure, and he lives with his family in another house in town.

In post-disaster projects, people often realize that they can achieve improvements in their lives through working together. In Salamá, something of a movement developed implementing mini-projects. Vegetable gardens were planted; water runoffs from wash basins made, even a drinking water system was installed. The visit to Juana and Moisés, the leaders of the movement who are now over 80 years old, was a special moment. Their house looks great and is the centre of a large and much extended family compound. Juana stressed that during the conflict, the movement stopped as they were accused of being subversive and communists. Raquel, a younger sister aged 78 (see Figure 9.9), also mentioned that they were observed and harassed during the conflict. Neither sister understands what a communist is, and why their community activities and hard work could possibly have been viewed as dangerous. Domingo vividly remembers the reconstruction and emphasizes that some of his companions, people he had not known before, have become his friends and he still has contact with several of them. He equally laments that with the conflict, the movement died and it was no longer possible to have meetings.

Figure 9.9 Raquel Moya and her house, 2013

Everyone we visited in the 2013 study reminded us of the fact that further projects and activities could not be carried out because of the intensification of the conflict. How a conflict can affect lives and livelihoods comes through strongly in the story of Demetrio.

Looking for Demetrio

Demetrio was a self-builder who became the best mason in the project (see Figure 9.10). Bumping along the earthen road, cracked and rutted from the rains, we stopped several times to ask people where we could find him. Finally, we were able to locate Demetrio's house and entered the compound hesitantly. A charming and vigorous elderly man looked at us and said, 'Kurt, these 36 years later'. What a re-encounter! As the post-earthquake mood gave way to intensification of the conflict, many of the people who stood out in society became suspect and their lives endangered. In the case of Demetrio, he sold the adobe house he had built and fled with his family to the capital city after army-backed killers had been looking for him. In urban exile, he and his family lived marginally, as he could not apply for any job, even eating from the garbage dump to survive. He had lost everything. However, the Peace Agreement of the 1990s brought changes to conditions in the country. He and his family returned to the village to begin afresh, building an adobe house. Guatemalan society slowly recovered from the years of conflict and reconciliation began and still continues to this day (see Figure 9.11).

Figure 9.10 Demetrio's house in San Miguel, 1977

Figure 9.11 Demetrio, 2013

Conclusion

The adobe reconstruction project in the district of Baja Verapaz was a quick response after the great earthquake in Guatemala, something that is rarely seen nowadays! Within six months of the earthquake, the first permanent houses were finished and 24 months later, there were 150 houses inhabited. It is the story of knowledge in the hands of the people, where they learned how to use their traditional materials, adobe and clay roofing tiles, in a manner that could resist earthquakes. Important to being able to carry out and complete the project was decentralized organization whereby everyone from the project director to the masons were together in the field and had decision-making power. Ultimately, the project included 39 groups scattered over 24 different locations, most of them remote from one another and from the district capital. As the project progressed, the use of adobe and the participatory approach spread to other parts of the country, and the neighbouring country, El Salvador.

It is an unfortunate fact that today with all the advanced communications technology and the physical possibilities of moving ahead fast, projects are developing slower. The organizational setup of this project and the freedom with which the local management was able to work is not possible to repeat today. Organizations are afraid to take decisions, there are complicated structures between the donor networks, and a growing fear of committing errors slows down actions. It seems that a growing part of the funds have to be used to back up the infrastructure of the organizations, decision channels have become more formal, and personal commitment of the engaged actors has often been replaced by bureaucratic 'professionalism'. The experiences in the tsunami projects, for example, and particularly after the Haiti earthquake, are not encouraging.

The project was not without challenges. Today, many people would like to build with adobe, even those in the urban environment. However, lack of money means they must take out loans and incur debt, and they explained that the loans are linked through government regulations, to the purchase of certain modern construction materials at particular businesses. This modern 'trap' is causing one of the great changes in the building tradition.

The level of political tension and repression in the country during the late 1970s and 1980s was high and many community projects had to be cancelled before they could start. Moreover, within the Catholic Church and Caritas itself divisions grew between followers of liberation theology and the traditionalists, and diplomatic skill was needed by all players. The project was walking on an edge between the progressive ideas of empowering communities and the power of veto within Caritas, let alone the physical threat posed by the military.

In those days in Guatemala and many other places in Latin America, there was fertile ground for the creation of grassroots movements. The political awakening of the masses, combined with a Catholic Church influenced by the second Vatican council that opted to support the creation of cooperatives and self-help groups to improve the living standards of the people, allowed for progress in many directions. Neighbourhoods rallied to push governments to improve services and educational facilities and demanded democratic participation. The Guatemalan government reacted with panic; influenced by the Cold War, they associated this movement with communist aggression and reacted with terror. Fifteen years of internal conflict with more than 100,000 people killed has stifled all grassroots activity, and even now the fear keeps neighbourhoods from gathering.

The outstanding aspect of visiting this project 36 years later is that it has been possible to see first-hand the sustainability of the houses passed through generations and surviving earth tremors. However, due to the political tension and subsequent conflict the proactive community grassroots movement was lost.

References

Comisión de Reconstrucción y Rehabilitación de la Zona Afectada, Proyecto Experimental de Vivienda (1970) Manual para la construccion de viviendas con adobe, Oficina Nacional de Desarrollo Comunal, Dirección de Promoción, Peru.

Morales, R., Torres, R., Rengifo, L., and Irala, C. (1993) 'Manual para la construccion de viviendas de adobe', Comites Romero [website] <http://www.comitesromero.org/tarragona/fichas/casa_adobe_texto.pdf> [accessed 25 April 2014].

About the author

Kurt Rhyner developed Grupo Sofonias, a non-profit organization with active bases in Nicaragua, Ecuador, Haiti, and Switzerland, and affiliated organizations in Namibia and Cuba. He is involved in the conception of projects, analysis of technologies and materials appropriate to specific situations, financial analysis, executive management, backstopping, and evaluations.

CHAPTER 10
Honduras: 'La Betania', resettlement of a flooded neighbourhood

Kurt Rhyner

Abstract

This project concentrated on building a new community with families who had lived in a high-risk area of Tegucigalpa, the capital of Honduras. After Mitch, land pressure increased. The growth area of Tegucigalpa was towards the north, where a new industrial area was being developed, however no suitable plot could be found at an affordable cost. The government decided to dedicate a farm in this area to build a satellite town. EcoViDe and the Betania grassroots committee were the first ones to decide to move there. After careful planning, construction could start 18 months after Mitch; it took another 18 months to finish 317 houses with assisted self-help. Every family contributed 150 days of labour. A 2008 survey and a 2013 visit showed satisfaction among the beneficiaries. The drawn-out time of insecurity without land had formed a strong community organization in Betania and the people learned to fight for their dream.

Keywords*:* Hurricane reconstruction; Land issues; Planning coordination; Community building; Assisted self-help

Introduction

Hurricane Mitch hit Honduras at the end of October 1998 and the strongest rainfall ever swelled the rivers until they swallowed whole communities lining their banks. Some 200,000 houses were destroyed or severely damaged, on top of an existing housing deficit of 700,000. Total damage was estimated to be close to US$4 billion, which is more than two-thirds of Honduras' annual gross domestic product.

Honduras is located in Central America, a subcontinent that suffers repeatedly from natural disasters, specifically earthquakes, tropical storms, hurricanes, and floods as well as droughts. As Julian Salas (2008: 17) states,

> It is difficult to find any comparative geographic area on the planet with such a concentration and diversity of natural phenomena that can cause disasters of such magnitude. The reason is the direct relationship between mountainous areas and volcanic and seismic episodes.

http://dx.doi.org/10.3362/9781780448398.010

Honduras is listed as number 14 in the world's ranking of countries at greatest risk from three or more types of hazards (World Bank, 2005).

The project analysed in this study focused on building a new community with families who had lived in a high-risk flood area. Tegucigalpa, the capital of Honduras, is embedded between hills and virtually no level plot of land can be found. After Mitch, the pressure for land increased and several NGO resettlement projects bought unsuitable land. The growth area of Tegucigalpa was towards the north, where a new industrial area was being developed in the Amarateca valley. When the national government decided to dedicate a farm in the foothills of Amarateca to develop a satellite town, EcoViDe and the Betania grassroots committee were the first ones to decide to be included.

After careful planning, construction started 18 months after Mitch, and in another 18 months 317 houses were built with assisted self-help. Every family contributed 150 days of labour. A 2008 survey shows exceptionally high satisfaction among the beneficiaries. This was confirmed in a 2013 visit during interviews with residents. This undoubtedly is a positive outcome of the drawn-out period of insecurity without land, when the donor agency was threatening to withdraw its support and EcoViDe was able to form a strong community organization in Betania and the people learned to fight for their dream.

Planning and organizing the intervention

As soon as the waters receded many families decided to return to their houses, which had been devastated by the flood on a low lying river bank known as La Betania. It is often the poorer segments of the population that live in less than solid houses on steep hillsides or near rivers that turn periodically into ravaging monsters. However, it was clear that they should eventually abandon this area due to the high recurrent risk of flooding.

EcoViDe, a national housing NGO, was active in emergency relief and immediately after the hurricane undertook management of one block of an emergency shelter put up by the Honduran government with relief aid. Together with EcoViDe, the residents set the goal of building new houses somewhere else. Around 300 families were actively involved in these discussions. Through the EcoSur network, EcoViDe came into contact with the Swiss Red Cross who was interested in financing a large reconstruction project, with co-financing from Chaîne de Bonheur, a Swiss charity organizing an appeal on national TV.

International pressure to build houses was felt by all the actors, with donor agencies wanting to see results and the communities also eager to start construction. Despite pressure from the donor side, the Betania team decided to look further. In 1995, the government had commissioned a study that defined the valley of Amarateca, to the north of the capital and on the country's primary highway, as the growth area (Universidad Politécnica de California, 1995). Amarateca is a flat wide valley with soft hills on either side and new industrial complexes were under construction, thus it seemed to be the ideal place for resettlement of mostly unemployed poor families. However, no suitable plot could be sourced at an affordable cost. The government, in coordination with Spanish aid, finally decided to build a satellite town on a government-owned farm in the foothills of the Amarateca valley. A local engineering company was given the contract to develop an integrated settlement plan. EcoViDe and the community of Betania immediately went to visit the site and they were the first to commit to this plan and choose their 'neighbourhood' within the designated land.

EcoViDe had sought planning expertise from EcoSur network partners and developed organizational and architectural designs together with the beneficiaries, who had by then formalized their grassroots organization. As the search for land took more than a year, this phase was done carefully and beneficiaries had the opportunity to participate fully in the dialogue. Once the government had sourced this land for the relocation of a total of 3,200 families, the Betania team quickly moved to adapt their design and place it in the area chosen which was slightly away from other projects.

In close dialogue with the community and government planners, a proposal was made that required only minimal earth moving and had a natural rainwater runoff system, something crucial in this hilly area. The design of the houses aimed to improve earthquake resistance by avoiding large rooms and designing simple roof structures. The urban plan was admired by all who came into contact with it, including government planners who had based their urbanization on straight streets and cost-intensive terracing of some 1,500 plots for their own programme.

Before the government assigned the land to the project, they began to flatten out the hilly terrain and terrace the hillsides. This was supposed to not affect the site demarcated for Betania, designed to be developed without major earth moving or retaining walls. After large parts of the land had been cleared and the vegetation removed, the government's Department of Ecology stopped the project and put a ban on any new development of land. This obliged the Betania project to change their plans and integrate into the terraced part of the project. Thus, an excellent urban design based on respectful treatment of the environment had to be abandoned and the houses built on terraces.

Figure 10.1 Guided self-help construction

Figure 10.2 Roof construction

The resettlement site more than 30 km from old Betania posed a serious challenge for organizing self-help construction. It was obvious that daily commuting for the brigades of self-builders consisting of up to 50 people was not feasible. At the edge of the resettlement site (later called 'Ciudad España' as the Spanish government sponsored much of it) stood an abandoned brick yard and EcoViDe got permission to use it. In the large chambers of the kiln, they installed dormitories and a kitchen. In the drying area, they installed equipment for the production of hollow concrete blocks and micro-concrete tiles (MCR). Other projects transported workers daily back and forth losing hours underway and spending on transport. The Betania group frequently worked overtime in a drive to finish their job.

The beneficiaries had to subscribe to 150 days of labour and the neighbourhood committee organized the weekly brigades who worked under the guidance of contracted masons (see Figures 10.1 and 10.2). The project provided food for the workers. This rather flexible organization allowed people to take advantage of periods of unemployment to forge ahead or to engage in temporary jobs and work slower; when the first families had complied with their duties, others had fallen behind. The houses were handed over to the beneficiaries in lots and only after they had complied with the programme.

Figure 10.3 Building the house is a family task

Technical solutions, time frame, and funding

Technical solutions, training, and production

A massive construction project like Betania relied on an easy and quick delivery of building materials. It followed one of the most common construction methods for walls, known as reinforced masonry with hollow blocks. The only walling material that was available and affordable at the time was hollow concrete blocks. Timber was readily available which made it a logical choice for the roof structure. For roof cladding, the choice was micro-concrete roofing tiles, a technology promoted by the EcoSur network and EcoViDe and produced locally. The alternative would have been imported metal sheets with a shorter useful life.

EcoViDe installed a production unit for hollow concrete blocks and for micro-concrete tiles in the old brick yard; products were supplied directly to the construction site with a trailer and a tractor. This on-site production was a decisive factor in assuring the supply chain and to lower costs. Timber and other external materials were bought in bulk and stored in one of the large chambers of the brick yard. This production and supply unit was staffed with paid workers who were mainly from Betania. The men in block and tile production received training that later would become a livelihood for most, and all families participated in house construction and learned some construction trades (see Figure 10.3).

The house design was based on combining the different rooms in a certain way to allow a very simple roof construction and to enhance earthquake resistance. The foundation and structure in reinforced masonry was designed to allow for later vertical expansion to two or even three levels.

The workmanship was satisfactory, as several self-builders had some prior construction experience, while others learned and the rest simply helped with the tasks. The location on the hillside overlooking the valley gave it a special character, and the creative design of the houses marked a strong difference to the uninspiring rectangular houses of the next two projects. The beneficiaries of the other projects soon called Betania 'the residential neighbourhood', which is the local synonym for 'higher level'. This helped to maintain the enthusiasm of the self-builders who pulled through the 18 months with few of the social problems usually connected with a relocation programme of urban dwellers. Fewer than ten families dropped out and they were quickly replaced by others. The monthly general meetings basically dealt with social issues and improving the quality of the work, but the technologies and the designs were never questioned.

Time frame

In any reconstruction project, time seems to be the overriding issue. Cooperation between EcoViDe and the community began immediately after the hurricane and first contacts with the Swiss Red Cross were established before the end of 1998. General planning happened in the first half of 1999 and the overall project received financial approval some 6 months after the disaster. Physical planning could not start until the end of 1999 when land was assured. EcoViDe and the Swiss Red Cross signed a contract in November 1999.

Although the site was assured by the government, construction could not start until an overall plan for the satellite town was approved. By early May 2000, EcoViDe/Betania was the first project to establish itself on the new terrain by building its base of operation, and in July it started the production of materials on site. Construction of houses began on 1 August and the last house (of 317) was finished on 15 November 2002, four years after the disaster. The first houses were finished before the next project began. The land issue and the disorganization of the government were such that no medium-sized or large project near Tegucigalpa was faster to provide permanent shelter with basic infrastructure (water, electricity, accessibility).

Funding

Finances for the construction were available long before it could start. Aid flowed through a complex multinational and multilateral donor network to the largely non-governmental relief and development agencies. While the main donor did not contemplate purchasing land, some international actors offered finances and pressured for action even on inappropriate land. The need to act quickly, logistical difficulties, and ineffective management by an overwhelmed Honduran government resulted in an improvised and uncoordinated effort. These factors tended to pitch NGOs against each other to compete not only for donor grants but also for land and beneficiaries. The EcoSur network was able to convince the donors to allow for the needed time.

The flow of finances was never a problem. Tight budgetary organization and an intricate controlling system allowed for periodic analysis done by the EcoSur backstopper. A hike in cost of only 2 per cent had been predicted several months before completion of the project and despite strong inflation during the period of implementation this was a correct prediction and allowed the project to come in on budget. The average cost per house in Ciudad España was reported to be $6,470 or $157.70 per m². In Betania, the cost was only $105 per m² for similar or better standards of construction.

No conclusive information is available on the total cost of the construction of this satellite town, but it can be safely assumed that the physical infrastructure has cost considerably more than the actual house building. The terracing of the hillsides was an exercise that could have been minimized by better planning, as EcoSur had proposed for the Betania project.

User survey in 2008

In 2008, a sociological study conducted interviews and analysis with 30 families randomly selected from the 317 houses in the resettlement project (Belli, 2008). The survey revealed that after living there for five to six years, 80 per cent of the inhabitants rated the project as very good and 20 per cent as good. All 30 interviewed families were happy with the solution, 23 per cent had some minor observations about construction details. Unemployment is considered the overriding problem but interestingly, security and violence were rated a far distant second, whereas these generally dominate in Honduras.

People highly valued their success in improving the community through communal action, and the forming of a strong neighbourhood committee (Codel) through which they collected funds for collective improvements. The first important task had been to activate an old well and connect it to pipes, so they had running water more than a year before the government provided the service. After EcoViDe had built a community centre, the people built a fence around it and added concrete footpaths to all houses. No serious problems between neighbours were reported, people felt safe and the police station confirmed that Betania was the most peaceful among the neighbourhoods in Ciudad España.

Everybody mentioned that the social work provided by EcoViDe and the Red Cross before and during constructions had been done well and they could not name real threats to the community. One person responded, 'We do not see any big threats; we do have some problems with the administration of the water service but at the house level, we are happy and proud to have an excellent quality house'.

About ten families had changed their roof, replacing the tiles with metal sheeting as it seemed that some houses suffered leaks. Also, a few families had made minor adjustments to the house, mostly building a fence or wall and adding a room. These works were all done by the house owners themselves or by contracting others in the community using the methods and materials of the original reconstruction. The construction training thus proved useful. Several men from the community were working in construction projects outside Betania. Overall, the job market in the valley was not as good as expected and the industrial development was slow.

Revisiting in 2013

During the 2013 visit, it became obvious that the results of a similar study would not differ substantially. All 20 people interviewed expressed degrees of satisfaction with the project and their living situation. Minor negative observations concerned details or specific preferences. Most interviews were conducted with women of different ages, as 70 per cent of the house owners are women; their responses are particularly worthwhile as it is the women who carry out the tasks of running a household. They also had been actively involved in the organization of the project.

User satisfaction

All houses in the project are inhabited, about 80 per cent of them by the original beneficiaries. Several houses have been expanded to include a small shop for selling products or doing handwork such as welding, upholstery, and tailoring. The construction with cement blocks is solid and needs little upkeep. The houses were handed over without rendering and but most families have done this now and made them look more attractive.

About 15 per cent of the families have changed the roof, as they said the micro-concrete tiles had let water through. Most of them were able to repair the roof through better placement of the tiles, but others decided to opt for metal sheets, as used in their former dwellings. According to the interviewed sample, some roof changes were also due to lack of maintenance, when people did not recognize the benefits of the roofing material, and did not maintain and care for them adequately. The only producer nearby closed down, but tiles are available within the neighbourhood as people who changed their roof to metal sheeting often sell their tiles.

The urban layout imposed on the project by the government makes access for people with disability rather difficult in most houses. Only a few houses have easy wheelchair access. Most houses are accessed through stairways or steep walkways.

Figure 10.4 A lively well-kept neighbourhood

Everybody felt that they have houses of good quality, safe from future natural events, and secure from the usual risks of theft. This has much to do with the social work at the initial stage of the project, long before the actual construction period. Several people stressed the fact that 'they were prepared' and had formed strong social networks long before the project was finished.

The local police chief highlighted that Betania and neighbouring Suyapa, also developed by EcoViDe, were the most peaceful and best prepared parts of Ciudad España (see Figure 10.4). Especially in the first years, when the new town suffered heavily from violence, like most towns in Honduras, the difference was great. Later on, it seems that prevention work by the police has pacified most neighbourhoods. The police chief himself moved his family to Ciudad España and whenever he is due to move to another town, the Patronato (residents' organization) intervenes to keep him in the community. Right now they are in such a situation as apparently policemen in other towns are trying to be transferred to 'peaceful Ciudad España'. While alcoholism is a problem in Ciudad España, as well as drugs, it seems clear that the level is lower than in other towns, and the police stressed that in Betania and Suyapa the level of drug use is much lower still. The AA (Alcoholics Anonymous) was a driving force in the project since the beginning, and managed to build a meeting place with their own means.

Beneficiary targeting

Most houses are still inhabited by the original owners; so far only a few have died. About 15 per cent have rented the house out, as their work schedule in Tegucigalpa makes travelling difficult. A factor contributing to this high percentage is that the houses of old Betania in Tegucigalpa were not destroyed and some families still have a usable house there in what remains a risk area. This is a flaw committed by the government, as there was an agreement that all buildings in Betania would be destroyed as the zone was declared high risk, and a park with sport fields was to be created. However, the authorities never acted on it, and new dwellers have built their shacks in old Betania. In turn several families who owned damaged structures in Betania repossessed them before squatters could occupy them.

As a result, more families live in this high-risk zone today than prior to the disaster. The project had handed a detailed map of the area to the government, and this is now used to monitor its development. However, it is unlikely that it will ever be vacated; in floods like the one caused by Mitch, it will have to be evacuated temporarily.

In the new settlement, no house sales have taken place, as the contract stipulates that the property cannot be sold for 20 years. However, some houses, probably between five and ten, have changed hands. This is possible under a legal statute in Honduras which differentiates between possession and property. In those cases, only the possession is transferred in a simple civil contract. After 20 years, the new owner can legally register it as their property. While it was not possible to get figures, people suspect that the prices were substantially higher than the value invested by the different actors.

Some 3,200 house were planned on the plots provided by the national government, but only 1,350 have been built as the Honduran Red Cross ran out of funds. The legalization of land titles is slow, only 223 completed, the remaining 94 are still pending. Apparently they are the only inhabitants of Ciudad España with titles out of 1,350 houses built. The government tried to hand the land over to EcoViDe who would then have to undertake the legal steps to land entitlement and charge the beneficiaries for it. However, EcoViDe wisely declined. For all other projects, the land was granted to the Honduran Red Cross and they have not yet begun the process, ten years after reconstruction finished.

During our visit, the Betania representative used the opportunity to apply pressure on the government. He telephoned the general secretary of the Ministry of Finance announcing that an international mission was visiting the project. He was advised to visit the lawyer in charge together with a delegation of beneficiaries to apply pressure and to make a similar visit to the Ministry – the way business is done in Honduras. Thus, people do not have to pay taxes, but they have to spend time and fares to apply pressure. During previous attempts to secure land titles, the lawyer had tried to collect money from residents; however, the group learned that the lawyer gets his honorariums through a global government contract, so they did not need to pay. This is another result of the good organization and local empowerment facilitated by the approach taken by EcoViDe and EcoSur, the community leadership was able to bypass problems and produce results.

Replication

EcoViDe replicated the approach in Supaya on the opposite side of the valley with similar levels of success. There is an architectural unity in the valley of 'Ciudad España' that separates it socially and visually from the other projects. The project director and community leader recalled an interesting anecdote:

At the beginning technicians of other projects criticized and sometimes even ridiculed EcoViDe because they were planning such a different house-type with irregular roof shapes. All the others planned a rectangular house with a simple two-pitched roof. When Betania was under construction, and before others had really started, the Queen of Spain visited the project. After all, the town had been named 'Ciudad España' because Spain financed most of it, with the exception of Betania. Overlooking the valley, the Queen made comments on the visual attractiveness of Betania, expressing her satisfaction that Spanish aid was moving away from the ugly monotonous architecture of most social projects. Everybody remained silent and she likely never knew the truth, but they all quickly changed their concept and design and introduced more variety in other projects. Some have introduced interesting roofs, one project decided to use clay tiles instead of metal sheets. All this has improved the presentation of Ciudad España, which does not look like a poor people's town.

EcoViDe later developed another project with 100 houses including basic services like water, sewage, and connection to the electricity grid. They profited enormously from the experiences in Betania and used similar mechanisms of organizing the community and its involvement in daily decisions. In the last decade, the situation for housing projects has changed drastically. Very few donor agencies are interested in financing houses, unless it is reconstruction after massive disasters like the Asian tsunami or the earthquake in Haiti.

It is harder for individuals to replicate the approach and technology. Land is not easily available for new construction, even worse than at the conception of the project. In Ciudad España all land belongs to the government and it is not for sale. Whilst the Betania project filled all plots, many other projects did not. These empty areas are now being invaded, partly by the offspring of families living in Ciudad España. Most build houses in adobe or provisional wooden structures. It is yet to be seen how the government will react to these attempts of 'soft invasion' (see Figure 10.5). Fifteen houses are under construction on these plots and around 30 more plots have been marked with sticks and some with a simple fence as a statement of intent. Affordable land is often only found far away from towns and services, which again increases the costs of construction and lowers the attractiveness of the house for beneficiaries who have to spend a lot of time and money commuting.

Figure 10.5 Illegal but apparently tolerated, 'soft invasion' with low-cost housing

In Honduras it is almost impossible for most people to get a housing loan, and high interest rates discourage the few who could. When finance is available, it is always as credits, making it impossible to reach the poorest segments of the population. If all or most of the credits have to be paid back by the beneficiaries with interests similar to bank rates (which in Honduras exceed 10 per cent), only families with a regular income are eligible. But they do not have time to participate in construction themselves, which makes the house more expensive if constructed using the original project techniques. Thus, it is difficult to find a balance between donor requirements that beneficiaries must be poor to qualify for such projects but also able to service a debt if they wish to extend or replicate the original construction method.

On all those points, Ciudad España is a positive model but difficult to implement somewhere else. Thus, good planning of one neighbourhood managed to influence the design of the new town. However, we have not seen similar results in other projects.

About 90 per cent of all residents have made some changes to their house. The first and most obvious is that they put a fence or a wall around the property, something that is needed if you have valuables inside the house. Much of it is to decorate the house; rendering, colourful paint and decorative plants are common. This was done little by little over the ten years of its existence, according to available means. Many then extended the roof to cover an additional area and have built walls to create an additional room. There are 12 houses that have been extended to the full size of the plot (15 x 8 m). Four have built a concrete slab over the house and a second floor above, and one has three floors. They all used one of the two dominant walling materials of the area which were also used by the project, hollow concrete blocks and fired clay bricks.

It is interesting that nobody has destroyed walls but built vertically and horizontally onto the existing layout which was designed to allow this. The project has educated and trained a number of masons among the beneficiaries and many who are capable of building. All families financed their improvements themselves or with informal loans or donations from relatives in the diaspora. The three-storey house belongs to a lady who opened a small meat business in her house which grew into a market stall; she is obviously doing good business.

Technical performance

The techniques and materials used are standard in Honduras and resist heavy rains. Roof cladding with micro-concrete tiles was chosen as it provides a better indoor climate than the prevailing metal sheets. In the majority of cases, the tiled roofs have proved durable, but in a small number of houses when torrential rains combine with heavy winds, leaks do occur – a fine mist penetrates through voids between tiles causing a moist environment in the house. This has been attributed to problems with the locally produced micro-concrete tiles during a period of the reconstruction project when quality monitoring was not maintained. This has affected some houses where the tiles are slightly irregularly shaped. No other technical problem has been reported. The concrete of walls and roof tiles is long lasting and timber was carefully chosen with no reports of insect damage.

Not many standards were imposed by government and the building code was not up to date. The project team applied accepted international standards. One could argue that they are on the high side, thus imposing higher costs. As some families have built a second floor and in one case even a third, as expected, the standards applied were definitely correct. However, the most important issue in any construction project is good workmanship and quality control, and this was fully implemented in the project.

Based on the interviews, the families who expanded their house did follow the same general rules, building walls of concrete blocks or clay bricks within a structure of reinforced concrete (see Figures 10.6 and 10.7). As families had participated in construction they were well aware of the requirements. Recent inspection showed that some of the changed galvanised iron, roofs have minor failures in cladding, but the winds in this valley are unlikely to be strong enough to actually cause damage.

Figure 10.6 People have made additions but the architectural unity is preserved

Figure 10.7 Several owners have made additions, up to three storeys

As plots were terraced, it was difficult to position the houses in ways that would facilitate extensions, which was less than ideal. The rain water flow was not well planned and after the first rains the government had to build concrete access ways to the houses with a runoff system for the water. It was also not possible to use plots up to the retaining walls, as the refill was not always well compacted. In fact during reconstruction two houses presented failures even before they were inhabited and had to be partially demolished and rebuilt. Afterwards, the government agency improved compaction and no more problems have arisen; families have since used this space for extensions.

Livelihoods

At least 20 men have found work in the construction sector, at least of them three of them as small entrepreneurs. They have all learned or improved their skills through the project. Several more held temporary jobs in construction. After the disaster more jobs in construction were expected by EcoViDe and EcoSur, as the extension of Tegucigalpa was planned in this direction. The insecure political situation of Honduras, however, has prevented this from happening for the time being. Industrial development of the area has recently stopped; two factories were closed. Officially, this is because the government raised minimum salaries, but more likely due to political unrest (including a coup d'état).

Unemployment is high in Honduras and Ciudad España is no exception. Official figures vary, but at least 30 per cent are underemployed. Most wage earners of Ciudad España work in industries of the Amarateca valley, less than 10 km away, while others travel to Tegucigalpa, 30 km away. Transport is good from Ciudad España towards local centres and Tegucigalpa, and relatively quick. Twenty-six buses run daily between Ciudad España and Tegucigalpa, passing though Amarateca. This also provides jobs for drivers and support personnel.

A new house with good walls and a concrete floor definitely reduces the household work usually done by women. Running water and a functioning sewage system also contribute to a reduction in household tasks. Many women feel that the social organization created during the reconstruction has levelled the balance of power. About 70 per cent of the houses are assigned to women – as they are usually considered the heads of households when couples are unmarried – and this definitely had an impact. In some cases, men feel mistreated after a separation, as they lost all rights to a house they had built with their sweat equity.

As part of the project every family had to pay 2,400 Lempiras (about $150) into a common fund. With this fund they improved local infrastructure. A well was re-fitted to provide water to their households while the public network was not yet in place and later they built a solid fence around the community centre and paved the pathways to the houses. All that work was done with community labour and materials paid by the fund until it was depleted. The social organization (Codel) supervised and audited the fund. The community centre was built with a donation from the Red Cross, again with families providing labour. There are two bodies for popular participation in Honduras: *Patronatos* and *Codeles*. *Patronatos* are the official representatives to the local government. They are legally constituted and have definite bargaining power with local and national government. *Codeles* are like block committees that organize cleanliness, security, and neighbourhood assistance in their area. Both are elected democratically by the community to defend their social interests. The *Patronato* of Ciudad España is lobbying for more industries in the zone. While they are somewhat disillusioned with the perceived poor management by the authorities of the water supply; they continue to push for a better supply.

An environmental awareness among inhabitants has developed through the project, with respect to materials used, and that residential areas should not be sited in flood risk zones. The fact that the community now lives in an attractive landscape, surrounded by pine forests had a profound impact on many. During interviews, respondents always mentioned that they are happy to see their children grow up near a natural habitat, far away from the slum environment from which they came. They know the danger of erosion, and housing 'invasions' mentioned earlier only take place in plots suitable for construction. Ciudad España presents itself as a clean place with minimum littering. Garbage collection has been set up by the municipality twice weekly.

But there are also active recycling businesses around PET, aluminium, and other metals providing a small income for some unemployed. The police also play a role in community education as they are very active in prevention issues that include not just violence, but also littering.

Conclusions and lessons learnt

Immediately after the hurricane the goal was to start reconstruction fast but land issues did not allow that. This gave the project time to prepare conditions through good planning and extensive social engagement. People had time to reflect and organize themselves in a community committee able to take over much of the organizational tasks when construction started. One could say that delays imposed by outside factors were a blessing in disguise.

The leadership of the NGO had experience in housing development, and they sought additional expertise, provided by the EcoSur network, with planning and backstopping. When the government decided to donate land for a satellite town, they were ready to act and with the organized community a firm decision was taken within days. When the government changed the allocation of land reassigning them a different plot, they were able to respond creatively.

Design and technologies responded to the needs and aspirations of the people, and they have subsequently injected life into the new community. The production of materials on-site provided income and skills and was a positive experience, although briefly there was a slip in quality in the production of roofing tiles. The introduction of the roof tile technology was stopped as there was no further market, but the experience was largely positive as the tiles outlast metal sheets that would have been used otherwise.

Tight budgetary control and financial backstopping allowed the project team to execute the full plan with only a marginal overrun, contrary to all other NGOs involved at the site who were not able to implement the numbers of houses promised. The project did not spend money on transitional shelters, those affected arranged shelter themselves until they could move into their new house, an important lesson for successful post-disaster rehabilitation.

The follow-up after the construction phase has resulted in physical and social progress of the neighbourhood and contrary to all other projects in Ciudad España, most beneficiaries of Betania have received their land titles. The long-term view shows that relative to neighbouring projects, the Betania community has continued to develop and grow. We believe that this is due, in most part, to the way EcoViDe helped the community come together in the reconstruction phase. Ciudad España is currently part of the municipality of Amarateca and dreams of becoming a municipality in its own right. The community of Betania, together with their immediate neighbours from Suyapa are leading the *Patronato* of Ciudad España. They are now organizing themselves to move their *Codel* one level up and become a *Patronato* of their own in order to be more flexible, influential, and forward looking.

References

Belli, Charlotte (2008*) Impacto Social de los Ecomateriales*, EcoSur, Proyecto Betania, Honduras.

Salas, Julian (2008) Risk Assessment of socio-natural disasters in Central America and the Caribbean, *Open House International,* 33(1).

Universidad Politecnica Estatal de California (1995) *Plan conceptual y lineamientos de diseño del Valle de Amarateca, Centro de diseño, arquitectura y construcción,* Tegucigalpa.

World Bank (2005) *Conclusions and the Way Forward in Natural Disaster Hotspots, A Global Risk Analysis,* Disaster Risk Management Series No 5, p.132, The World Bank, Washington DC.

About the author

Kurt Rhyner developed Grupo Sofonias, a non-profit organization with active bases in Nicaragua, Ecuador, Haiti, and Switzerland, and affiliated organizations in Namibia and Cuba. He is involved in the conception of projects, analysis of technologies and materials appropriate to specific situations, financial analysis, executive management, backstopping, and evaluations.

CHAPTER 11

Nicaragua: Reconstruction with local resources in an isolated region

Kurt Rhyner

Abstract

The project was to provide solid shelter for extremely poor people who had lost their shack in Hurricane Mitch and had no means of building anything but another shack on a plot that eventually will be inundated again. The international NGO Casa de los Tres Mundos bought a piece of land outside the risk zone. It teamed up with Sofonias Nicaragua who are experienced in rural construction and production of building materials. They started a social programme, uniting extremely poor families with low social skills. These participated in a planning exercise to design houses and the neighbourhood. The architects developed a ground-breaking concept: modular floor plans with many different shapes of roof, creating the feeling of a naturally grown neighbourhood. The houses were built through assisted self-help. After 12 years, the project has developed into a community with basic services and most houses are in good repair.

Keywords: Hurricane; Solid reconstruction; Creative design; Assisted self-help; Nicaragua

Introduction

Hurricane Mitch hit Nicaragua in October 1998. The country was totally unprepared. The president decided not to communicate the urgency of the approaching hurricane in order not to 'create panic among the population'. Malacatoya was one of the worst hit villages in the country. As it is surrounded by a river, a swamp, and Lake Nicaragua, most of the houses were flooded. The precarious situation became worse when the dam was opened to prevent it from bursting. The river going through Malacatoya swelled another two meters. The country declared a national emergency; the army flew people out of Malacatoya and delivered food to the cut-off population. Outlying villages were in worse condition, especially the poorest shacks on the river banks. Many of the dwellings near the river had been swept away. The more formal houses and those further away from the river were damaged but not lost. Affected families built provisional shacks on their plots with debris and plastic sheets. The municipal government of Granada as well as several NGOs decided to focus their relief efforts on Malacatoya.

http://dx.doi.org/10.3362/9781780448398.011

A few weeks after Hurricane Mitch devastated Nicaragua, journalist Jose Luis Hernandez visited the area of Malacatoya; he did so again in 2013, at the request of the research team. He remembers the precarious ferry crossing back in 1998 when only to mention Granada implied disaster and more so when you said Malacatoya:

> Emergency brigades could only mobilize if they were accompanied by more than four vehicles, all 4-wheel drive. The area was completely desolate of trees. There was nobody in the streets, other than the work teams one encounters along the road, mainly from different non-governmental institutions that had arrived to help those that were affected. I remember that although they had cleaned the road out of the city of Granada, the condition of the ferry over the Malacatoya river was unknown, but luck was on our side and we were able to cross without a problem. On the other side of the river circumstances appeared to worsen. What was formerly an environment of green rice fields now looked like a black and white painting, abandoned and flooded. We arrived at the communities to distribute food and clothing. The families were shell shocked due to the loss of their property and loved ones.

Resettlement

Shortly after Mitch, Casa de los Tres Mundos (La Casa), an NGO working on promoting cultural projects in Granada, contacted Sofonias Nicaragua (SofoNic), to work together on resettling and rebuilding people's homes. SofoNic is an NGO from the neighbouring department of Carazo with decades of experience in disaster-resistant house construction, appropriate materials production, and reconstruction projects.

The new project, in Los Angeles, resettled people who had lived along the riverbanks, up to 7 km away, and had lost their homes in the disaster. They were resettled on a piece of land on the edge of Malacatoya bought by La Casa. Most were agricultural workers on large farms, mainly rice growing and cattle grazing. Some of them also had their own small plot or were members of a cooperative. The affected population needed houses, so the project focused on providing solid and decent permanent shelter for extremely poor people who had lost their poorly built houses. La Casa and SofoNic were prepared to assist the population with funding and technology.

A post-project evaluation report by SofoNic carried out in 2007 (Belli, 2008: 12) drew attention to this aspect in its conclusion that 'beyond construction of houses a fundamental objective of the project was to achieve the social organization and integration of the families, who have distinct customs and habits, which today is evident in the various organized activities with a vision toward the future'.

Traditional construction is mainly of timber with a metal sheet roof, sometimes with a stone or brick wall as a footing. However, due to deforestation there was literally no more timber available locally. The popular choice for walls would certainly be hollow concrete blocks or burnt clay bricks, but they were costly and had to be brought in over the bad roads. It was important to produce as many houses as possible within the project budget.

The search for a solution

It was necessary to find local solutions to enable rapid construction of permanent dwellings that would be safe. The only locally available materials were rocks of all sizes in the Malacatoya river and banks of sand and gravel. It was decided to build the foundations and walls with cyclopean concrete made of rocks, gravel, sand, and cement, known as *calicanto* in Spanish. SofoNic had much experience with this walling technology in projects in Guatemala and on a larger scale in the Dominican Republic. It basically consists of concrete poured into a formwork, but with the addition of rocks of different sizes. The rocks, which were abundant in Malacatoya, replaced more than 50 per cent of the concrete and the result was a solid wall at a very attractive cost in terms of material and labour. Production was ideally suited to beneficiaries working in small groups. It used a lot of unskilled manpower; in this case, much of it was womanpower. About half of the building labour was done by women, and most of the leaders in meetings were women. The roof structure and cladding were placed by a professional team with the help of groups of beneficiaries. A workshop for the production of micro concrete roofing (MCR) tiles operated on site. Everybody agreed early on, that they would put their own labour into the project; they were prepared to build themselves with the assistance of masons and technicians. The use of *calicanto* in this particular project fostered participation and strengthened the teamwork and relationships of people who formerly did not know one another, as they came from eight different hamlets along the river. It was the beginning of a new community.

In terms of infrastructure, the water network was extended to the site by the municipality, the project built latrines, and the electricity network was also extended to the site; for the latter, individual households had to register with the utility company to get connected. Part of the project was also to build a community centre which could also be used as a nursery, as well as construction of a health clinic which would also serve neighbouring communities. The nursery was one of the first buildings in Los Angeles, and during the second part of the project it served as a community meeting place. The health clinic was built after the houses, using largely the same materials, but with professional labour resulting in much better quality. Later, La Casa built a lovely playground in front of the school with funds provided by the Ministry of Education. It also put up a bakery and bought some land where a few families have founded a cooperative and are now growing basic foods. This did not greatly change the income-generating activities of beneficiaries, who remained mostly involved in farming, and occasionally looking for temporary jobs in towns or in neighbouring Cost Rica.

Not only were technical solutions needed but organizational challenges had to be faced too. From the beginning, SofoNic recognized that resettlement brings together people who are experiencing post-disaster trauma and who do not know one another. Thus they coordinated with the psychology department of the national university and integrated socio-psychological students into their technical team. The students were deployed to the remote areas; they slept in the humble dwellings of the potential beneficiaries and really got to know rural life; for most of them it was a totally new experience. They provided the project team with detailed data on the economic and social situation of the families, and above all they were able to put 'real life' into the data; they often became 'advocates' for the families. Two of them were contracted by the project and they stayed on to completion. Because of this positive experience, it has become standard practice in most projects of SofoNic.

A confident and secure start of the rehabilitation phase

The intervention was able to start 6 months after the disaster due to the local strength and experience of the two NGOs. The planning phase started after 8 months and was finished 13 months after Mitch. The planning process was drawn out, as finances were not yet secured, and the team took this as an opportunity to involve the beneficiaries in a step-by-step procedure. Construction began 14 months after the hurricane and the 130 houses were formally handed over 32 months after Mitch.

The German partner of La Casa, Pan y Arte e.V., was quick to provide funds for purchasing land outside the risk zone and for planning costs. SofoNic worked on a project proposal which was presented to the European Union for co-financing and was approved at the end of 1999, 12 months after the disaster hit. The manager of La Casa made several other funding applications within and outside Nicaragua. This proved to be important as it gave more flexibility to the overall programme at a later stage. Acquisition of the land was crucial and enabled a confident and secure start of the rehabilitation phase after the emergency relief. Land and finance are the two fundamental requirements for permanent housing solutions.

A process of participation

A pre-selection of seven damage clusters, areas that had been inundated and were considered vulnerable, were targeted for an assessment. Sociology students visited all affected families and gathered data on their personal situation. Most of those families were living on the river banks, next to the plot they rented (or in some cases owned). Potential beneficiaries were engaged in a planning exercise for the new houses and at the same time to design a low-risk and pleasant neighbourhood. SofoNic assembled an interdisciplinary team of colleagues from the EcoSur Network, of which SofoNic is a founding member, and set to work surveying the land and meeting with the beneficiaries. For the actual design of the settlement, SofoNic drew upon the talents of two colleagues from the EcoSur Network, Nolasco Ruiz, a civil engineer and Eduardo Camero, an architect. The settlement design had to take into account the possible runoff paths for rainwater, a difficult task on the flat plot. SofoNic organized participatory design sessions for the houses with the potential beneficiaries, students, architects, and planners. They also discussed the roof variations and ensured that everyone was pleased to include an individual touch. After every round of discussions the team tried to interpret the ideas of the people and in the third round everybody agreed on two basic housing models.

During the initial stage the action became a grassroots movement, as the implementation began with a social programme, seeking to unite extremely poor families with low social skills. Everybody agreed rapidly on guided self-construction and each family agreed to work four days per week.

Part of the decision-making was to decide on the level of finishing of the houses. The communities opted for the concept of 'unfinished houses' consisting of solid walls, roofs, and floors, but no doors or windows, chosen in order to augment the number of houses to be built within the available budget. This decision was made before the actual selection of the beneficiaries, and it increased the chance of a house for everybody.

The selection of beneficiaries took place after that. Anonymized survey sheets were evaluated by community leaders, the organizations involved and the municipality. The criteria were vulnerability which included the location where they lived, their economic situation, and the number of family members. At this time it was assumed that all preselected families were highly motivated to move to a secure location, however, later it turned out that some of the families were receiving pressure from their fundamentalist preacher not to accept an offer that would have them live together with people of different beliefs. This caused some problems which were never resolved, as they never integrated well into the work groups, were unstable in their attendance and three families moved in but never really settled into the community. But it would also have been unfair to remove them from the project.

Participatory design

The disaster specialist, Ruiz, made a thorough analysis of the surrounding area and the project site and devised a system that would channel the rainwater from the practically flat piece of land, but at the same time allow adequate distribution of the plots. The few existing trees were incorporated into the urban design, important for shade in this extremely hot environment. Martin Melendez, then director of Grupo Sofonias Nicaragua, communicated a clear message to Camero, the architect: 'We want a very simple design as the masons do not understand plans and the workforce are going to be the beneficiaries themselves. It has to be cost saving at all levels. The houses have to be cool and safe. They have to be all identical in size and cost, but look different. We want an attractive neighbourhood that does not 'smell of poverty.'

This set of tasks seemed contradictory. 'Identical in size and cost but look different' being the toughest requirement. Camero decided to go back to basics and asked himself which part of the house creates the major visual impact. The answer was a surprise: 'In small buildings it is the roof that makes the decisive impact!' He started thinking about different roofs on top of identical houses. From observing traditional Nicaraguan houses he knew that roof shapes were far from monotonous. A standard in popular rural dwellings is a double-pitched roof over the main part of the house, and a single pitched roof added on to cover the kitchen. Camero realized that this was an element that should be incorporated into the design and eventually it led him to the final result.

It was this intense interaction among project managers, social workers, and builders that led Camero to arrive at a concept that everybody felt was a breakthrough:

A module of 3 x 3 metres would be the basic unit, and each one of these units would be covered with a single pitched roof. There were several ways to combine the different units and it created a variety of roofs. If a house consisted of six such units, theoretically there could be hundreds of different roofs, always on top of the same floor plan! Of course most of those shapes were impractical from a technical point of view, but plenty of room remained for creativity.

Figure 11.1 Drawing of house plan showing the design principle of having the same floor plan but different roof shapes

Figure 11.2 Aerial view of the houses showing the variety of design

It was during the third round of meetings that Camero revealed the three different floor plans, each with several roof options. In this round of discussions, two of the models were chosen which were almost identical and in practical terms, they became one (see Figures 11.1 and 11.2).

On-site management

SofoNic deployed a team composed of an architect, four master masons, and two sociologists (former students who had participated in the survey) to direct the action. The beneficiaries were organized in teams of eight families which assured five or six workers every day for the building work. Roof construction and cladding were done by a team of professionals and helpers from each group.

A model house of each of the two designs was built and used as an office and living quarters for the technicians. The fact that the team lived in Malacatoya from the beginning made communications easier and helped to understand the community and many of the behind-the-scenes activities.

A visit after six years

In 2007 SofoNic commissioned a multidisciplinary case study of the project. Since construction, the new community had not experienced flooding. In addition to the original development, an informal settlement has been established at the edge of the terrain, while on the other side a Spanish NGO-funded project has built more formal houses.

It was discovered that the houses were solid and technically appropriate. It was concluded that the physical goals of the project were met: more than 130 families have a solid house in a low-risk location and improved access to social and educational services. However, many of the beneficiaries had problems adjusting to a wall which made it difficult to drive a nail into because of the rocks.

Generally, maintenance was poor and some roofs were in a deplorable state. The high rhythm of production during construction caused fluctuations in the quality of sand delivered to the tile production, and this in turn caused variations in the quality of the tiles which were not properly detected and acted upon. At the moment there are no replacement tiles available in the village; they would have to be purchased in town. While many roof coverings have been replaced with corrugated galvanized iron sheets, the architectural novelty of the roofs continues to define the built environment (see Figures 11.3 and 11.4).

Nonetheless, almost all houses are occupied by the original owners or by their families. Only three houses are empty due to economic emigration to Costa Rica and it seems that another three have been sold. A few families are not living permanently in their house and spend part of the year in shacks to attend their plot of land, close to their harvest. Two of them were interviewed and both expressed their satisfaction with the house and relocation, but find it easier to stay at their plot during the intensive workweeks. This is a practical and common solution for a problem that cannot be resolved otherwise. People have land far away and in a risky location; they move to town where there are services and schools for their children. The man migrates a few weeks per year to his land or to where he finds a temporary job.

There were considerable differences amongst the houses, some were in good repair and have been improved, whilst others looked dirty and unkempt. The visiting team observed that there seemed to be a basic difference between the more 'worldly' families who formerly lived in or near town and invested in their house, as compared to most families from remote places who did only minimal maintenance. However, they found it difficult to establish what role poverty plays in this case and even more difficult as to what might be due to suspected religious influences.

The project stressed the social integration and a democratic decision-making process to an extent that is not typical of a disaster-reconstruction project. In fact, it became a development project. However, some evangelical preachers opposed the community aspect of the project from the beginning and some of their followers were among the participants that were challenging to work with. During construction, many attempts were made to integrate them and to conform to their rules, for instance, no radio would be played where they were working as their pastor opposed any music except gospels. On this return visit, it was observed that the poorly maintained houses belonged to those participants. The extremely low social skills of many families and the influence of those preachers who were competing for their flock potentially lowered the success rate of the educational process.

Subsequent campaigns by different political parties promising improvements reinforced a latent tendency to accept favours instead of acting on their own. Interpreted differently, the good social preparation of the community developed in a direction that had not been intended by the project, whereby the well-trained social movement had learned to play the favours of politicians and competing NGOs. Where are the limits between empowerment and dependency? In political terms, one calls it lobbying: trying to get external support for what you want implemented.

It is debatable whether this is a completely positive development. The project managers had tried to motivate the beneficiaries to take things into

Figure 11.3 Typical rural scene with the houses after a few years

Figure 11.4 Some families try to make some extra cash by setting up shop from their homes

their own hands and not concentrate on lobbying for help. However, they have gained support and thus there is some positive physical result.

While public areas such as the park, school, and health centre were in good condition and well-maintained, concern about controlling the water runoff was lacking. The layout of the village was done in a way to guide rainwater through the streets out of the inhabited area. However, in this flat land with a clay soil it is normal that over time water will form puddles, but there is little preoccupation by most families to dig ditches that would help drain the standing water more effectively.

The current situation

Jose Louis recalls his 2013 journey to Malacatoya, full of curiosity about what he would encounter.

> The journey to Malacatoya at this time was very different, with summer houses along the lake shore with modern infrastructure interspersed with humble dwellings with families carrying out their daily tasks. We encountered a detour and a large earth-moving machine ahead, something that appeared unusual but proved to be a good sign. The Treasury had allocated funds to improve the roads and drains so that Malacatoya and neighbouring communities would not be cut off during the rainy season.

> As we approached the river, we were happy to see the ferry was in good condition to take us across and waited only a few minutes. On board a young man continually tossed a net into the river as we moved toward the other riverbank. During a crossing that took only eight minutes, the man was able to catch several fish. The smiling fisherman told us that the catch is for his wife who makes delicacies for sale.

> Although the poor road conditions continued, we knew that within a short time this situation would improve. Upon arrival at Malacatoya, one of our team commented that many things were the same as a dozen years ago but the buildings were new. Entering the first streets of the community it appeared to be just another Nicaraguan town, yet there was something particular, houses having a common look about them, without being identical. The climate is oppressive because of the humidity combined with the heat at mid-day, the streets are in poor condition, and run-off water from each of the houses circulates in a free manner wherever nature provides an opening.

Resettlement also requires infrastructural improvements and enhancements that tend to emerge over time. Transportation is one key aspect and a bus system now extends to the site and the government is improving roads. The school and preschool have full-time teachers. The health centre is staffed on a part-time basis; the new settlement is becoming a rural centre.

Opinions of beneficiaries

Two selected interviews are highlighted as they convey the key points reflected in the many visits and chats with residents. The first, to the house of Fátima Jaime, gave a good impression, where one sees the results of working as a family. Besides cultivating rice on a small property, they have established a small shop in the house that sells various products. Fatima and her family lost everything in Hurricane Mitch, which led her to become part of the Los Angeles project. Now that 12 years have passed, she says she is pleased to have moved there as she now has a safe place to live. 'I lived in Malacatoya close to the river. I was a young girl and for me it was horrible when we returned to the community and saw that everything had been swept away by the river. I was already married at the time but we did not have any children yet. We needed a house and when we learned about the survey they were making, little by little we became involved in the project.'

Figure 11.5 Fatima in her house, 2013

Although she did not know anything about construction, she worked in building her own house. She still remembers the entire process from start to finish.

> At first I thought that I would not be able to do anything, as I had never held a shovel to mix mortar. But after I saw the other women involved, I decided that I was capable and realized that I could help in everything. This was good because now I still use the techniques that I have learned from the project.

> I feel happy in my house now with my children and husband, who works in agriculture. We have a small shop, our chickens, and we continue going

ahead (see Figure 11.5). With time some things in the house have worn out. At first, the tiles cracked one by one on their own and we had problems when it rained. The only solution was to buy corrugated galvanized iron sheets and now we have a better roof. The walls have also had problems, in some parts the plaster has fallen, so we have repaired it.

In front of the house of Fatima is the dwelling of Maria Isabel Rodríguez, a housewife now in her forties. From the outside, her house appeared to be in optimal condition, and the floor and the patio were very clean. As we came closer, we could see that a new room was added one or two years ago. Maria Isabel likes to sit beside her father and enjoy the comings and goings of the neighbours who greet her from the street. The two adults were accompanied by a young grandchild using a computer in the living room.

> I lived in Tepalon when the hurricane passed. It was terrible. I remember that after Mitch we were taken to a refuge, and even in the refuge the water came up to our waists. To imagine how it would be in the community made it even worse. Everything was destroyed; the houses were swept away by the currents of water.

> When they talked to us about the project, I didn't want to get involved because I thought it would be very difficult. Besides, I would have to move from the community and be with people I did not know, but some of my family insisted and I accepted. I attended the meetings, and then we began to work. At times I worked and other times I had to harvest melons so I paid a youth to help us in the construction. At other times my father worked and so we continued until we finished. During this time I learned many things that I still remember now. For example, I still know how to mix mortar and you can see this part that I repaired myself,

and she proudly pointed to a small wall at the edge of her house.

Figure 11.6 A well-maintained house

Figure 11.7 Houses are in good repair

When asked what it means to own a house that she has built herself after all these years Maria Isabel answered:

> Look, each day I thank God. I am eternally grateful to be far away from the river. Some years ago, even my daughter came to my house for refuge

because the river swept away her house. Here I am secure, calmly living my days and nights far from the river. Some weeks ago, I decided to install a small stall on weekends, and sell *fritangas* (fried food) in front of my house. In the evenings a lot of people come to buy; it helps me with a little money, aside from our harvest. Now, my father and I are planting some vegetables but the land is not ours; we are renting it. So, we hope that the harvest will be good so that we can pay the rent and that a little profit remains for us.

María Isabel draws attention to the development that the community has achieved among themselves as a result of the social cohesion achieved during reconstruction, such as the introduction of electricity and drinking water: 'Installing the drinking water system made the whole community work together. Men opened the trenches and women helped in any way they could. When such things happen, we unite so that everything will be better.'

Figure 11.8 Community buildings are well maintained and their tile roofs are in good shape

General observations

This case study of Malacatoya can draw upon information and observations from on-site visits in 2007 and 2013. In summary:

User satisfaction in the case of resettlement is reflected in the relief of residents to be able to live in a risk-free area. As they built the houses themselves, there is an inherent satisfaction, often pride. There is a tendency to accept flaws and imperfections as part of the experience. That they have a new community, have learned to live together, and continue improvements to their life are witness to the intense socio-psychological support during the project. In Malacatoya, there are no great tensions or divisions between the families and their grassroots organizations are strong. Some families are renting or owning land in the place where they lived before and they have to walk there or migrate periodically for the peak season. But for the remainder of the year they are in a better location, closer to potential jobs, and much better for social integration like schooling, health facilities, and shopping.

Interestingly, the good social preparation of the community and the skills they acquired to express and negotiate their needs developed in a direction not originally intended by the project. The leadership learned to play the favours of politicians and competing NGOs. While some families immediately began to upgrade their houses, putting on doors and windows and painting them, others sought to convince La Casa to give them further assistance, and eventually succeeded. After all the houses had been furnished with doors, the organization also financed cement floor tiles to cover the concrete slab.

Beneficiary targeting was 'right on', focusing upon people who lived along the banks of the river and had lost their homes and sometimes family members. The use of socio-psychological university students was a clever move. Selection data was gathered in a creative manner by the student team, who visited the affected families and conducted interviews that provided clear data from which the final choice of potential beneficiaries was made. In 2013, most houses are still lived in by the original beneficiaries.

Replication is most evident in the organization, urban planning and architectural innovations. This has been incorporated by SofoNic in subsequent housing projects in different departments of the country. As to replication of the materials used for the houses, this is less evident.

Because of the lack of materials available after Mitch and the urgency to resettle people and provide housing, it was necessary to find local solutions to enable quick construction of safe permanent dwellings. The decision to use the system of *calicanto* took advantage of the rocks and sand available nearby. This highly participative technology fomented and intensified the teamwork of people who did not formerly know each other. It was the basis of a new community.

The roofing technology, while theoretically replicable, has not been drawn upon as the production facilities were removed to another location after project completion. However, the onsite production of the roofing tiles enabled the project to finish in time and the people to occupy their permanent houses within a couple of years after the disaster. Nevertheless, during execution of the project, a neighbouring project with a Spanish organization decided to use the roofing tiles and called upon SofoNic for technology transfer. The community centre and the health clinic are also covered with tiles and they are in good shape (see Figure 11.8). The alternative would have been using imported galvanized iron sheets, which was not desirable from a development point of view and there was hope to establish a culture of local production. Naturally, the tiles are cooler and longer lasting when produced and placed well.

Technical performance has been variable. In all cases, safety is guaranteed; the houses will not be swept away. However, the theme of maintenance becomes a crucial factor in whether a house performs well and stands the test of time, as seen on both visits. It was noted during the 2013 visit that poorly maintained houses belonged to those few people who were challenging to work with and not motivated to learn during the execution of the project, reiterating the findings of the 2007 survey.

However, it is clear that quality is also a critical issue when construction relies heavily on the voluntary labour of beneficiaries. The technology chosen needed many helpers and only a few qualified workers; this was ideal for integration, but not necessarily for quality of workmanship. Also, the cost of transporting the families every day and to provide lunch on site was as much as paying helpers would have been. The option of building temporary shelters, however, was discarded earlier on as people wanted to stay in their huts and travel daily. On the other hand, full integration into the work process now enables beneficiaries to make small repairs, plaster a wall or fix a door.

Livelihoods tend to emerge as the new community establishes itself. As most residents of Los Angeles are agricultural workers, the local partner Casa de los Tres Mundos purchased nearby land for some people to farm. However, most still commute to their original plots near the river to cultivate land they own or rent.

A new community must find ways to access items of daily use, and several families have increased their incomes by setting up shops with miscellaneous articles for daily needs and special delicacies for the weekends.

Moreover, different political parties, competing for votes, financed sports fields. Thus, some members of the community concentrate on asking for aid instead of taking initiative themselves.

Conclusion

Fifteen years have passed since Hurricane Mitch swept through Central America, Nicaragua and Honduras being particularly hard-hit. Post-disaster resettlement in both countries was carried out by members of the EcoSouth Network which enabled a quick response with very experienced local organizations rooted in society. This strength cannot be underestimated. Their networking at the local level enabled managerial and organizational coordination beyond the dreams of many large international organizations. There was little fear of working together, or of getting along with organizations with other experiences. It also paved the way for post-project review and monitoring of resettlement projects.

Reference

Belli, C. (2008) 'Impacto social de los ecomateriales', [website], EcoSur, <http://www.ecosur.org/images/stories/documents/la_betania_impacto_social.pdf> [accessed 15 April 2014].

About the author

Kurt Rhyner developed Grupo Sofonias, a non-profit organization with active bases in Nicaragua, Ecuador, Haiti, and Switzerland, and affiliated organizations in Namibia and Cuba. He is involved in the conception of projects, analysis of technologies and materials appropriate to specific situations, financial analysis, executive management, backstopping, and evaluations.

CHAPTER 12

A roof for La Paz: Reconstruction and development in El Salvador after the 2001 earthquakes

Claudia Blanco, Alma Rivera, Jacqueline Martínez, and Jelly Mae Moring

Abstract

The 2001 earthquakes in El Salvador amplified the poverty in the country and modified its geography. The damage to housing, education, health, road infrastructure, sanitation, environment, agriculture, and fisheries exceeded the available resources and responsiveness of public and private institutions. La Paz was one of the districts that was most affected by the earthquakes, with damage to 64.9 per cent of all homes.

FUNDASAL's Post-earthquake Housing Reconstruction Programme (the Salvadoran Foundation for Development and Low-cost Housing) was not simply a response to the damage that the earthquake caused, or just another housing reconstruction programme, but rather a process aiming to reduce exclusion and vulnerabilities. It was a process of investigation, rebuilding of the social fabric for the victims and their relationship with their surroundings, strengthening citizen participation, and enabling communities to rediscover their potential. The house served as a thread that connected the different processes – from the tangible to the more abstract.

Keywords: Reconstruction; community development; 2001 earthquakes; La Paz; mutual aid

El Salvador and the 2001 earthquakes

With a population of 6 million and an area of 21,040 km², El Salvador is the smallest and most densely populated country in Central America. The country is divided into 14 states and 262 municipalities. El Salvador has recently emerged from decades of civil conflict and is prone to natural disasters such as hurricanes and earthquakes. The country lies along the Pacific 'Ring of Fire' and is thus subject to high seismic and volcanic activity. A total of 55 earthquakes have occurred between 1573 and 2001, and an estimated 70 per cent of the territory is vulnerable to seismic events (CEDES and FUSADES, 2007).

http://dx.doi.org/10.3362/9781780448398.012

On 13 January 2001, an earthquake struck El Salvador with a magnitude of 7.7 degrees on the Richter scale, at a depth of 39 km; it lasted for 45 seconds. The epicentre was offshore in the Pacific Ocean yet it was felt throughout Central America. The earthquake devastated the country, heavily affecting the departments of Ahuachapán, Cuscatlán, La Libertad, La Paz, San Miguel, San Salvador, Santa Ana, San Vicente, Sonsonate, and Usulután. Significant damage occurred in Colonia 'Las Colinas' in Santa Tecla municipality in La Libertad, where a major landslide buried around 200 homes.

Exactly one month later, on 13 February, as the people of El Salvador were still digging out from the destroyed buildings, a second earthquake occurred with a magnitude of 6.6 degrees and a depth of just 13 km. It lasted for 20 seconds and was centred in the town of San Pedro Nonualco in La Paz. While the first earthquake affected the entire country, the second hit a less extended area specifically in the departments of Cuscatlán, San Vicente, San Salvador, and La Paz. Many of the buildings damaged by the first earthquake completely collapsed during the second.

The two earthquakes left at least 1,200 people dead, more than 8,000 people injured and a million homeless. Twenty per cent of houses were damaged, with 12 per cent either completely destroyed or declared uninhabitable. Damaged infrastructure included 40 per cent of hospital capacity and 30 per cent of the nation's schools. Around 1.5 million people, 25 per cent of El Salvador's population, suffered grave losses from the earthquakes (Villacis, 2005). Total economic losses were estimated at US$1.6 billion, equivalent to 12 per cent of the country's GDP in the previous year (CEPAL, 2001). In terms of housing provision the country moved back two decades. The country had a total housing deficit of 550,000 units in the year 2000 and this increased to 718,000 units after the earthquakes (DIGESTYC, 2001).

The department of La Paz was one of the worst affected with 59 per cent of the housing damaged. Almost half of the population was in poverty in La Paz prior to the earthquakes (DIGESTYC, 2000); this increased substantially in the aftermath. More than 300,000 people were affected, and the damage amounted to a total of $85.1 million (PNUD, 2001).

The Post-earthquake Housing Reconstruction Programme

FUNDASAL (the Salvadoran Foundation for Development and Low-cost Housing), a not-for-profit NGO, began responding on the day the first earthquake occurred. The situation in the field was noted and steps were immediately taken to access international funds. With funding from the German Development Bank (KfW), FUNDASAL developed the Post-earthquake Housing Reconstruction Programme or PRVPT (*Programa de Reconstrucción de Viviendas Post-Terremoto*) in response to the 2001 earthquakes in the department of La Paz.

The main aim of the PRVPT was to restore and improve the housing conditions of those affected by the earthquakes through the strengthening of citizen participation and the organization of the various actors involved in local development. The programme was implemented in three phases from June 2001 until March 2005 covering a total of 18 out of 22 municipalities in La Paz. The first phase worked on rebuilding houses, compost latrines, and drinking water systems. The second phase focused on strengthening the organization and interrelations between communities and local governments. The final phase established continuity mechanisms and identified shared needs with a wide consensus of representatives in La Paz.

The programme took a holistic approach from the outset. Knowing that the concept of habitat goes beyond the home and its living environment, FUNDASAL incorporated economic and social interventions in the PRVPT aside from physical reconstruction. A noteworthy aspect was the methodology of mutual aid to carry out the construction work which gave impetus to the organizational processes. FUNDASAL emphasized participation as the ultimate goal of their projects, not only as a means for building works but to promote community integration. The basis of this methodology is the formation of work teams, with a representative from each beneficiary family, who are trained in construction techniques to facilitate the maintenance or future expansion of their home. In the PRVPT approximately 1,200 teams were organized. The beneficiaries and communities worked together in the construction phase and were involved in the decision-making processes.

The **physical components** of the programme – housing, compost latrines, and potable water systems – contributed towards the reduction of the housing deficit caused by the earthquakes and helped improve living conditions by addressing infrastructure repairs or upgrades. There were three different housing systems that were constructed depending on land tenure.

Almost 6,500 houses were built on a mutual aid basis of which 3,373 were constructed with concrete blocks, 1,297 with concrete panels, and 1,802 houses with removable steel structures. Over a thousand compost latrines were built and accompanied by posters, manuals, and training given to families for their maintenance and use. In addition, six piped drinking water systems were built to improve water supply from deep wells or springs, benefiting 943 houses or almost 5,500 people. The physical components form the basis around which the organizational processes and participation were integrated and strongly influenced the families to improve their living conditions.

The **social components** aimed to create mechanisms for citizen participation to enable the local communities to take greater responsibility for the development and management of their communities and municipalities. These comprised organization, capacity building, encouraging interaction among the 130 communities, and the creation of nine water committees. The training process in mutual aid led to the identification of community leaders and group representatives and an assessment of the situation and drafting of the training plan with them. Mechanisms for interaction between communities were established and commitment letters signed with municipalities. Shortly thereafter, they saw the need to bring these community organizations

• *Concrete block housing*, a basic unit of 27 m² for families with secure tenure. Consisting of concrete block walls and micro-concrete tile roofing, it provided one living room and two small bedrooms.	 **Figure 12.1** Concrete block housing
• *Concrete panel housing*, a building system that was used for the first time in El Salvador for mass housing projects, as it was previously used only for demonstration or technology showcase purposes. FUNDASAL's Materials Production Centre (CPM - *Centro de Producción de Materiales*) exclusively produced the building materials, a result of research on earthquake-resistant construction systems. It is a concrete panel unit of 27 m² for families with secure tenure.	 **Figure 12.2** Concrete panel housing
• *Removable steel structure housing*, a unit of 37 m² with a steel structure and galvanized iron and aluminium sheet lining suitable for dismantling. With this system, families who lacked secure land tenure were able to obtain a house. PRVPT was the only reconstruction programme in El Salvador that overcame the challenge of meeting the needs of the most vulnerable families from housing programmes.	 **Figure 12.3** Removable steel structure housing

together, paving the way for the creation of ASPODEPAZ (Association of Residents of La Paz), a formally established organization that advocates for habitat improvement.

The **economic component** comprised a start-up fund to support small businesses for female-headed households, people who were not eligible for credit from financial institutions, the elderly, and people with disabilities. The seed fund was $57.14 per family for them to invest in projects that would allow them to generate income. Families used the fund to carry out projects such as the expansion of small businesses, street vending, selling food and other goods, etc.

Looking back at the impacts of PRVPT

FUNDASAL staff revisited 15 communities in the department of La Paz 12 years after the 2001 earthquakes occurred and approximately nine years after the completion of the PRVPT to investigate the impacts of the reconstruction programme. Interviews and focus group discussions were conducted with 23 representatives from the beneficiary families as well as local leaders of La Paz.

User satisfaction

Most of the beneficiaries described their happiness and satisfaction with their homes by comparing their current situation to the circumstances in the aftermath of the earthquakes when their houses were either damaged or destroyed. Having a safe place to call home in the midst of such calamity was a goal or a dream for the beneficiaries, made possible by the PRVPT. Having a secure house was a priority need that has been met. They value their house because for them, it is not only a place to live in but also a safe place for their families to be together. So far none of the houses built by the programme have been damaged by subsequent earthquakes in El Salvador. Most of the people interviewed agree that the materials and design give them security and comfort. They also appreciate the quality of the materials and the construction in comparison to what they had before. One resident from Concepcion Jalponga of Santiago Nonualco municipality reiterated, 'I feel like it is mine, the walls are more secure and more presentable'.

The type of building materials used helps to moderate the hot climate of the area. They feel that their houses are secure in terms of withstanding extreme weather events and in providing a safe space and privacy. The design is favourable for the local area as it incorporated local building traditions and, where feasible, allowed space for future expansion. A 32-year-old woman from Caserío El Socorro of San Luis Talpa municipality, who lives in a concrete block house mentioned during the focus group, 'I like my house because it is a place where my family has a covered patio; we have expanded it and kept it nice'.

Some beneficiaries felt that some things could have been done differently, e.g. the divisions between rooms could have been made from another material, not just for the durability of the material but also to create contrast with the rest of the building materials. They wanted to have a space for a covered patio, although they were aware that there was little money available for each house, since the goal was to reach more people who were in similar or worse conditions. This was pointed out in the focus group by one beneficiary from Caserío Los Laureles of Santiago Nonualco municipality who said, 'I like the house. It is really secure but it would be better if it was higher and with a covered patio'. For the rural communities in La Paz, the covered patio (or open-air covered patio) is a space for the family to share as well as an outdoor resting area that can be shared with the neighbours. Therefore, it is a very important and significant place for the design of family houses.

Figure 12.4a and Figure 12.4b A concrete block house in San Miguel Tepezontes municipality that was extended in the back with the construction of a covered patio and the main room was modified to put up a shop as a means of livelihood

With respect to their health, the people interviewed felt that their housing conditions have helped to improve the health of the entire family, and reduced the incidence of sickness caused by dust or extreme changes in climate. The compost latrines contributed significantly to reducing the bad odours and presence of disease vectors such as flies. Moreover, the kitchen helped to give families a space exclusively for cooking and the improved stoves prevented a build-up of smoke, thus reducing the incidence of respiratory diseases.

In terms of reducing expenses, the interviewees said that they seem to be spending less, but they have no evidence because they do not keep records of their expenses. Nevertheless they believed that the houses and other components of the programme have directly contributed to saving them money such as savings on firewood expenditure by using improved stoves, and savings in water consumption with the introduction of water systems. However, there were some components such as drinking water, electricity, public lighting, toilets, and bathrooms, among others that were not included in the initial stages. These components were implemented later through collective efforts by communities or families and financed by the households themselves. When the programme began these components were not considered and the focus was mainly on housing provision, but upon seeing the need and urgency they were incorporated into complementary projects.

Since the beneficiaries participated in the construction, they know their houses have a strong structure and foundation and are confident that they can withstand earthquakes. They also think that the type of materials used and their ability to acquire them through the CPM was an advantage, in addition to knowing how to use them. Mr Santos Agustin Maldonado, a 58-year-old resident of Hoja de Sal village at El Copinol in Paraíso de Osorio municipality, described the impact of the project on how they view their houses,

> FUNDASAL taught us to value the brick that we lay, the iron that we bend, and I think that has helped us to really value and cherish what we have. We are going to see our houses improved in some way, with

the materials that we have. Some managed to build their little covered patio, and those who have been blessed in their lives have been able to upgrade it with brick. The project has completely improved people's quality of life.

Beneficiary targeting

Most of the beneficiary families still live in their houses, and there are some who have made modifications to provide space for small stores or shops in order to earn income. A young man from the Edin Martinez community in San Rafael Obrajuelo, who has panel block housing, pointed to his shop saying, 'I built this little shop which is our means of subsistence'. There were also some families who transformed the space that was originally intended as a kitchen into an extra bedroom as the household size had grown and a new living space was needed, hence moving the kitchen outside the house and building a small extension for safekeeping.

During the field visits, it was not possible to identify exactly how many houses had been left or sold by their original owners. Nonetheless, in the opinion of the people interviewed, the number is very small, and in those few cases, one major reason cited was the infiltration of gangs – a nationwide problem that has increased in the years since the implementation of the project – which is a problem deeply felt in almost all municipalities and departments of El Salvador. Rural and urban communities have been affected by common crime and gang operations which caused families to seek other places to live for fear of being attacked or killed.

Another reason why a small number of families left their homes is the need to relocate to other areas to find employment. Population growth and the insecurity of agriculture as a main source of livelihood meant some families needed to look for different sources of employment in other municipalities or even in other departments. These two aspects have emerged and grown in recent years, but were not contemplated in the original design and construction of housing.

Moreover, there are still some families who have not resolved the issue of land tenure. There are cases in which an inheritance has not been legalized in due course because families could not afford the cost of acquiring the property titles.

Replication

Some houses had been expanded using the same materials and techniques; in other cases, people have used low-cost materials such as sheet metal or adobe and *bahareque* (mud and pole). Significant modifications to houses include: rear extensions to create an extra bedroom; building a hallway; building perimeter walls; using ceramics for finishing; having French windows, balconies, false ceilings, paved yards, different doors, garages, etc. The materials used to make these modifications varied depending on the area and the resources available to the families. For example, in the Tihuilocoyo Cooperative most of the houses that have been extended used the same building materials, which families bought at the CPM in Zacatecoluca municipality. Others have built walls with red bricks, but used the same tiling for the roof, while others have built walls with *bahareque* and sheet metal. A few of the families have used other types of materials for modifications such as replacing cement floors with ceramic flooring or different paint on the façade. Some families modified the existing roof or the roof extensions, replacing the tiles with galvanized metal sheet as this was more readily available in the area.

Figure 12.5 Concrete panel houses in the Edin Martinez community: house on the left – no changes made since its handover; house on the right – painted façade, doors and floor changed

Around five removable steel structure houses were also visited, which are still located in the places where they were originally built. Small changes were made such as improving the floor and installing another type of windows. One of the five families visited in San Miguel Tepezontes municipality was able to buy land in another area and move the detachable steel house to the new plot, modifying half of the walls with concrete block and utilizing the rest of the removable materials for extensions.

One significant aspect that has been widely replicated is the practice of mutual aid, a collaborative effort of people to work together on certain problems. The municipalities have taken this methodology of work to execute other projects, such as upgrading the streets or building community centres. They recognize that mutual aid facilitates teamwork among the communities and reduces financial costs in the long term. The families themselves have also implemented it in small projects or activities they ran and funded on their own. Mr Carlos Ramos, the mayor of San Pedro Masahuat municipality, further described the value of mutual aid saying, 'It serves as an important organizational fabric and it has been applied in other activities, not just in housing, but also in environmental risk management, raising public awareness

Figure 12.6 Unmodified removable steel structure house in San Miguel Tepezontes municipality

or in an organization's work to empower the people. Mutual aid has served us until today and we try to apply it in the various projects that the municipality carries out'.

Technical performance

Most of the respondents believe that the construction system and the materials used were ideal for the area where they live. In communities with hotter temperatures, mostly in the coastal areas, the construction materials have helped to mitigate the heat, making the homes more comfortable and pleasant for families to live in.

According to the local authorities that were interviewed, the FUNDASAL project made a great contribution to permanently resolving the housing deficit in the project area. More widely there are still families who were affected by the 2001 earthquakes who have chosen to build houses made of sheet metal, adobe, and *bahareque* with no technical assistance, and many times have had to rebuild or improve their homes when damaged by hurricanes or strong winds. Meanwhile, with the houses built by FUNDASAL, they have not heard of, nor in their visits to communities have they seen, any which have collapsed or had serious structural problems. This was echoed by Mrs Marvin Morena Martel de Canales, mayor of Santiago Nonualco municipality, who stated, 'I don't know of anyone who has reported that a FUNDASAL house has had any fault'.

However, some PRVPT houses were lost or damaged during Hurricane Stan in 2005 and Hurricane Ida in 2009. These two hurricanes brought torrential rains and very strong winds which caused significant damage throughout El Salvador. In the project areas, the river overflowed causing heavy floods that undermined the foundations of houses and washed them away. Others were inundated and sustained limited damage that was eventually repaired. Mr. Carlos Ramos, Mayor of San Pedro Masahuat municipality, had witnessed the houses being swept away by the floods during Hurricanes Stan and Ida. He remarked, 'The ground collapsed when the river flooded and it was strange to see the houses were intact as they were swept away. Despite that, this showed us that the quality of materials used was good'. This phenomenon could not have been foreseen by the programme, as the damage to river banks and the deforestation of the woodlands happened years after the housing reconstruction.

With respect to the design of the houses, the beneficiaries felt that it was a participatory process in the sense that families' preferences were taken into account to define the location and orientation of the house within the plot even though designs were the same for all beneficiaries. These designs were done with a type of incremental housing in mind, which would facilitate future expansions made by families. Mrs Rosa Maria Morales de Diaz, the director of *Casa de la Cultura* in Paraiso de Osorio municipality, added, 'I think the houses are well-made and flexible because you can easily make extensions'.

In terms of maintenance, the families employ certain measures for the proper use and upkeep of their houses. They tend to do this as their finances allow and agree that the primary task is the cleaning of the interior and exterior parts of the house which they do on a daily basis, painting the façade as necessary, checking roofs, replacing windows and doors, etc. No significant problems have arisen in terms of providing maintenance since the materials are accessible, and the technologies used are known by the families since they learned during the construction process how to replace or improve parts of the roof or wall.

A majority of families are still using the improved stoves, drinking water systems, and compost latrines properly with monitoring from the Health Units of the areas. The drinking water systems are still in operation, as well as the Water Committees created for their management.

Livelihood development

The PRVPT has contributed greatly to the construction and commercial sector in general in the aftermath of the earthquakes and still contributes to this day though to a lesser extent. The families became more interested in the construction technologies used by FUNDASAL in the programme, and are still using the same techniques in building works. Other families, when expanding or improving their homes, have chosen to buy the same building materials that FUNDASAL used in its houses. They have been able to find these materials easily through the CPM in Zacatecoluca municipality, where people can get what they need or learn about new construction techniques.

An excellent case of lasting benefits of the PRVPT in the commercial sector is the Tridimanía cafeteria, located in Santiago Nonualco municipality, which has provided food services to participants since the start of the programme and during the different activities carried out by FUNDASAL in the department of La Paz. Prior to the PRVPT, they only had a space of approximately 25 m² and this has now grown to an area of 200 m². The Tridimanía cafeteria improved its sales strategy and, thanks to the programme, earned recognition from other institutions and was able to go to other municipalities within La Paz which helped them to expand their coverage and improve their income. Mrs. Ana del Carmen Vaquerano de Guzmán, manager of the cafeteria, indicated that 'Around 60 per cent of the improvement in our business has been due to the work that FUNDASAL gave us during the project and even beyond that. Other institutions have gotten to know us through FUNDASAL and we now work with other NGOs and government agencies in providing food services'.

Moreover, the infrastructure projects brought benefits to the livelihood of the beneficiaries. One resident from Hoja de Sal village pointed out, 'I live in one of the most remote villages of the area and the road that FUNDASAL repaired has facilitated access both for products that we need for farming to enter here as well as for us to get our agricultural products out'.

The installation of the drinking water systems contributes to the reduction of the workload borne by women in rural areas as they no longer have to carry water home and can spend their time and efforts on other activities, for personal development or recreation. The improved stoves also helped improve living conditions as they reduce the firewood used and the time and effort spent collecting it, which then reduces environmental impact.

Another significant contribution is the change in the balance of power between men and women. Important in this respect is the female leadership of ASPODEPAZ – *Asociación de Pobladores del departamento de La Paz* (Residents' Association of La Paz), the community water committees, SECOME – *Semilla Comunitaria para el Mejoramiento Económico* (Community Fund for Economic Improvement), and ADESCO – *Asociación de Desarrollo Comunitario* (Community Development Association). All communities have ADESCOs which are formally established community associations. The women leaders of these organizations have developed the capacity to lead, manage, and represent the interests of their communities. ESFORCI – *Escuela de Formación Ciudadana* (Citizenship Training School) is an establishment where they could develop these and other abilities and many of the women who attended ESFORCI courses currently occupy important and influential positions in their municipalities.

Many beneficiaries who received the start-up fund have joined up to form solidarity groups called SECOME that provide small credits to members for them to invest in small businesses and generate income. Beneficiaries formed productive enterprises for the sale and purchase of meat, seafood, clothing, and food they processed, among other activities. More than 1,000 such enterprises have been established, many of them by women. The number of SECOME members and the amount of capital has remained steady. The impact of this initiative is evident in the form of an improved quality of life of their families, especially their children, since they have invested their earnings in their children's education.

The respondents used a metaphor drawn from agriculture to describe what has happened after the PRVPT. They stated that FUNDASAL planted a seed with the reconstruction programme which provided the houses, latrines, and water systems. SECOME and ESFORCI then watered and fertilized the seed until a little plant emerged which gradually grew and is today starting to bear fruit. Those little plants are the community leaders, young people, and children. They are aware that as representatives of their municipalities they have a very important responsibility to ensure that all their work continues beyond the programme. Mrs. Rosa María Morales de Díaz added, 'I believe that I grew and learned a lot about leadership [through the project]. Since we have been trained as leaders, we know that we have a commitment to the communities, and thankfully, FUNDASAL believed in the leadership of those people who then began a process of growth'.

Figure 12.7 ASPODEPAZ lobbying for decent housing for low-income families

Formal agreements and working arrangements with local municipalities have been created in order to give a political voice to the communities. This was done through ASPODEPAZ who coordinates with the mayors and local legislative representatives in La Paz to influence policies for the benefit of the communities. The mayor of Santiago Nonualco, Mrs. Marvin Morena Martel de Canales, pointed out:

> The agreements that the mayors and communities had publicly signed together at the start of the municipal administration had incorporated issues that mattered to the people and had become part of our local development plans. For instance, risk management and disaster prevention issues or support to agriculture which we recently addressed (...). I do everything I can to fulfil these agreements.

ASPODEPAZ has also advocated for the protection of natural resources and lobbied for the approval of the proposed Social Housing Law, and is part of the National Commission of Residents (CONAPO) which campaigns for the proposed law.

FUNDASAL has had limited involvement after the housing reconstruction programme, and since then the communities have taken the lead and responsibility in making changes to their society and improving their living conditions.

Conclusions and lessons learned

Based on the observations made during the field visits, interviews, and group discussions, five findings stand out with regards to the overall impact of the programme:

Replication of technical capacity: The families still apply the knowledge they acquired for the maintenance and extension of their homes. Through FUNDASAL's Materials Production Centre, the use of the same quality building materials and housing construction techniques is maintained.

Construction technology: The housing systems that were built were not only an innovative solution to the housing deficit in the region after the earthquakes, but they continue to fully contribute to reducing the vulnerability of households and families against earthquakes and other extreme natural hazards. Moreover, the housing designs of concrete blocks and concrete panels facilitated the extension of the housing units, allowing adaptability to the dynamic circumstances of each family. The steel structure houses have allowed families without land tenure to continue living in the same place and make modifications to these units. This technology also showed flexibility for families to disassemble and reuse the same materials for rebuilding on a new plot.

Mutual aid: The methodology of mutual aid promoted community integration and solidarity among the beneficiaries involved in the construction of housing and community infrastructure. Because of its benefits, the methodology has been widely replicated and applied by local institutions in implementing community projects. Using this methodology also facilitated the identification of leaders, giving impetus to the organizational processes that were promoted in the communities.

Contribution of the seed fund to strengthen families' livelihoods: The seed fund was an added benefit for the programme to help increase the opportunities for an improved quality of life by supporting initiatives for the sustainability of families' livelihoods.

Strengthening of citizen organization and participation: The sustainability of the PRVPT is based on the strengthening of local organizations and the generation of permanent mechanisms to coordinate the stakeholders in La Paz. The leadership training helped to create new relationships between local governments and community-based organizations in the development of strong citizen participation. With the establishment of ASPODEPAZ and its coordination work with local governments, continuity and long-term actions in La Paz are ensured. ASPODEPAZ has facilitated negotiation and consultation between and among communities, municipalities, and departmental levels and thus plays a key role in highlighting the problems of the region as well as in constantly advocating for their solutions.

FUNDASAL's Post-earthquake Housing Reconstruction Programme in the department of La Paz demonstrates how successful community development can result from rebuilding after a devastating earthquake. The reconstruction of houses and health infrastructure was implemented through citizen participation and organization. The interrelationship of people, partnership building, and coordination with local governments were promoted and these mechanisms triggered development strategies in the region and helped to rebuild the social fabric of communities.

FUNDASAL found that in the initial stages, the conditions in the aftermath of the earthquakes determined priority needs and the type of intervention to implement. Looking back at their experience, they would have wanted to include additional interventions in the reconstruction programme. Over time the economic, environmental, social, and demographic changes in El Salvador have created other problems at local, regional, and national levels that have affected impoverished families which had not been foreseen at project inception. Hence, new projects may include components that would respond to societal changes in the long term such as improving access to and extension of water systems, working with youth and children, or integrating community facilities such as community centres and green public spaces, among others. FUNDASAL still continues to work in La Paz; however, it does not work on the same scale or with the same features as the PRVPT, but rather as an advisor, facilitating community organization and strengthening ASPODEPAZ as an organization that represents all the communities from the 22 municipalities of La Paz.

One aspect that needs to be explored further is how to boost the interaction between residents or community organizations in other regions of El Salvador to form alliances for broad citizen participation with greater capacity and strength. This is crucial for the residents and communities to be able to develop proposals for habitat improvement in all of its components such as legalization of tenure, environmental management, vulnerability and risk prevention, provision of basic services, access to materials and technical assistance, financing, and access to resources according to their real needs.

References

Comisión Económica para America Latina y el Caribe (CEPAL) (2001), 'El Salvador: Evaluación del terremoto del martes 13 de febrero de 2001'., San Salvador, El Salvador.

Consejo Empresarial Salvadoreño para el Desarrollo Sostenible (CEDES) and Fundación Salvadoreña para el Desarollo Económico y Social (FUSADES) (2007), 'Riesgos Naturales y Vulnerabilidad', *Gobernabilidad Ambiental para el Desarrollo Sostenible*, Edn 1a: 37–43, [website] <http://www.cedes.org.sv/index.php/publicaciones/category/8-gobernabilidad-ambiental-para-el-desarrollo-sostenible.html?download=7%3Aparte-5> [accessed 17 April 2014].

Dirección General de Estadísticas y Censos (DIGESTYC) (2000), 'En cuesta de Hogares y Propósitos Múltiples (EHPM) año 2000', El Salvador, Ministry of Economy.

Dirección General de Estadísticas y Censos (DIGESTYC) (2001), 'Censo de Viviendas afectadas por la actividad sísmica en El Salvador año 2001', El Salvador, Ministry of Economy.

Programa de las Naciones Unidas para el Desarrollo (PNUD) (2001), 'Informe sobre Desarrollo Humano: El Salvador 2001 (IDHES 2001)', p. 50, Cuadro 2.17: Población damnificada por los terremotos del 13 de enero y 13 de febrero de 2001, <http://www.pnud.org.sv/2007/component/option,com_docman/task,cat_view/gid,10/Itemid,56/?mosmsg=Est%E1+intentando+acceder+desde+un+dominio+no+autorizado.+%28www.google.com.sv%29> [accessed 29 April 2014].

Villacis, C. (2005), 'Latin American cases: Hurricane Mitch (1998), flash floods and landslides in Venezuela (2000), El Salvador earthquakes (2001)' in *Recovery and Reconstruction Reports of the Worldwide Disasters and their Comparative Study*, [website], Asian Disaster Reduction Centre, <http://www.adrc.asia/publications/recovery_reports/pdf/Mitch.pdf> [accessed 24 February 2014].

About the authors

Claudia Blanco is an architect and has been with FUNDASAL since 1998, working on issues related to the low-cost housing sector. She is involved in the execution of projects, research, analysis and evaluation of housing and neighbourhood improvement programmes, public policy advocacy, and advice to social movements in the struggle to improve their habitat.

Alma Rivera is the head of FUNDASAL's Planning and Research Unit managing the project systematization processes, facilitation of social community development projects, and research.

Jacqueline Martínez is a sociologist and has been involved in the research and implementation of social community projects.

Jelly Mae Moring is a Research Officer in the International Programmes department of the Building and Social Housing Foundation (BSHF).

CHAPTER 13

Peru: Building on the vernacular

Theo Schilderman and Max Watanabe

Abstract

After an earthquake hit Ica in 2007, Practical Action supported owner-built temporary shelter and permanent core housing, using an improved vernacular building technology – quincha. Continuing to work with affected groups following the emergency and through to reconstruction stimulated participation, helped to define local needs and resources, and enabled training. Although the project worked with beneficiaries selected from a larger area, that wider community remained passive and did not come together to initiate additional activities after reconstruction. When improved quincha technology proved cost-effective and performed well, it was replicated elsewhere, but not within the neighbourhood. When people there extended their core houses, they did so with government funding which they could now access, but only where construction methods used bricks and concrete. For government to accept improved quincha technology as an option, the project required greater advocacy from the start.

Keywords:Vernacular construction; Participation; Training; Self-help

The 2007 earthquake and its impacts

On 15 August 2007 at 18:40, a strong earthquake struck the coastal region of Peru, just south-east of the capital, Lima. Measuring 7.0 on the Richter scale the epicentre was situated off the coast, 60 km to the west of the town of Pisco, and lasted over three minutes. The quake was particularly devastating in the Ica region, but also impacted surrounding regions. The most heavily affected provinces were Ica and Chincha in the Ica region, and Cañete in the Lima region. Official figures established the impact as: 596 casualties; 1,289 wounded; 431,313 people suffering damage or personal injury; 219,326 affected in other ways; and 91,240 destroyed dwellings (INDECI, 2009).

The INDECI (Institute of National Civil Defense) report blames negligence by builders for the bulk of destruction and damage, as well as casualties. It explains that many builders did not use the structural reinforcements required or follow industry norms; built informally in risky locations; had too little construction knowledge; or used inadequate materials or technologies. At the same time, the report points to another important correlation: that the greatest destruction and highest casualties occurred amongst the poorest

http://dx.doi.org/10.3362/9781780448398.013

sections of the population. Peru's society is very unequal, but all people including the poorest need to protect themselves and their property from the impacts of climate, disasters, and violence. Low-income households tended to use the materials most readily available. Many built using adobe, which was the principal factor in the destruction and death caused by the quake. In the affected coastal region, many of the poorest were migrant labourers, who descended from the Andes to make a living in commercial agriculture, a growth sector in the coastal plains. According to Castilla (2009), the sector employed 70,000 workers, in 'poorly paid, low quality work'; some earned as little as S/580 (about US$200) per month, which is below the poverty line in Peru.

Figure 13.1 People living amongst the remnants of their adobe houses, putting up reed mats as temporary walls for shelter

The impact of the quake was felt very strongly in the 'social interest popular settlement' (UPIS) of El Carmen, near Chincha, where it destroyed or severely damaged most of the houses (see Figure 13.1). The majority of the 280 households of El Carmen were on very low incomes. Their homes, therefore, could not withstand the force of a 7.0 magnitude quake: 70–80 per cent collapsed or had to be demolished (Guzmán Negron, 2009). The state promised grants of $6,000 (Nuevos Soles) (about $2,000) through the Fund for the Reconstruction of the South (Forsur) to make a start with reconstruction, but to access those, affected households needed title documents. In El Carmen, most households did not have these, as they were living on large farms. These *haciendas* have a single owner and registered title that can include as many as 400–500 houses. In the earthquake zone, only 10 per cent of occupants were fully registered owners, and only 30 per cent of those were in a position to comply with registration quickly. In addition to this issue, the national Civil Defence organization launched a strong campaign against building with adobe, and as a result many people destroyed adobe houses that could have been repaired or reinforced with the grant (Guzmán Negron, 2009). A land title was also an essential requirement to be able to access government-sponsored housing schemes such as *Mi Vivienda* and *Techo Propio*. The latter scheme also required that applicants constituted a family unit, received less than S/1,620 (nearly $600) income per month, had received no other state housing aid, did not own other property, and were registered as qualifying due to earthquake damage.

The quake did not just affect buildings, but livelihoods too. In the informal settlements, many people had home-based enterprises (HBEs) that disappeared with their houses. Leticia Quispe lives in El Carmen. She and her husband had put all their savings into their house, for which they were still paying off a mortgage, when it crumbled before their eyes in just three minutes. Leticia lost not just her home, but also her work place and source of income: a *wawawasi* (nursery) that she was running in a room of her house (Practical Action Latin America, 2008).

Reconstruction supported by Practical Action

International NGO Practical Action had been active in Peru for over 25 years when the earthquake struck, and had worked on a range of reconstruction and disaster risk reduction projects since 1990. It could, therefore, build on substantial experience. As a development (rather than humanitarian) organization, it typically focused more on permanent reconstruction than on temporary shelter, and on mitigating the negative impacts that disasters and climate change could have on development.

After the 2007 earthquake, however, it became involved in Chincha province at a much earlier stage than is typical, working from November 2007 until February 2010. This took place in the rural and peri-urban districts of El Carmen and Sunampe, with a joint total population of 33,000, of whom around 14,500 were living in urban areas. Before the earthquake, 61 per cent of homes were not connected to a water supply, 54 per cent were not connected to sewers, and 79 per cent had no electricity. These types of area were largely overlooked by other agencies, which tended to focus on larger cities. Most of the beneficiaries were poor migrants, who had arrived from the Andes over a decade ago to look for work in agriculture; 70 per cent of them were female-headed households.

Initially the selection of beneficiaries involved community leaders, who knew their neighbours and their needs best; at other times the selection process involved 'victim committees' or 'reconstruction committees'. The criteria used for preliminary selection were the state of damage to a candidate's house; their socio-economic status; access to a plot; and their willingness to learn, self-build, and participate in communal activities. The selection was then finalized by a joint committee including the Lieutenant Governor along with representatives from the municipal council, the irrigation commission, the local councillor, and democratically elected representatives of the neighbourhood council. The beneficiaries selected had previously built with adobe which had not withstood the quake; their land tenure situation was informal; and for that reason (and others) they were not eligible for a Forsur reconstruction grant. In Chincha, 24,599 houses needed rebuilding, but only 6,780 households had been able to access the $2,000 government reconstruction grants, less than 30 per cent of those in need.

In an initial phase, Practical Action supported the construction of 1,365 transitional shelters and 33 temporary classrooms, as well as water supplies, and the restoration of less severely damaged houses. The walls were built using the *simple quincha* technique, a vernacular technology that consists of a basic round wood frame, filled in with a patchwork of smaller sticks or bamboo, plastered with soil (see Figure 13.2).

Figure 13.2 Traditional *quincha* house under construction in the Alto Mayo of Peru

The transitional shelters were finished with reed mats and plastic sheeting (see Figure 13.3) instead of soil, or reused materials from the damaged houses and some cement mortar for the footings. *Quincha* has a much better record in resisting earthquakes than adobe or *tapial* (rammed earth). Gutiérrez Aliago and Manco Rivera (2006: 128), for example, compared the seismic behaviour of quincha, adobe, and tapial, to conclude in relation to *improved quincha*: 'the structure is very solid and possesses unmatched flexibility to absorb seismic forces'. Roofs were made from bamboo and reeds, covered with a plastic sheet and a layer of mud mixed with straw or wood waste, to improve durability and thermal performance. These shelters were intended to last at least five years.

Figure 13.3 Interior of a temporary shelter

Practical Action's early involvement laid the foundation for subsequent reconstruction work. From the start, the NGO worked with communities, local building artisans, and local authorities, strengthening their disaster awareness, organization, skills, and capacities. Their participation was important to develop appropriate projects, manage them, handle logistics, and be involved in monitoring. This included providing support in developing strategic plans for the risk management, reconstruction, and development of both El Carmen and Sunampe.

In the next phase, 257 permanent core houses were built, as well as a further 44 permanent classrooms. This took place mainly on land donated by the former agricultural cooperative, for which the communities subsequently achieved title registration. These houses were built with walls of *improved quincha*. The first reconstruction with *improved quincha* by Practical Action during 1990–1992 in the Alto Mayo region of Peru used a timber pole frame (Schilderman, 2004). However, making strong connections between round poles can be problematic. Reconstruction in Chincha, therefore, opted for a stronger, sawn, treated timber frame, set in concrete footings, and well connected to the roof structure. These buildings had infill walls of cane and mud that were plastered with a gypsum-cement mortar (it hardly ever rains in the coastal zone of Peru); doors and windows were also made of sawn timber.

Roofs were made from sawn timber beams covered with bamboo and reeds, levelled with mud and a sheet of plastic, with a final layer of gypsum-cement mortar (see Figure 13.4). In El Carmen, the municipality contributed the aggregates to the construction and some water. Households formed collective

Figure 13.4 *Improved quincha* houses during construction

working groups of between five and seven families, and worked with local artisans. The working groups received weekly training on site to enable them to build well. Tasks were allocated according to existing capabilities. Each group had a coordinator who received more thorough training. The housing units measured 32 m², incorporating just two rooms, which was considered adequate to start with, as well as cheap enough to allow as many families as possible to be reached with the available budget. It was always the intention that these would be extended, and the 120 m² plots and ample training provided for this. By 2011, 125 (of the 280) households had already extended their dwellings (Ferradas Mannucci, 2011).

All this happened in a context of fragile governance in the province, with three local authorities being forced to step down and replaced in Sunampe, for example, which hampered collaboration with those authorities and the strengthening of their capacities.

Looking back

In late 2013, a project team returned to Chincha to investigate the status of the reconstruction work approximately four years after its termination. They focused on the district of El Carmen, where the project had been most active.

User satisfaction

The vast majority of beneficiaries greatly appreciated their *improved quincha* houses. Their participation in the project had created a sense of ownership; in the words of two: 'I liked it, because we got support, and the house was the result of our own efforts', and: 'If I had to do it again, I would do so'.

People also appreciated that, during the planning process, after starting off with a number of standard designs, the NGO showed enough flexibility to accommodate individual household requirements, resulting in greater variety. As some remarked: 'People indicated where to put doors and windows', (P. Chávez Cartagena, personal communication, November 15, 2013) or, 'The original model had no bathroom, but my mother requested one, and the NGO included it' (M. Felipa Robles, personal communication, November 14, 2013).

Some people liked the house because it was simple, made from local materials such as *quincha* and cane. One of the builders involved said people liked the quality of the work, and praised the NGO for its steadfast support. Several beneficiaries also remarked that the *quincha* houses were cooler in summer and warmer in winter than other types, due to the materials used, the height of the rooms, and good ventilation provided. This had led to health improvements, particularly for children who previously suffered from frequent bronchial illnesses: 'We used to go to the clinic daily, mainly with coughs and flu, caused by the cold and dust. Now, I do not go any more, and the expense has reduced. People also felt very safe in their houses.

In fact, the safety provided by the houses was one of the most widely appreciated benefits. A night-watchman expressed this as follows: 'I feel at ease and safe. I go to work without worries, because I know that, if there is a strong quake, it will not kill my children, because the materials used are light. My wife and children also feel safe. If there is a tremor, they stay inside and go back to sleep once it has passed.' The owner of an extended house expressed similar feelings: 'If there is a quake, the *quincha* part is the safest. I know nothing is going to fall there, not even the plaster. If I am in the brick section and a tremor starts, I move to the room built with *improved quincha.*'

When asked whether something should have been done differently, most beneficiaries could not think of anything. One person replied that while his internal plaster kept well, on the outside it got damaged by young people with skateboards and footballs, and needed some repair. There was also some concern that the roofs, covered with bamboo and reeds, would not last. Others said the house was a bit small for their household, and that they would have liked an additional room. The houses are still mainly used to live in, but many would have liked to open a shop or enterprise in the house, and some have in fact started to sell groceries, or occasionally to process food for sale along the street. This function perhaps should have been considered in the design phase.

There was consensus amongst beneficiaries that project staff had been very open to listening to their demands and concerns. However, people were anxious about participating in the various stages of capacity-building, though this was done progressively, because of the novelty of the technologies. In the words of one participant: 'Often, some people criticized aspects. Instead of that, we could have made better use of the support, and been better organized. It was the fault of the community that it was not unified.'

Some beneficiaries had changed or improved their houses using their own means. These included aesthetic changes such as tiling or painting, or changes to internal walls, to make better use of the space. Others had replaced wooden doors and windows with metal ones, for greater security. Some households found the house large enough and did not add anything, but others had added a room, often not in *quincha* but in brick, using a government reconstruction grant. Where this was done, however, the family often slept in the *improved quincha* section, or went there when tremors started. As one respondent said, 'The *quincha* houses are very safe. Those built with modern materials are also resistant, but during earthquakes of great magnitude, they will collapse and kill people'.

Beneficiary targeting

Four-fifths of the inhabitants of El Carmen lost their house during the earthquake. There was, therefore, no shortage of people in need of a home. By providing relatively simple core houses, many were able to benefit from this project. After four years, nearly all of the beneficiaries still live in their houses, and many have made alterations and additions, showing a sense of ownership and intention to stay.

In fewer than 10 per cent of cases, the original inhabitants are no longer there, and reports from respondents still living in the area are often rather vague as to the reasons for this. A few families seem to have moved out of the neighbourhood because they found work outside Chincha, and have subsequently rented out their house. It seems that, where letting occurs, it is often to family members at below market rates, in order to have someone trusted look after the house in the owner's absence. In a couple of cases, ownership has been passed on, or the house is shared with family or children (e.g. two elderly people who died left their houses to family members).

There are conflicting reports about the number of beneficiaries who have demolished their house, (ranging from one to three). This seems to have happened after they subsequently were able to access one of the two government housing funds (*Techo proprio* or *Mi Vivienda*) or subsidies from the municipality or central government. Some community members were unhappy about this, and felt that those families in greater need, who had no access to those state programmes, should have been prioritized over those who had already been helped by Practical Action.

Most respondents did not know anybody who had sold their house, but one said he knew of a lady who had sold it because she moved to Lima. However, respondents noted that the *improved quincha* houses are in demand: 'People have come wanting to buy the houses, because they are safe and appealing, but the beneficiaries do not want to sell', and 'Others have asked about the model and the budget for an *improved quincha* house. That is because they know its qualities, and everybody now wants to be protected against earthquakes'.

Replication

After the project was completed, there was no more building with *improved quincha* in El Carmen, although the technology was replicated elsewhere, including in the other project area, Sunampe. There were two main reasons for the lack of replication within El Carmen: suggested building codes for *quincha* were not adopted by the municipality; and once the project ended, inhabitants got access to government housing funds and subsidies, which required the use of bricks and cement (see Figure 13.5). As one builder said, 'The state obliged us to use these materials'. Later, the government began presentations about *improved quincha*, encouraged by Practical Action. In these presentations they expressed the intention that the state grant would extend to allow building with *improved quincha*, but this remained an intention only. A further reason may be that the lack of status of *quincha* persuaded some residents to build something more modern looking. Where they did not have the means, some have even gone as far as painting brick masonry on a plastered *quincha* wall (see Figure 13.6).

Figure 13.5 Extension of a well-finished *improved quincha* house with one part made of bricks and a structural frame of concrete

Figure 13.6 Painted *improved quincha* house, including an 'imitation-brick' lower part

Towards the end of the project, several people experienced a good harvest which allowed them to invest a bit more (Guzmán Negron, 2009), and in general the economy in the region was improving. A similar aspiration for people to move towards modern construction was noted after reconstruction in the early 1990s in the Alto Mayo region of Peru. A form of *improved quincha* was used in the reconstruction then as well; and while this way of building continues to be replicated in rural areas, in urban areas about a third of beneficiaries have now changed their *improved quincha* house for a concrete and brick one (Guzmán Negron, 2010).

Through the project, people have become more aware of disaster risks and the earthquake-resistant qualities of *improved quincha*. Homes built with adobe are demolished and replaced with brick, but *quincha* homes are left standing, and owners just build extensions using bricks and cement. There are a fair number of such extensions in El Carmen, to provide the houses with bathrooms, kitchens and other rooms.

Most people are still believed to have the skills to continue building with *improved quincha* in the future. One said, 'Should I have the means, I would do so with [*improved*] *quincha* rather than bricks, because that is what I know'. Some think that what prevents others from replicating *quincha* technology is a lack of capacity building: 'Very few have copied us. They did not have the skills, because they did not get extensive training. We beneficiaries did not share our skills with others, but used them for ourselves only. Besides, *improved quincha* requires delicate and complex work. Those people want to do something rapidly, with their cement and steel.' Project staff confirm that building a brick wall is quicker than constructing and finishing a wall with *improved quincha*. CARE (2011), took up building with *improved quincha,* and found that it takes more qualified manpower than building with adobe.

Some respondents mentioned that building with *improved quincha* had been replicated elsewhere in the province (e.g. in Elia Rebatta, Chacarilla, and Sunampe) and someone else had heard of over 40 houses being built near Ica. This happened mainly for financial reasons, as people there had no access to government grants and subsidies. Some of them did come for help: 'Individuals nearby asked Practical Action for advice or sometimes trained community members supported them.' The NGO was always ready to offer qualified manpower, and its engineers trained five people from each of several nearby municipalities, after their mayors had become interested in the technology (Guzmán Negron, 2009). However, there is no documentation of cases and numbers replicating individually. NGOs followed suit too. CARE (2011) started to promote the *improved quincha* technology more strongly, once Practical Action's work had made the technology acceptable, and built 33 houses in Pampa Mendoza (part of El Carmen). Caritas Ica (2009) built 24 in the settlement Tierra Prometida (El Huarango), in the district of Ica. And Paz y Esperanza (2010) built 32, with GIZ (German Agency for International Cooperation) support, in Santa Lucia, in the Independencia district of Pisco province.

Technical performance

The houses built with *improved quincha* have stood up well during the several tremors that occurred since. Plaster may have cracked occasionally, but inhabitants had the skills to repair it themselves. The population ascribes this success to the process followed: the selection of a technology based on previous studies and performance, the use of good materials, and sufficient training and supervision by qualified staff. Thus, notwithstanding being built mainly by beneficiaries themselves, the houses were of good quality. Beneficiaries of the *improved quincha* technique also thought that the money was used wisely: 'One notices that there are good reasons for the quantity of cement used. The work has been efficient; money was spent where it was needed.' The direct participation of beneficiaries in design and construction has created confidence and trust.

Some beneficiaries have modified the *improved quincha* houses, but without affecting their structural integrity, e.g. one person has put in a much higher door, to get better ventilation. Others have replaced the gypsum plaster with a cement plaster, to prevent damage and improve appearance. There have been no real maintenance problems, as residents know how to perform the necessary tasks, and the materials are available and relatively cheap. The use of *improved quincha* has saved residents money in comparison with modern construction methods, where it would have been necessary to hire a builder and buy expensive materials. As one respondent remarked, 'If there are tremors, plaster may crack occasionally, and we repair it ourselves. I also painted the house inside and outside'. In fact, the majority of people have painted their houses in order to make them more attractive (see Figure 13.7).

Figure 13.7 Several houses in a row that have been well finished, the farthest with 'imitation-brick' paint and metal windows

Most materials and equipment needed to build with *improved quincha* are easily accessible, although price increases have started making it difficult for some households. This is why timber may pose problems. Some would prefer to use eucalyptus poles instead of the much more expensive sawn timber used in the project, but they are aware that insects will attack the poles, whereas the sawn timber comes treated. Even buying good sawn timber can present problems, as no one in the community really knows how to select the right timber, and they have seen other building sites where the sawn timber is getting warped.

Many people knew from the outset that they were going to expand their house from the initial size of 32 m². This was facilitated by the original design and by placing the core house at the front of the plot, so that any extensions were made towards the back. Whilst extensions were generally not of *improved quincha*, residents took care not to reduce the integrity of the core.

Those interviewed thought that the houses performed so well because during construction they followed guidelines established by the project.

People were also appreciative of its participatory methodology, and the support provided: 'The engineer we had was very good, he did the work with us.' This is in a context where it is very common that people build themselves without guidelines or support.

Livelihoods, empowerment, and resilience

In many households, incomes have increased thanks to work in the construction sector. In Peru, there has been a construction boom since 2008 when the sector grew by 18 per cent; a trend which has continued. Thanks to the training received in the reconstruction project, many beneficiaries have now found work in the sector. Employment rates and incomes in agriculture have increased too. Within the house, domestic tasks have become easier, which has led to some savings. A major factor in this is that the houses are now connected to the water network, which saves women a lot of time compared to fetching water at communal water points, or waiting for a municipal tanker. Improved stoves introduced through the project were also valued: 'There certainly is a reduction in women's work. We were also taught to make improved stoves. Using those, costs have diminished.'

The position of women in society in relation to men has also changed as a result of the project. Women were equals of men during capacity building as well as construction. One member of a focus group remarked, 'Women put a lot of effort into the reconstruction. Before, their role was seen as cooking. Now we even see women managing heavy machinery, or being leaders. And where we had to have a requirement to have at least one token woman on political lists, parties are now actively looking for women to have on their lists.'

As a community, however, there were no further initiatives or communal development activities. There have been improvements in infrastructure (e.g. roads have been tarmacked and pavements built) but this was carried out by the municipality or as a result of central government support for areas affected by the earthquake. While the project did empower its beneficiaries, within the wider community apathy prevailed, with most people waiting for the municipality to initiate activities. In the words of one beneficiary:

> There is much we would like to change, but people here need to be united. In other places, I have seen whole communities support each other and progress. Within the housing project, we did get together, helped each other, and thus advanced more quickly. As beneficiaries, we even managed to build a community hall. But the wider community did nothing; they just want things to come easily.

The authorities seemed more interested in getting people's votes than in providing some real support. And when people approached them with initiatives of their own (e.g. water purification) they were ignored.

Thanks to the project, people have become much more aware of risks, and feel that should any similar disaster happen in the future, they would be more resilient and better able to manage. They are confident that their *improved quincha* houses are safe, and know how they could further improve them. They also have the capacity to negotiate with the state for money, and with contractors on building contracts: 'We are taking things more seriously with these new building works. Now we can access *Techo Proprio* there are various enterprises coming forward, and we negotiate directly with them.' Beneficiaries are now also more eager to formalize their housing situation: 'People are now planning to have proper sanitation; before, that was not considered important. They are getting titles to their property and paying property taxes, and with that can access *Techo Proprio* programmes.'

Key lessons

Practical Action provided support to communities in El Carmen and other parts of Chincha from the emergency phase right through reconstruction. This continuous presence had several advantages, as the early work laid the basis for reconstruction. It allowed links to be made with community-based organizations and local authorities, needs and resources to be explored and understood early on, and a process of participation to begin. This was followed by thorough training on identified skills gaps and also facilitated the re-use of some materials and components. All of this allowed budgets to go further.

The project was essentially self-build and low cost. Building with *improved quincha* does create quality housing but is time consuming, and this may have hampered replication. It is assumed that time is amply available in rural areas, however, this hypothesis may be less valid in a changing context. This is particularly true in peri-urban areas where the availability of time is determined by the dynamics of paid employment locally – be it in commercial agriculture or elsewhere – and an increased participation of women in the labour market.

Second, questions remain over beneficiary targeting. This is partly because some beneficiaries were able to access government grants and subsidies later on, and with those were able to build more modern extensions. Some in the community now say that it would have been preferable to solely target affected people who would not have qualified for such assistance. It is not clear whether this would have been achievable at the relevant stage of the selection process, when those government schemes were not yet active in El Carmen.

Third, there is the issue of post-project apathy in the wider community, even where those members who had benefited from the reconstruction project had been very active and empowered as a group, to the extent of building a community hall. These observations may present a case for agencies to work with all inhabitants of a geographically delimited community, irrespective of their level of need, in order to build a strong overall group that can continue to move the community forward. However, the complaints of the type mentioned in the previous paragraph suggest help should be provided to individuals within such groups according to need.

Finally, agencies need to consider whether they want to work with government systems or in parallel to them. In the case of this project, specialists as well as residents agree that the *improved quincha* technology has a proven resistance against earthquakes. It is very telling that residents move from brick extensions to the *quincha* parts of their houses at the slightest tremor. However, the government generally prefers, and reserves its funding for, brick and concrete houses. There has been one pilot project in Ica where the state bank, *Banco de Materiales* (Materials Bank), funded 200 *quincha* houses, but their normalization and inclusion into regular housing finance programmes is an ongoing topic of discussion. The perceived status of bricks and concrete leads many people to aspire to them, with a desire to be seen as modern, despite their much higher cost and lower safety.

An agency can work with a government to try to make an improved vernacular technology such as *improved quincha* part of the system, which would allow much wider replication as it would qualify for government funding. However, in many cases this would require the development of standards or specifications, and just after a disaster is not an ideal time to do this, as it tends to be time consuming. It may also require greater investment in training, to ensure that skills are more widely available. Additional training materials may have to be developed and become part of relevant curricula, and training may need to be recognized through certification. Furthermore, this approach would require much stronger advocacy to be built into projects from the start, and perhaps stronger governance than that present in Chincha province.

In contrast, working in parallel allows agencies to move forward with the job, and achieve quicker results. Given the pressure to build houses quickly, this is an important consideration. Furthermore, the results of working in parallel, as we have seen in El Carmen, may well be very satisfactory to most beneficiaries, as well as agencies and donors. We have also seen, however, that working in parallel can limit replication; in this particular case as eligibility was restricted to those with no access to government funding and who were unable to afford brick and concrete housing initially.

References

CARE (2011) 'Reconstruyendo Hogares: Modelos de vivienda rural del proceso de reconstrucción de la zona afectada por el sismo del 2007 en el Perú', [website], CARE, http://bvpad.indeci.gob.pe/doc/pdf/esp/doc1946/doc1946-1.pdf [accessed 1 May 2014].

Caritas Ica (2009) 'Caritas Ica inauguró 24 módulos de vivienda en El Huarango – Tierra Prometida', [website], Caritas, <http://www.caritas.org.pe/documentos/noticis_en_red_2009.pdf> [accessed 1 May 2014].

Castilla, J.V.L (2009) 'Agroexportacion, empleo y género en el Perú. Un studio de casos', [website], CIES, DFID and ODI, Lima, <www.iadb.org/intal/intalcdi/PE/2010/04779.pdf> [accessed 26 February 2014].

Ferradas Mannucci, P. (2011) 'Participative reconstruction and risk reduction in Ica', *World Reconstruction Conference Innovation Competition*, Geneva.

Gutiérrez Aliaga, L.M.C. and Manco Rivera, M.T. (2006) 'Caracteristicas sismicas de las construcciones de tierra en el Perú. Contribucion a la enciclopedia mundial de vivienda', [website], PUCP, Lima, <http://tesis.pucp.edu.pe/repositorio/handle/123456789/158> [accessed 26 February 2014].

Guzmán Negron Negrón, E. (2009) *Sistemas constructivos empleados en la reconstruccion posterior as sismo des 15 de Agosto del 2007*, DFID and Practical Action Latin America, Lima.

Guzmán Negron Negrón, E. (2010) 'Peru; The long-term impact of short-term reconstruction work' in M. Lyons and T. Schilderman (eds), *Building Back Better: Delivering People-centred Housing Reconstruction at Scale*, pp. 307–343, Rugby, Practical Action Publishing.

INDECI (2009) 'Resumen Ejecutivo: Lecciones Aprendidas del des Sur – Sismo de Pisco' (posted 15 agosto 2007), [website], Instituto Nacional de Defensa Civil (INDECI), Lima, <www.indeci.gob.pe/publicaciones/resumen_lecc_apren/2_info_gral.pdf> [accessed 26 August 2014].

Pazy Esperanza (2010) 'Construyendo Hogares', [website] http://www.pazyesperanza.org/pe/hacemos/hacemos_programas_ica.htm [accessed 14 May 2014].

Practical Action Latin America (2008, unpublished) *Housewives down to work*, [website] http://redesdegestionderiesgo.com/Item/1583 (accessed 26 February 2014).

Schilderman, T. (2004) 'Adapting traditional shelter for disaster mitigation and reconstruction' in *Building Research and Information*, 32(5): 414–426.

About the authors

Theo Schilderman is a Senior Researcher at the Building and Social Housing Foundation (BSHF), a consultant, and lecturer. He is a Dutch architect with 40 years of experience in low-income housing and post-disaster reconstruction who has worked for Practical Action, COOPIBO, and the IHS in the past, both in developing countries and in management. He was the editor, with Michal Lyons, of *Building Back Better* in 2010.

Max Watanabe is a sociologist working for Practical Action Latin America for the past decade. He is the coordinator of the Risk Reduction and Climate Change Adaptation Programme, involved in research, project design and implementation, and monitoring.

CHAPTER 14

Conclusions: How does our approach to reconstruction need to change?

Theo Schilderman, Eleanor Parker, Matthew Blackett, Marion MacLellan, Charles Parrack, and Daniel Watson

Our research into the long-term impact of reconstruction provided new learning, leading to some suggestions for future changes to reconstruction and recovery and our ways of working. We were also able to identify gaps where we need to broaden our understanding, perhaps through future research. However, it is worth noting again that our review of case studies was based on qualitative information only. Numbers interviewed in each case were relatively small, and, therefore, did not produce statistically viable quantitative evidence. As far as possible, we verified individually obtained information through triangulation. We also compared our findings with those of two parallel research efforts with a similar focus. That said we are aware that these case studies are looking back at reconstruction over a very variable timespan, ranging between 4 and 35 years, making comparison of long-term impact difficult even between them. Moreover, they took place in widely differing contexts, and every new crisis is bound to be different again. The positive lessons that have come out of this research will, therefore, always need to be adapted to new disaster situations. Bearing in mind these restrictions, we can see some of the findings from the literature reviewed in Chapter 1 confirmed in our case studies. Other literature findings are harder to verify, partly because our sample of cases may not have covered them sufficiently, but also because these findings may have been evident in the short-term impact and changed in the longer term, a phenomenon confirmed in the research by Duyne Barenstein in Chapter 3.

What earlier findings does our research confirm?

This section returns to the literature review contained in Chapter 1, and reviews its findings in the light of the case studies researched. Where in the following section we refer to countries or regions, these are meant to describe the respective case studies for those locations only, as described in the chapters of this book, and not to be mistaken for general findings about overall reconstruction in those locations.

The importance of beneficiary participation in the design, implementation, and monitoring of reconstruction from an early stage, and to make enough

http://dx.doi.org/10.3362/9781780448398.014

time for it, stated in sections about user satisfaction, replication, and livelihoods of Chapter 1, is confirmed by most of our case studies and cannot be stressed enough. Doing so integrates local culture, housing experience, and skills, perhaps most clearly shown herein in the example of Gandhi Nu Gam, India. Participation allows local needs and priorities to be taken into account by agencies. As a result, it makes their designs more flexible and adaptable and, therefore, easier to tailor to families' individual needs, either from the start, or during extensions, as evidenced in Peru. Successful participation creates the 'ownership' that helps residents continue to develop and improve their housing, and is often key in replication. Participation and the social capital it can create can be empowering and enable communities to tackle other and bigger issues in the future, as was shown particularly in El Salvador.

User satisfaction can vary over time. Where there is initial beneficiary unhappiness/dissatisfaction with aspects of the design or construction, householders will change such aspects where they have the means, and ultimately become more satisfied, as Duyne Barenstein described in Gujarat, and projects we studied in, e.g. Peru and Indonesia. But this is noticeably harder for the poorest; several case studies refer to the poor being unable to make changes or extensions, or doing so in poor quality. On the other hand, householders may also gradually become more dissatisfied with their house, e.g. because technical faults start appearing over time.

Choosing the right technology is crucial, as it influences both replication and technical performance. Even where design may be participatory, projects sometimes are more prescriptive where it comes to technology choice, often with good intent for reasons of disaster resistance. Where technologies proposed are too alien, people struggle to implement them well due to lack of skills, and replication is limited, as was the case with the concrete ribs on roofs in Vietnam, the rat-trap bond masonry in Sri Lanka, and flat concrete roofs in India. If the technology is too expensive, many will not be able to continue building in the same way; resistant construction needs to be affordable to beneficiaries in the longer term, not just with the help of disaster aid. Many of our cases show examples of people extending their houses in haphazard ways after the reconstruction phase, due to lack of money. In several of our cases (Guatemala, Pakistan, Gandhi Nu Gam) reconstruction with improved vernacular technologies proved to be worthwhile, as they tended to be cheaper and easier to learn and replicate than modern technologies. One problem, though, is that the vernacular is often not incorporated in building codes, which means it is not supported by government initiatives, as in Peru and Guatemala. In practice, however, these cases have proven to stand up well against natural hazards and the wear and tear of time and climate, in the case of Guatemala over 35 years!

The issue of skills is closely related to that of technology choice. Beneficiaries and local artisans are more familiar with vernacular technologies. Projects can help to build on and adapt those skills; this is easier when existing technologies are improved, than when new and perhaps more modern ones are introduced. Often, training provided in relatively short-term reconstruction activities is inadequate for radically different technologies to get a foothold, as happened in Sri Lanka. In Pakistan and Vietnam, where thorough training was given to local building artisans, and agencies had a much longer presence, the innovations persisted. It was also noticeable in Habitat for Humanity projects after the tsunami, and in many of the Latin American cases we studied, that the guided sweat equity contributed by beneficiaries to reconstruction gave them the skills to maintain and repair their homes themselves. Donor-driven and usually contractor-built projects that focus much more often on modern technology tend to leave far fewer skills behind, which generates problems in the future when beneficiaries will be forced to spend more on repairs or extensions.

Building codes can be overrated as the prime means to achieve quality and disaster resistance. Yes they can work well, as in the case of Gujarat and also recently in Concepción, Chile. But often they do not apply or do not impose disaster-resistance on non-engineered structures, as in Aceh. Or they are poorly understood by lay people and where they are poorly implemented and inspected, vulnerability can remain high. Yet, beneficiaries greatly value the safety that good construction can offer. Our cases have proven that disaster resistance can be achieved by the right vernacular technologies, with often minor and cheap improvements, e.g. in Peru – where people sleep in or move to the improved *quincha* part of their house rather than in their more modern extensions – and in Guatemala, and through retrofitting in Pakistan and Vietnam. In many of those cases, building manuals were made available locally, which proved invaluable for the correct take-up of those technologies. Unfortunately, those solutions are not covered by prevailing codes, and not trusted by building professionals whose vocational curriculum did not cover them – this will need to change. Gujarat and Pakistan are cases where codes were changed relatively quickly to accommodate improved vernacular construction to the mutual benefit of all.

Where housing is built informally, as is the case in the majority of the South, quality and disaster resistance will need to be achieved without reliance on enforced building codes; by generating local awareness, skills, and knowledge. Several of the cases we studied, e.g. Vietnam, Pakistan, Peru, and Guatemala, have shown that this can be achieved through appropriate communication, training, technical assistance, and supervision on building sites. In regions exposed to frequently occurring hazards, such as typhoons in Vietnam, we are starting to see that those investments in quality are reducing the costs of future repairs, enabling some people to improve their livelihoods. Where this investment is somewhat lacking, e.g. in MCR tile production in both Honduras and Nicaragua, poor quality and associated vulnerabilities can result.

Projects often have a tendency to focus too much on housing and not enough on infrastructure and community facilities; we saw examples of this in Tamil Nadu, described by Duyne Barenstein, Sri Lanka, and with Habitat for Humanity's projects. When infrastructure is lacking or arrives late in relocation sites, significant discontent can result; though sometimes, communities manage to self-mobilize to overcome such problems of their own initiative, as they did with water supply in Honduras. Some agencies may fail to account for local culture and habits, in particular those associated with sanitation or kitchens, leading to inappropriate designs. Where improved infrastructure or facilities are provided beyond beneficiaries' pre-disaster levels, beneficiaries tend to be satisfied, sometimes healthier, and often benefit from savings in time and money, as we found in Peru and Pakistan.

Similarly, many projects do not pay enough attention to livelihoods. Houses are rarely designed, and sometimes plots are inadequate – e.g. in Maharashtra and Gujarat – to accommodate livelihood activities, and in the case of relocation, livelihoods may be lost altogether. This has led some beneficiaries to divert cash given for shelter into cash for livelihoods, with a negative impact on their housing reconstruction. In a few extreme cases in Sri Lanka, we saw a few beneficiaries sell off their houses in order to revive their businesses. Frequently, beneficiaries have incorporated livelihood activities such as shops and workshops in their house or on the plot at a later stage; this has been facilitated by adaptability of design and adequate plot size. But perhaps projects ought to have been designed to accommodate this from the start.

Reconstruction can stimulate the local economy, especially in construction. Many of our cases made deliberate efforts to buy or produce locally, boosting materials production and trade. Beneficiaries trained by our projects found subsequent lasting work in construction and/or maintenance in about half of the cases. To an extent, however, this depended on how the economy fared after reconstruction. In some cases, e.g. in Sri Lanka and Nicaragua, where construction fell back to levels that existed before the disasters, the additional jobs could not be maintained, whereas in India, El Salvador, and Peru, for example, some project beneficiaries found permanent work in construction. A contributing factor in both former cases was the introduction of an innovative technology with insufficient take-up post reconstruction, and, therefore, less demand for those new skills.

Few projects described in the literature ventured beyond construction in their livelihood support. This was slightly better in our projects. One constraint may be that agencies who know about construction are not necessarily very knowledgeable in other sectors of the economy or in small enterprise support. Our projects met with variable success when supporting other economic activities, as in Aceh, but the start-up funds provided in El Salvador had a much more positive impact, e.g. establishing over 1,000 micro-enterprises, the majority by women, producing meat, seafood, processed food, clothes and other things. The more holistic approach to recovery, preferred in Gandhi Nu Gam, was very successful. All involved were aware that to halt out-migration to urban centres as the only option for advancement, local livelihoods needed to be boosted as part of the recovery, and they did so in agriculture, through traditional crafts, in vernacular construction, and tourism.

Where does long-term impact differ from the short-term?

In the projects reviewed there was little evidence for beneficiaries not occupying the allocated houses or vacating them after some time. In Maharashtra, Duyne Barenstein found no evidence of people returning to their original villages, and indeed some villages not originally designated for relocation chose to anyway in order to reduce the risk to which they were exposed in their traditional settlements. We found that relocated beneficiaries sometimes abandoned their houses for other reasons, e.g. the offer of a job elsewhere, in Peru and El Salvador, marriage in Aceh, or emerging crime in El Salvador. And some of the cases studied by Duyne Barenstein and Maynard, e.g. in Sri Lanka and Gujarat, found that relocated communities suffered from reduced access to education and employment and less community cohesion.

The negative consequences for relocated communities can be magnified early on but may not always perpetuate in the long term. If relocation is tackled carefully, and with the participation of beneficiaries, it can work. Important factors controlling success are: proximity to the previous settlement, as described by Duyne Barenstein in Gujarat; good transport links, as in Honduras; and the adoption of a holistic approach that includes livelihoods, as in Gandhi Nu Gam, India. In Nicaragua, where some beneficiaries were relocated relatively far from their original lands, they built temporary huts on their fields to stay in during peak farming times while they tended their crops. As long as people do not lose their livelihoods, beneficiaries often manage to improve what they did not initially like. Finally, relocation sites can be significantly safer than the original site, provided comprehensive risk assessment is undertaken and critical infrastructure, such as drainage, is not neglected. This did not happen in some cases, e.g. in our study of Honduras, and in Tamil Nadu and Gujarat, studied by Duyne Barenstein, and Sri Lanka, assessed by Maynard, where some reconstructed houses suffered flood damage after relocation.

Poverty is a key factor in replication. Where reconstructed housing can only be afforded by the majority with assistance from disaster aid, replication is often limited or 'diluted', diminishing quality and increasing risk. What can make a difference, though, is to suggest a range of low-cost, effective improvements that can be implemented, as shown in the reinforcement of houses in Pakistan, or give people access to small flexible loans. As stated by e.g. Rhyner, loans for housing are a known problem in developing countries, where mortgage finance is almost impossible for the poorest to access. In Vietnam, the Vietnamese Bank of Social Policy managed accessible loans which greatly helped replication. In other countries, such as Peru and Guatemala, some finance also became available, but this had a counterproductive effect as it excluded the use of the improved vernacular construction used by the projects, and thus limited those who could replicate to the somewhat better-off. The cost and affordability of reconstruction are crucial issues that future projects should consider carefully: are they aiming to solve a problem temporarily, by helping some disaster-affected people rebuild a house, or in the longer term by providing them the potential to continue to build safely in that region, at an affordable cost? Agencies should consider how safe houses need to be, against how many beneficiaries a project aims to reach within a set budget. Some of our cases, e.g. in Peru, El Salvador, Guatemala, Nicaragua as well as the Habitat for Humanity projects, have opted for core houses with good disaster resistance, in an attempt to reach as many as possible. Beneficiaries saw the value of reaching many victims, but some struggled to extend the cores to the same standard.

Poverty is also a factor in beneficiary targeting and who ultimately benefits from reconstruction. There is evidence in the literature (Lyons and Schilderman, 2010) that the rich and more powerful in the community often benefit more, and Duyne Barenstein, in her study of a range of Indian cases, offers some proof of that. There is less evidence in the projects studied, as these were generally successful in targeting the less well-off; some agencies involved made an effort to have beneficiaries participate in defining a transparent selection process or in defining appropriate selection criteria. Others, such as Habitat for Humanity, made deliberate efforts to reach the marginalized and disabled, whilst others aimed to address the gender balance, and often succeeded in empowering women, e.g. in Aceh and most Latin American cases. On the other hand, the case of Peru did show that targeting some people in affected communities and getting those to work together well, whilst not working with the remainder, did prevent a spirit of joint action developing at the level of the larger community. Perhaps, if agencies were to go for more integrated projects, developing a common plan and with some services that benefit all, and then targeting housing support according to individual needs, a greater sense of agency could remain for the future development of the community.

Insecurity of tenure is a big constraint to reconstruction, particularly in urban areas. It is a key reason for many agencies to focus on owners only, with proven property titles, in what is these days called owner-driven reconstruction. Lack of tenure tends to delay reconstruction, make finance and infrastructure inaccessible, and discourage the occupiers of the land to invest much in building a structure that might be bulldozed later on. It is also likely to minimize replication of the good examples set by projects. Some of the cases studied, e.g. in Sri Lanka, wanted to commence reconstruction quickly and, therefore, focused on owners. But other cases, e.g. in Peru and Habitat for Humanity projects, are starting to show that it is possible to improve the tenure situation, e.g. through empowering communities to take action. Where waiting for land issues to be resolved took time, that was often used to accommodate the participatory planning process for the project, e.g. in Honduras. Where that seemed unfeasible to lead to rapid results, one option offered in El Salvador was that of a house that could be disassembled and rebuilt elsewhere.

Can reconstruction generate greater resilience in the longer term? We found only sporadic evidence in the literature of empowered communities continuing development work after reconstruction finished. There is more evidence in our research, in about half of our cases, particularly in Latin America and in Gujarat. In Peru, where the project target groups were part of a larger neighbourhood, their enthusiasm to undertake further work was met by apathy in an environment where most people were waiting for politicians to resolve their dreams. Poor local governance can be an important constraint too, particularly if that involves oppression, as happened in Guatemala, and too much political wrangling or bureaucracy. The most resilient communities amongst the cases studied are probably those in El Salvador, where reconstruction was led by a development – rather than humanitarian – organization that opted for a longer-term presence, which supported a community umbrella organization to get a voice, and Gandhi Nu Gam, India where a holistic approach strengthened the community across the board.

New findings of long-term impact

Adaptability of the reconstructed house is hugely important to beneficiaries. Many of them have shown great resourcefulness in adapting houses that originally had some shortcomings, e.g. offering a core to a growing family with changing needs over time. Many households have extended houses, or converted rooms to other uses, such as shops or small workshops. This is facilitated by designs that allow flexibility and expansion, by placing houses close to the borders of plots to allow adjacent extensions, and by allocating plots that have sufficient space, as in Gandhi Nu Gam, India and Peru.

We did notice that many beneficiaries extended their houses with cheaper materials and often in haphazard ways. In some cases, they reused materials of a temporary or transitional shelter for that purpose. The resulting extensions are frequently unsafe and unappealing. This problem could be reduced by more joined-up thinking and organization between transitional shelter and permanent housing. The challenge is that this usually involves different agencies. In one of our cases, one agency kept working with the same communities in Peru through both these phases, and they used a similar technology, different levels of *quincha*, throughout. Feedback here suggests that the early involvement helped to get participation and partnerships started, leading to successful permanent housing designs, needing less training later on as beneficiaries had learned from transitional construction, and reusing some appropriate materials and components effectively and safely.

The aesthetics and appearance of a house are important to people. In Sri Lanka, houses were reconstructed with unplastered brick walls that many perceived as a 'poor man's house'; some beneficiaries went on to plaster their houses later. But in another case in Peru, beneficiaries were unhappy with plastered *quincha*, which some then painted over to look like unplastered bricks. Peru and Sri Lanka are countries with very similar levels of income and development, yet how people want their house to look is culturally specific. This shows that a good understanding of the local context and housing culture, as well as involving beneficiaries in design, are very important.

Beneficiaries value ease of maintenance, leading to time and cost savings in some cases. Where maintenance was required, it was sometimes neglected, and as a result the house's performance reduced over time, e.g. most beneficiaries in Sri Lanka did not regularly protect their brickwork with sealant, leading to occasional water damage, and houses in other projects sometimes were noted as being urgently in need of a coat of paint or repairs to plaster by the review team. Information and training about proper maintenance may need more attention from project teams. The issue of available time, related to the labour intensity of technologies, is important in this respect too. Agencies sometimes assume that time is freely available; self-building by beneficiaries can help to reduce costs and thus reach more people, and generate useful skills. In urban areas especially, time is often scarce, as many people are struggling to make a daily living, and there are no clear slack seasons, as in agriculture for rural communities. We noticed that this hampered the spread of improved *quincha* in the more urban context of Peru, but even in rural Nicaragua time was a factor in the lack of replication of cyclopean concrete walls.

Some of the longer-term impacts of projects are determined by the beneficiaries themselves, but agencies have a role to facilitate the best possible outcome. Projects with a more holistic or integrated approach, such as Gandhi Nu Gam in India that focused not just on housing, but also on incorporating services, restoration of social networks, and livelihoods support, for example, tend to be more successful in the long term. The added services have often improved people's health, or saved time and money that could be re-invested elsewhere. The livelihoods support has increased income that has contributed to house improvements and extensions. Stronger social networks have given voice to communities.

It is questionable whether transformational change can really be achieved within the time span of two to four years of the average reconstruction project; be it in technology, financing, market development, regulation, livelihoods development, or community empowerment. To achieve such change is typically more the realm of development organizations, willing to commit to a longer presence, than of humanitarian organizations whose remit is much more limited. The long-term commitment of agencies and subsequent changes facilitated is evident in e.g. Vietnam, in technology, financing, and regulation; in El Salvador, with respect to financing, livelihoods development, and empowerment; and in Pakistan, in technology and market development. For replication to happen beyond the originally targeted communities awareness-raising is required, along with appropriate information, capacity-building, and advocacy, probably in collaboration between various agencies and institutions. This has started to happen in the above cases, but most projects are not designed to do so. Elsewhere, agencies have retired and changes that might have seemed promising did not take hold, e.g. in technology in Sri Lanka, Nicaragua, and Maharashtra, with changes in sanitation and the introduction of solar power in several locations being abandoned.

Apart from a longer-term view of the recovery of affected communities, there also needs to be a greater focus on disaster risk reduction (DRR), and, related to that, climate change. For natural hazards to have less impact, better houses need to be built during the normal construction process, not just in occasional reconstruction. Reconstruction projects must also consider DRR and all possible future risks when designing and implementing technologies. Several cases demonstrated resistance to recurrent hazards – earthquakes and cyclones but they sometimes failed to take account of other hazards that could occur, particularly flooding. As a result of climate change, floods and storms may increase, both in numbers and or magnitude. Mitigating disasters up front can be a lot more cost-effective than having to reconstruct repeatedly (World Bank, 2010), but it requires more investment and change for resistant housing to become accessible to all. The government of Vietnam has made a step in the right direction in making finance more accessible. It also requires DRR to be affordable, perhaps done in small steps, such as in Pakistan and Vietnam, and incrementally. This is probably less than ideal in the eyes of structural engineers, but is bound to have a larger uptake.

What does this mean for future reconstruction?

The oldest case study we assessed was reconstruction after the earthquake that devastated parts of Guatemala in 1976. It happened in a global context where reconstruction was dominated by an agency-driven approach with a focus on sound engineering and design and the use of rules and regulations as well as contractors to guarantee quality and disaster resistance so as to minimize future risks. The resulting designs were often ill-suited to local culture, climate, and resources. It was an expensive approach which left many disaster victims uncatered for, who per force rebuilt themselves as best they could. What our case study illustrated in Guatemala was noticeably different to the norm in that it focused on those self-builders, provided little cash for construction, but crucially gave them the knowledge to build back safer themselves. Other countries took note and replicated various aspects of this project; sadly, in Guatemala itself, the empowerment the project had started to generate was subsequently curtailed by an oppressive regime.

The first Habitat Conference in Vancouver also happened to be in 1976. Practitioners and researchers such as John Turner (1976) argued there that most housing, especially in developing countries, was realized through self-built or self-managed construction by residents themselves, and that this was not a burden but a resource to be cherished. Turner also argued that housing was equally important as a process – since that empowers people – as it was a product. Prior to this, the state had been seen as the primary provider of housing to the masses but, for many reasons, had failed to reach the population in sufficient numbers, much like agency-driven reconstruction. The Conference urged governments and agencies to turn away from previous policies, in favour of policies that enabled popular construction. This then gave rise to sites and services and slum upgrading programmes, support for housing co-operatives and community contracting, and innovative forms of financing such as CLIFF (Schilderman, 2010).

Whilst individual NGO-driven projects took this thinking on board in small-scale projects, it took the reconstruction sector a lot longer to adopt this new perspective at any scale. Perhaps that is due to some extent, to many of the key players in reconstruction being humanitarian rather than development agencies. The first large-scale attempt at Owner-Driven Reconstruction happened after the 2001 earthquake in Gujarat; parts of that experience are described in Chapters 3 and 5 of this book. The early focus on 'building back safer' emphasized resistant housing, then started to shift towards 'building back better', wider definitions of which go beyond housing as a product and start considering process as well as community, services, and livelihoods, unfortunately now perhaps a term that is being over-used and seems to be developing many definitions. The narrow definitions of 'building back better' do not differ that much from 'building back safer', though they may vary as to how that safety can be achieved.

Influenced initially by a greater attention to DRR, instigated by the likes of UN-ISDR (United Nations International Strategy for Disaster Reduction), and increasingly also Climate Change Adaptation (CCA), some agencies have now started thinking about generating resilience through reconstruction and recovery. Like 'building back better', resilience appears not to have an agreed definition, but is often seen as an ability to resist, cope with and recover from the effects of hazards. The great advantage of pursuing resilience is that it enables people to become more adaptable and so less impacted by disasters in the long term, thus diminishing future needs for reconstruction, whilst building back safer achieves that only for a while, and only for those targeted. Achieving resilience requires much more integrated approaches to reconstruction that stress not just more resilient construction, but also community agency and empowerment, good governance, livelihoods improvements and diversification, risk awareness, and access to technology. Having the right processes appears to be the key to achieving resilience.

Many agencies that traditionally get involved in reconstruction struggle to go that far. They are under time pressure to achieve results quickly which may hamper good process, and their presence on the ground is limited; the cases we studied have shown that for agencies to have a wider impact a sustained presence is needed. Some agencies are limited by their mandates or rules about what activities they are able to undertake and in what ways. They are also afraid of their reputation and what a negative impact could do to fundraising, and are, therefore, somewhat reluctant to venture into the unknown, such as undertaking projects utilizing improved vernacular construction.

Where does that leave the people affected by disasters? Many of them will never have heard of resilience. The overwhelming impression that emerges from our research is their concern for safety and security. But a house that you can sleep safely in, as expressed by some beneficiaries, is only part of that concern; in many cases, the investment in better housing can only be realized if secure tenure is achieved first. Having income security is another one; for a few beneficiaries, it was so important that they went as far as selling their house to invest in a livelihood; and secure and growing incomes are essential to keep building well. A secure living environment, not marred by violence or oppression, is important to them too; we have seen some people leave a safe house, because they felt unsafe in their neighbourhood, and elsewhere their further initiatives as communities were oppressed by a regime weary of 'communism'. Poor people are faced with many insecurities in their lives; which ones predominate varies, and will need to be determined from case to case. What seems to be clear, though, is that policies and projects that tackle only a single one of them – unsafe housing – often only provide a short-term and incomplete solution, and can result in limited success.

There is, therefore, an overwhelming need for agencies and donors to move to more holistic or integrated approaches to reconstruction and recovery designed with the intended beneficiaries. That will not be easy for many, as their mandate and focus are often limited. It probably also requires a presence over a longer period than just building houses would take. Thus, some agencies may have to change, or seek to collaborate with others to enable them to undertake a programme not curtailed in coverage and time. In pursuing such an approach, they should not forget to integrate the other lessons of this chapter, in particular that outsiders should not presume to know best, but learn from local housing and experience, and that getting designs and plot layouts that are adaptable often gets better long-term results. It also requires participation, inclusion, and skills development of those affected by disasters, and generating the capacity to deal with future risks and climate change.

What future research may be needed?

Even given the studies evaluated herein, we still have only a limited understanding of holistic approaches to reconstruction and recovery, and there is a prime need to look further into examples and draw all the lessons from them we possibly can. As we have seen it took fully 25 years for the reconstruction sector to take steps to adopt the example set by the housing sector – in 1976 in Vancouver – to make a strategic move from an agency-driven to a more people-driven approach at scale – in Gujarat in 2001. Yet there have been smaller-scale examples of the latter approach all along, starting off with Guatemala. The same is the case with more holistic reconstruction, where we have to learn more from cases such as Gandhi Nu Gam, India or El Salvador, described in this book, or that of the coffee growers in Colombia, described elsewhere (Lizarralde, 2010).

Assisting all those affected to recover is a huge task that authorities and NGOs often struggle to undertake comprehensively. It will require us to gain a better understanding of what the possible impact is of targeting the vast majority of the affected with some aid, perhaps only a core house, against helping a selection with a more complete housing solution. Several of our cases seem to show that provided projects create the right conditions, core houses can work and be left to owners to expand and improve. If a more joined-up approach could be established between transitional shelter and permanent housing that would help too. A related issue to be explored further is perhaps whether projects should target communities or neighbourhoods as a whole, rather than those more affected, perhaps with different levels of aid, to build the agency required to maintain development momentum.

A few of our cases, most notably Pakistan, have shown that reaching large numbers also requires the construction market to function effectively. Tools such as Emergency Market Mapping and Analysis (EMMA) (Albu, 2010) now enable us to understand post-disaster markets better and take relevant action. But the role of the private sector can go beyond that of building or supplying materials towards financing reconstruction itself or delivering other elements of more holistic recovery programmes, e.g. in livelihoods support or education, areas where traditional actors in reconstruction are often weak. Future research could assess partnerships between the public and the private sector or NGOs and companies in such areas, and identify possible ways of applying this to reconstruction.

Quite a few agencies in our cases have tried to introduce technological innovations, for a variety of reasons: to achieve disaster-resistance, to build cheaper, to save energy or be more sustainable. We have seen many of those innovations not take hold. Some agencies have argued that a longer presence is needed; others claimed that it is more successful to simply improve the local examples of vernacular technology that have shown some promise and can be adapted for disaster resistance. Even that can meet obstacles, e.g. in government or risk-averse agencies. Whether such innovation can work in three to four years, and what is needed to make that happen, is another topic that merits further research. And where agencies do stay longer to advocate change, we need to learn more about how to do so successfully, and how such agencies can phase out and hand over to local authorities and/or civil society.

Our understanding of how reconstruction can help to overcome psychological trauma is still limited. In a few cases, e.g. Aceh, researchers have found that for some victims getting actively involved in positive action helped them to overcome their trauma. But we know little about how projects could do so most effectively, and our research did not focus on this aspect. Yet we know that trauma and depression as a result of great losses, and the alienating effects of relocation and sometimes reconstruction itself, can have devastating impacts on people's sense of security. The weakening of social networks that might have provided support also has negative consequences. This should be recognized in project planning and may require further research.

Finally, if we aim to pursue integrated approaches to reconstruction that might require a variety of agencies to work together more closely, we need to develop a greater understanding of the barriers that need to be overcome, how that might work and what enabling environment – at local, national, and international levels – may need to be in place. Developing that fuller understanding can start with looking at a number of holistic reconstruction case studies in more detail, as suggested in the first paragraph of this section, but is likely to need further research into key issues.

References

Albu, M. (2010) *Emergency Market Mapping and Analysis Toolkit,* Practical Action Publishing, Rugby.

Lizarralde, G. (2010) 'Decentralizing (re)construction: Agriculture cooperatives as a vehicle for reconstruction in Colombia' in M. Lyons and T. Schilderman, (eds) *Building Back Better: Delivering People-centred Housing Reconstruction at Scale,* pp. 191–213, Practical Action Publishing Ltd., Rugby.

Lyons, M. and Schilderman, T. (2010) 'Putting people at the centre of reconstruction', *PCR Position Paper,* Practical Action, Rugby and London South Bank University, London.

Schilderman, T. (2010) 'Putting people at the centre of reconstruction' in M. Lyons and T. schilderman, (eds) *Building Back Better: Delivering People-centred Housing Reconstruction at Scale,* pp. 17–23, Practical Action Publishing, Rugby.

Turner, J. (1976) *Housing by People,* Marion Boyars Publishers Ltd., London.

World Bank (2010) *Natural Hazards, UnNatural Disasters: The Economics of Effective Prevention,* The World Bank, Washington DC.

About the authors

Theo Schilderman is a Senior Researcher at the Building and Social Housing Foundation, a consultant and lecturer. He is a Dutch architect with 40 years of experience in low-income housing and post-disaster reconstruction, who has worked for Practical Action, COOPIBO, and the IHS in the past, both in developing countries and in management. He was editor, with Michal Lyons, of *Building Back Better* in 2010.

El Parker is Principal Lecturer in Natural Disasters at the Centre for Disaster Management and Hazards Research and Associate Head for the Department of Geography, Environment, and Disaster Management at Coventry University. She is an engineering geologist by background with a PhD in the impacts of climate change; her research covers multi-hazard and risk assessment, community-based early warning, and community preparedness for resilience and adaption to chronic and acute risks. She has been a lecturer for 15 years and course director for the undergraduate programmes in disaster management at Coventry for 10 years and has also undertaken numerous research and consultancy projects in that field.

Matthew Blackett is a Senior Lecturer in Natural Hazards and Physical Geography for the Department of Geography, Environment, and Disaster Management at Coventry University. He completed his PhD and post-doctoral position at King's College, London working in the remote sensing of earthquakes and volcanoes. He is now co-director of Coventry University's Centre for Disaster Management and Hazards Research.

Marion MacLellan is a Senior Lecturer in Development Studies for the Department of Geography, Environment, and Disaster Management at Coventry University. Her research interests lie predominantly in Sub-Saharan Africa, and in particular in human development issues – livelihoods, education in emergencies, children and orphans, AIDS, and disaster management. She is working with practitioners in the Democratic Republic of the Congo on the development of a network of disaster managers based in the global South and is external examiner for the postgraduate sustainable development programme in the University of Makeni, Sierra Leone.

Charles Parrack trained and worked as an environmental engineer, focusing on sustainability and community development. He leads the Post Graduate course in Shelter after Disaster at The Centre for Development and Emergency Practice (CENDEP), Oxford Brookes University. His research interests are based around the shelter and disaster area. Charles is Co-Chair of Architecture Sans Frontières–UK and has taught sustainable design and technology studios at architecture schools in the UK. He is a Senior Lecturer at Brookes and teaches design and technology on the architecture courses.

Daniel Watson is part of the Humanitarian Engineering and Computing Group, based at Coventry University. He has a wide range of professional experience, having worked in disaster preparedness, response, and early recovery throughout South and South-East Asia. Most recently, before joining Coventry University, he worked on a number of emergency projects in Northern Afghanistan. Through his work, he has come to recognize that there is a relative lack of longer-term evaluation of humanitarian and development projects, and that addressing this gap could have real implications for the design and implementation of subsequent projects. Daniel holds degrees in Disaster Management and Civil Engineering.

Appendix 1: Research methodology

Areas of investigation

The areas of investigation listed below have been discussed initially with research partners who showed an interest in participating in the research. In addition to that, they have been discussed with about 150 representatives of agencies and individuals involved in the researching, funding, and implementation of reconstruction and disaster mitigation projects, who are considered to be the potential end users of the research results. These discussions took place in meetings of the UK Shelter Forum in Oxford on 22 February 2013, and the international Shelter Meeting in Geneva on 25 April 2013. The questions listed below were given to all fieldworkers as areas to explore.

User-satisfaction

- Are residents happy with their houses, after having lived in them for a while?
- What do they particularly like about the house?
- What do they think should have been done differently?
- Have they actually made any changes in how their houses are being used?
- Have they made changes to the materials used?
- Did the increased safety of the houses reduce subsequent damage? Did that liberate money previously spent on repair or reconstruction costs?
- Has the health of residents improved? If so, in what ways? Did improvements in housing lead to reduced health bills?
- Do the houses adequately accommodate income-generating requirements of residents?
- Are the houses easily accessible for people with disabilities?
- How did the availability, accessibility, and abilities of project managers and staff affect how far residents felt their needs and requirements were met by the projects?
- If certain components (e.g. of infrastructure) could not be accommodated in the original projects, were these added later, and if so, how was this funded?
- What are the advantages and disadvantages of living in these houses compared to others that have used different technologies?

http://dx.doi.org/10.3362/9781780448398.015

Beneficiary targeting

- What proportion of the original beneficiaries, including family members who may have inherited the house from others who died, still lives in their properties?
- Did any of the original beneficiaries not occupy or abandon their house altogether? If so, what were the reasons for that? What happened to those houses afterwards?
- Did any of the original households resell their re-built properties? For what reasons? What was the resale value? What attracted the new owners to buy the houses?
- Are any households renting out their properties, or parts of those? For what reasons? What are the rent levels? What attracted renters to the houses?
- Are the beneficiaries using the houses for the intended purposes, or have they changed the functions of the house, and if so in what way?
- Did the beneficiaries have to pay taxes (for example land or council tax) upon acquiring the property? If yes, what are its impacts on the households?

Replication

- Have residents in the houses built by the projects continued to expand them or to build additional houses, using the techniques or innovations introduced by the projects? How were these works funded?
- Have residents expanded their houses, or community members built additional houses using designs and technologies differing from those introduced by the projects? If yes, what were their reasons for doing so?
- Have other individuals who were not beneficiaries of the projects copied the examples?
- Who could afford to do so and who could not?
- What limits the families to replicate this type of housing?
- Did those who did replicate have the knowledge and skills to continue building in the same way, and if not, where did they get the required help?
- Have other organizations replicated or disseminated the projects or some of their innovations? If yes, what enabled them to do so?
- Are the materials or equipment required to replicate or maintain the houses readily available?
- Has there been any uptake of the innovations into local building codes, local policies, etc.?
- Has the implementing organization incorporated the lessons learned into their other projects? If so, in what ways?
- Did awareness-raising and communication about safety in building raise general knowledge about the need for safer building after the project was over?

- Were financial mechanisms (such as access to credit for safer building) put in place by the project to facilitate the building actions? Did these continue to offer services to households after the project was over?

Technical performance

- How well have the houses stood up to the impact of subsequent hazards? What made them perform like they did?
- Are they sufficiently durable, e.g. did they withstand the weather or insect attacks?
- In relation to their performance, were standards or guidelines set by projects or imposed by authorities adequate, too high or too low?
- Did the residents make any alterations affecting the resistance or durability of their dwellings? If so, what were they, and explain why they made them.
- Has the design of the house and the plot layout facilitated or hindered extension? In what ways?
- Did the residents have any housing maintenance issues? If so, what are they? How are they maintaining their houses?

Livelihoods

- Have projects led to lasting benefits (jobs, increased incomes etc.) in the construction sector?
- Were projects helpful in reducing workloads of women?
- Did projects result in any changes in the balance of power (e.g. on the basis of gender)?
- Did the beneficiary community initiate and undertake other development activities after the reconstruction project? If so, what are these activities?
- Have individual residents and communities been empowered and become more resilient themselves? E.g. is there evidence of them negotiating with agencies or authorities on their own initiative?
- Are residents and their communities now better able to deal with risks and changes in the environment (e.g. due to climate change or erosion), the economy (e.g. collapse of markets), and the socio-political context (e.g. changes in power)?

Research methodology

The methodology aims to gather qualitative rather than quantitative information on how projects have changed since they were completed, and how that has impacted on their inhabitants and the wider community. The information was gathered using the following methods:

Interviews

In-depth interviews covering all areas of investigation mentioned above with a sample of minimum 15 people, matching the following characteristics:

1. Interviews with at least one representative of the local authority (e.g. a municipality) in charge of housing.
2. Interviews with at least two key informants within or close to the project area, such as CBO leaders, teachers, or church leaders.
3. Interviews with at least two local builders.
4. Interviews with at least eight direct beneficiaries, distributed as follows: one male and one female teenager (aged below 20), one male and one female young adult (aged 21–35), one male and one female older adult (aged 35–50) and one male and one female older person (above 51 years of age).
5. Interviews with at least two representatives of institutions in the region with an interest in housing that were not directly involved with the project but offer an outside opinion on how and why it may have been replicated or not.

Focus groups

Two focus group discussions; one group with only women and the other with only men. The rationale for gender-specific groups was two-fold: on the one hand, the opinions of men and women about what matters in housing are frequently different. On the other hand, a separate discussion would ensure that women's opinions are heard as in some cultures the presence of men might prevent free expression from women. Each group should include separate groups of male and female beneficiaries, including representatives of all the above age groups.

Observation

Observation of the reconstruction sites and new or rebuilt houses. These observations were recorded both in writing and in pictures and described physical changes to the houses or changes in their use. These covered, e.g. deterioration due to weather or insects; damage as a result of natural hazards or otherwise; extensions made by the inhabitants; improvements to the structure or appearance; replacement of elements or components by others; and changes in the functions of rooms or plots.

Data analysis

Researchers took detailed written notes and made recordings of interviews and discussions as a backup for their analysis and as a source of quotes for the report.

This research was qualitative and based on a relatively small number of interviews, discussions, and observations. There was, therefore, a risk that conclusions drawn from it would not be representative of the larger project. To reduce that risk, and increase the credibility and validity of the findings, researchers were required to use triangulation wherever possible. In triangulation, more than two research methods are used to confirm findings. For instance, a point derived from talking to a single beneficiary, could be checked by talking to other beneficiaries, by bringing it up in a focus group, or in interviews with local leaders. The latter two sources could also confirm whether the particular point occurs only once in a while or often. Certain items of information, e.g. on the quality of construction, can also be illustrated by pictures and double checked by talking to local builders. For this reason, it was advisable to organize focus groups after interviewing most individuals; this would allow points raised by individuals to be confirmed by a broader group. Triangulation could bring out points of agreement, but there might also be points on which the various sources of information disagree; if that was to happen, it would be important to mention this, and provide the varying points of view.

Researchers were advised to analyse the interview and focus group results using the five broad areas of investigation listed above, a challenging task as many of the suggested questions do relate to each other, and interviews would often flow from one to the other. They were to look for indicative rather than absolute frequencies with which certain points had been raised (numbers being insufficient for meaningful statistical analysis), in three categories: (1) raised frequently (by half or more of the interviewees); (2) raised sometimes (by at least two interviewees but less than half); (3) raised occasionally (by a single interviewee); these five lists of frequencies were provided as annexes to their fieldwork report. Focus groups would be used to check whether the frequencies found were broadly representative for the project as a whole.

Index

Abhiyan (NGO network) 46
Aceh 137–50
    achievements and outputs 140
    beneficiary targeting 141, 142,
        143
    community participation 148,
        149
    livelihoods 146–7, 148fig, 149
    local culture 149
    post construction assistance
        149–50
    project intentions and design
        138–9
    replication 143–4
    rural housing 9
    technical performance 144, 145, 146
    training 11
    urban better-off 7, 8
    user satisfaction 140–1
adobe construction
    adoption of norms 166
    advantages of 162
    beneficiary satisfaction 160
    as building material 154–7, 161
    factor in Peru devastation 218, 220
    rural preference for 165
    spread of use of 169
    training manual 166
Aga Khan Development Network
    (AKDN) 74
Agency for the Rehabilitation and
    Reconstruction of Aceh and Nias
    (BRR) 140
Alcoholics Anonymous (AA) 179
alcoholism 179
Amarasingh, S. 99, 102, 104, 105
Amarateca 172, 173

animals 47, 49, 86, 117
apathy, post-project 229
architectural unity 180, 183fig
'architecture of hope' 161
artisans 12, 41, 62, 74, 157, 234
Arup International Development
    (Arup ID) 21, 22–3, 29
ASPIRE tool 21, 23
Association of Residents of La Paz
    (ASPODEPAZ) 204, 211, 212, 213,
    214
awareness-raising programmes 128

'Baja Verapaz' project 153, 155, 157,
    159, 166, 169
'baseline' 2
beneficiary targeting 3, 6–7, 8, 238,
    248
'La Betania' 171–85
    beneficiary targeting 179–80
    funding 176
    grassroots committee 171, 172–3
    livelihoods 183, 184, 185
    planning and organization 172–4
    replication 180–2
    technical performance 182–3
    time frame 175, 176
    user satisfaction 177, 178–9
bhungas (Traditional circular house)
    79–82, 84–90, 92
biological filter septic tanks (biofil)
    145, 149
'buffer zones' 24, 138
Building and Construction
    Improvement Programme (BACIP)
    59, 62–6
    beneficiary targeting 68

capacity building 63
construction methods 66
lessons learned 72–3
livelihoods 71–2
replication 68, 69–70
skills training 63–4
technical performance 70, 71
user satisfaction 68
Building and Social Housing
  Foundation (BSHF) 2–3, 59, 118,
  129
building codes
  and disaster resistance 9
  and government funding 234
  local 73
  overrating of 235
  in Pakistan 61, 62, 65
bureaucratic 'professionalism' 169

Calicanto (cyclopean concrete) 189,
  199
Camero, Eduardo 191, 192
Canadian International
  Development Aid (CIDA) 126
capacity building 32, 74, 100, 203,
  223, 226
CARE 226
Caritas 153, 154, 157, 169, 226
'cash grants' 123, 124, 125, 131
cash-for-work programmes 147, 149
Catholic Church 154, 169
Chaîne de Bonheur 172
Chavarria, Guillermo 159
chowki 79, 82, 85 table, 86
Ciudad España 174, 176–82, 184–5
climate change 14, 115, 133, 219,
  241
Climate Change Adaptation (CCA) 242
climatic consideration, house design
  26, 27, 33
Codeles 184
Colombia 7
commercial interests, effect on
  livelihoods 12
communication 128

community engagement
  authentic 105
  at each stage 148, 149
  importance of 73, 132, 133, 177
  lack of 53, 55
  and mobility 29
  project management committees
    29
  self-help 29
community passivity 102
community trust 81
community-based organizations
  (CBOs) 99
compound walls 43, 46, 49, 54, 55
computer-aided design (CAD) 102
concrete block housing 204fig,
  206figs
concrete panel housing 204fig,
  208fig
conflict, effect of 167–8
construction materials
  access to 74
  core houses 26
  local sourcing 32, 139, 154, 189,
    199
  quality of 5
  and status 230
  used for extensions 91table
core houses
  adaptation of design to meet local
    needs 29–30
  family compound 164
  limitations of design 25–7, 33
  permanent 220
  plan 43fig
Cosgrave, J. et al 11
credit availability 129, 157, 166, 204
  see also loans
crime prevention 185
cultural requirements 4, 29, 41, 43,
  46, 49, 149
cyclone-resistant construction
  119–21fig
cyclopean concrete (*calicanto*) 189,
  199

Da Silva, J. 11
Daji- (Dhajji) (Katore) style
    construction 66
decision-making, participatory 4, 5,
    8, 35
Development Workshop France
    (DWF) 116, 119–27
    aim of 115, 117
    construction guidelines 133
    'Prevent Typhoon Damage to
        Housing' programme 118
    training in safe construction 121,
        125, 128, 129
disabled people 12, 102, 125, 127,
    178
disaster risk reduction (DRR)
    importance of 241, 242
    incorporation into housing
        planning 33
    in reconstruction 130, 131, 134
donor-driven programmes (DDP)
    98–9
donor-driven reconstruction (DDR)
    4, 10
'dual education programme' 157

earthquakes, effects of
    El Salvador 201–14
    Guatemala 153–70
    Gujarat 46–9, 77–95
    Honduras 171, 173, 175
    Indonesia 137, 143, 144
    Kashmir 61, 70
    Maharashtra 40–6
    Pakistan 60–75
    Peru 217–30
    risks of reconstruction 9
economic boost 11, 146, 236
economic diversification 90, 92, 93
EcoSur 173, 175, 176, 180, 185, 190
EcoViDe 172–3, 174, 175–80, 185
education
    access to 28, 29
    effect of greater income 212
    and new housing 34

El Carmen 218, 221, 222, 224
El Salvador 201–14
    beneficiary targeting 207
    construction technology 213
    earthquakes 201, 202
    economic component of
        programme 204
    gangs 207
    health improvement 206
    holistic approach 202
    house design and construction
        205
    livelihood development 210–12,
        213
    modifications 207, 208
    mutual aid 213
    participation 213, 214
    physical components of
        programme 202
    Post-earthquake Housing
        Reconstruction Programme
        202–4
    PRVPT 210
    replication 207, 208, 209, 213
    seed fund 213
    social components of programme
        202, 204
    technical performance 209–10
employment
    agriculture 207, 228
    local builders 125
    low-paid 31
    in reconstruction 30–1, 33, 34,
        139
    and relocation 24, 33, 207, 237
    and skills training 146
    unemployment 174, 177, 184
enabling mechanisms, governmental
    46
Engineers Against Poverty 21, 23
entrepreneurs 63, 64, 71–2, 75
environmental awareness 184
environmental sustainability 94, 140
equity, housing reconstruction 40,
    41

Escuela de Formación Ciudadana
(ESFORCI) (Citizenship Training
School) 211, 212
European Community Humanitarian
Office (ECHO) 126
extensions
and better organization 239
economic status owners 56, 109
for income generation 124, 177
prevalence of 49
quality 45, 143

Fadsar village 47–9, 55
female headed households 119, 204,
219
'filler slab' roofs 103
financial assistance 46, 74, 124, 125,
127, 129
First Micro Finance Bank (FMFB)
74
fishing 30, 50–2, 98, 105, 123
flexibility 92, 223
flooding
and climate change 241
construction guidelines 133
construction materials 103
El Salvador 209, 210
Honduras 171–85
platform construction 121, 125
seismic-resistant housing 66, 70
and site selection 24, 47, 48, 52
typhoons 117
focus groups 106
Footprints E.A.R.T.H (Environment
Architecture Research Technology
Housing) 78
Ford Foundation 124, 129
Forsur (Fund for the Reconstruction
of the South) 218, 220
Free Aceh Movement (GAM) 140
fuel consumption 28, 34, 71, 73, 211
FUNDASAL (Salvadoran Foundation
for Development and Low-cost
Housing) 201, 202–3, 205, 206,
209–14

galvanized wire technology (GWR)
66, 67, 68, 69, 71
Gandhi Nu Gam 77–95
analysis post occupancy 83–9
beneficiary targeting 90
changes in spatial typology
85table
community needs 80, 81
Harijan community 78, 79, 81, 90
holistic reconstruction 80–3
housing design 81
infrastructure reconstruction 83
livelihoods 92–3
migration 80
Muslim community 81
participatory settlement planning
81
replication 90–1
self-help construction 82
site plan 84fig, 85fig
site relocation 81
technical performance 91, 92
user satisfaction 89, 90
gender balance 101
gender equity 211, 228, 184
gender perspectives 101
German Agency for International
Cooperation (GIZ) 226
German Development Bank (KfW)
202
governance 10, 13, 222, 230, 239
Granada 187, 188
Greenpeace 149
groundwater contamination 27
Grupo Sofonias 165, 166, 191
Guatemala 153–70
beneficiary targeting 161, 162
capacity building 157–8
collective action 158–60
conflict 167–8
decentralized organization 158–60
earthquake fatalities 153
evaluation 160
financial assistance 157, 165
friendships 166, 167

infrastructure 158
internal conflict 170
livelihoods 166
quick participatory response
    155–6
replication 162–6
social movement 159, 160
technical performance 166
training of local people 157–8
user satisfaction 160, 161
Gujarat
building codes 235
holistic approach 77–95
increased value housing 55
local NGOs 47
'owner-driven' reconstruction 7,
    46
reconstruction after earthquake
    9, 46–9
rejection of relocation 46

health
access to healthcare 89, 189
children 126
destruction of coastal habitat 51
low lying land 52
negative effect on 6
public 27, 32, 94
and sanitation 206
and ventilation 26, 28, 206, 223
Hernandez, Jose Luis 188
Habitat for Humanity (HFH) 21–35
access to services 27–8, 29, 34
community engagement 29–31,
    34
house design and construction
    25–7, 33
methodology 22, 23
relationships with other actors 32,
    34, 35
site selection and settlement
    planning 23–4, 33
skills training 235
holistic and integrated approach
    80–3

ASPIRE appraisal framework 23
importance of 35
methodology 78
need for further research 243–4,
    245
PRVPT 203
relocation 33
and 'specialities' 132
success of 236, 240
home based livelihoods 109
Honduras 171–85
beneficiary targeting 179–80
building materials 175
financial assistance 181
funding 176
governmental disorganization 176
international building standards
    181
livelihoods 183, 184, 185
local infrastructure improvements
    184
planning and organization
    172–4
political insecurity 183
public transport 184
replication 180–2
self-construction 174
technical performance 181–2
technical solutions, training, and
    production 175
time frame 175, 176
training 175
unemployment 184
user satisfaction 177, 178–9
household costs, reduction in 206
household size 40
housing
affordability 7
compromise 7
core houses 6, 7
cost of 6
culture 153, 239
disaster resistance 9–10
government schemes 219
incremental 210

layout 141
  as part of whole 95
housing 'invasions' 98, 184
Hurricane Ida 209, 210
Hurricane Mitch 171–2, 187
Hurricane Stan 209, 210
Hussain, A. 63
hygiene awareness, promotion of
  27

IFRC (International Federation of the
  Red Cross/Crescent) 124, 125
in-situ construction
  community agreement 90
  design and livelihoods 11
  HFH approach 22, 23, 33
  and infrastructure 5
  quality of 47, 52
income diversification 105
income generation, home-based
  85–8
India 77–95
  analysis post occupancy 83–9
  beneficiary targeting 90
  changes in spatial typology
    85table
  community engagement 30
  community needs 80, 81
  Harijan community 78, 79, 81, 90
  holistic reconstruction 80–3
  housing design 81
  housing reconstruction 22, 24–35
  infrastructure reconstruction 83
  livelihoods 92–3
  migration 80
  Muslim community 81
  participatory settlement planning 81
  replication 90–1
  self-help construction 82
  site plan 84fig, 85fig
  site relocation 81
  technical performance 91, 92
  user satisfaction 89, 90
indigenous knowledge 73, 81
Indonesia 137–50

alterations to enable home based
  business 142
beneficiary targeting 141, 142–3
community centres trauma
  healing 146
community engagement 30
economic decline 143, 149
financial assistance 139
house layout 141
housing reconstruction 22, 24–35
infrastructure 140, 146
inspection training, local 144, 145
livelihoods 139, 146–7, 148fig
local suppliers, materials 32
maintenance 145
replication 143–4
technical performance 144, 145,
  146figs
training of survivors 139
user satisfaction 140–1
indoor air pollution 28, 63, 71, 73
infrastructure
  delays in 5
  importance of 235, 236
  lack of 7, 9
  social 23
  strengthening of 129
Institute of National Civil Defense
  (INDECI) 217
integrated approach 12, 28, 73, 74
international aid 10, 137

Jigyasu, R. 41
JUB ('Village Solidarity Network')
  139, 140, 149

Katore- or Daji- (Dhajji) style
  construction 66

La Casa (Casa de los Tres Mundos)
  187, 188, 190, 200
La Libertad 202
La Paz 201, 202, 213
land rights 24, 139, 218, 219, 238
landlessness 41, 47
language 29

leach pits 27
'liberation theology' 154
literature review 1
livelihoods
    community engagement 34
    consideration for 6
    holistic approach 35
    home based livelihoods 166
    importance of 236
    investigation into 3, 10–13
    post-disaster 149
    targeted assistance 12
loans 64, 124, 127, 165, 169, 182,
    237 *see also* credit availability
long-term impact 35, 237–41
Louis, Jose 195
Ludiya village
    community facilities rebuilding
        82
    Harijan community 90
    livelihoods 79
    Muslim community 90
    Panchayat (village council)
        building 82
    personal decoration of houses 82,
        83figs
    post-disaster 79, 80
    relocation 83
    settlement layout 79
Lyons, M. and and Amarasingh, S.
    99, 102, 104, 105

Maharashtra 7, 39, 40–6
Maharashtra Emergency Earthquake
    Rehabilitation Programme
    (MEERP) 40
maintenance
    basic 145, 210
    disaster-resistant 10, 90
    importance of 199
    lack of 107, 108, 178, 193, 240
    local workmen 127
    need for support 111
    reduced 68, 71, 109, 125
Malacatoya village 187

Malkondji village 42–6, 54
Manav Sadhna 77, 78, 79
Matara Trust 100, 101
Mayan people 153
medical bills, reduction in 71
medical care, access to 89
Melendez, Martin 191
microfinance programmes 27, 67, 74
military, relationships with 32
model house 156fig, 157
Morgan community 24
Multi Donor Fund 137
Muslim community 24, 78, 81, 90,
    102, 110
mutual aid 203, 208, 209, 213

Nasi Island 144
National Commission of Residents
    (CONAPO) 213
National Housing Development
    Authority (NHDA) 102
national government, relationships
    with 32
Negrón, Guzmán 4
Nias Island 137
Nicaragua 187–200
    beneficiaries' opinions 196–8
    beneficiary targeting 199
    flooding 187
    infrastructure 189, 195
    livelihoods 200
    replication 199
    resettlement 188, 189
    on-site management 193
    technical performance 199, 200
    traditional construction 188,
        189
    user satisfaction 198, 199
Nienhuys, S. 61, 66, 67
non-engineered housing 60, 62, 67
non-occupancy 7, 47

owner-driven programmes (ODP)
    46–7, 98, 99, 100
owner-driven reconstruction (ODR)
    disaster resistant housing 9

first 242
increased satisfaction 4
and infrastructure 94
livelihoods 11
and local skills 8
problem with 6, 7
post-tsunami 97, 98
and quality 10
Oliver, P. 95
Pacific 'Ring of Fire' 201
Pakistan 59–75
access to finance 74
accessible technology 73, 74
BACIP 62–5
beneficiary targeting 68
deaths 60
integrated design 73, 74
livelihoods 71, 72
local housing construction 60–2, 73
replication 68, 69–70
seismic resistance 65, 66–7, 68
technical performance 70, 71
user satisfaction 68
Pakistan Building Codes 61, 62
Pakistan Engineering Council 65, 71
Pan y Arte e.V. 190
participatory approach 190–2
assurance of safety 139
FUNDASAL goal 202
housing needs assessment 97
importance of 7, 233, 234
improvement in gender equality 147, 148
mechanisms for 202
people-driven 137
tokenism 105
workshops 101
participatory design 92, 93, 130, 133
Participatory Housing Approach (PHA) 77, 78, 93, 94
Participatory Rapid Appraisal (PRA) 22, 62
Patronatos 179, 184, 185
Paz y Esperanza 226

peace agreements 140, 160, 168
people-centred approach 93
People's Committee of the Commune 126, 129
Peru 217–31
beneficiary targeting 219, 220, 224, 229
and change 4
early involvement Practical Action 219
earthquake 217
extensions 225, 228
financial assistance 224, 225
health improvements 223
livelihood, empowerment and resilience 228–9
replication 225–6, 229
technical performance 226–7, 228
user satisfaction 222, 223–4
police, relationships with 32
political movements 169, 170
Post-earthquake Housing Reconstruction Programme (PRVPT) 202–3, 205–6, 207, 213, 214
post-reconstruction evaluation, importance of 132–3
post-reconstruction assistance 149, 150
poverty
beneficiary targeting 238
effect of disasters on 1, 202
income generation 124
and loans 118
and reconstruction 10
and replication 8, 237
Practical Action
Peru 217–30
Sri Lanka 97–112
preventive strengthening 126–7
production, facilitation of 129
professionals 54
psychological support 190
public health 27, 32, 94
public works, tendering 121

quincha (traditional mud and pole construction), improved 220, 221–7, 229, 230

radio 65, 70
rapid housing need assessment methodology 101
rat-trap bond approach 102–3, 104fig, 105, 106–7, 108, 109–11
Reconstruction of Aceh Land Administration System (RALAS) 24
recycled materials 144, 185
Red Cross 172, 175, 176, 177, 179, 184 *see also* IFRC
reinforced concrete 43, 66, 67, 71
Rejuvenate India Movement 78
relocation
    advantages and disadvantages 24
    community engagement 172–3
    and dissatisfaction 5
    effect on livelihoods 11
    enforcement buffer zone 98
    health risks 52
    holistic approach 33
    long term impact 237
    non-occupancy housing 7
    rejection of 48, 50, 138
    requested 41
    traditional settlement plan 83
removable steel structure housing 204fig, 208
replication 8
    and accessible technology 74, 108, 109, 111, 165, 234
    awareness raising 240
    financial constraints 128, 230, 237
    participation and 234
    time constraint 229
research methodology 3, 247–51
resilience 111, 129, 242
'resource person' 65
respiratory diseases 74
respondent groups 106

retrofitting 9, 68, 82, 235
risk awareness 9
roofs 125, 192, 193, 194figs
Ruiz, Nolasco 191

Salamá 154, 155, 157, 158–60, 166
Salas, Julian 171
Salazar, A. 41
Salvadoran Foundation for Development and Low-cost Housing (FUNDASAL) 201, 202–3, 205, 206, 209–14
sanitation 6, 27, 28, 34, 229, 236
scaling up, cost sharing 35
Sedky, N. 63
seismic vulnerability 59–75
    local housing construction 60–2
    seismic resistance 65, 66–7, 68
self-relocation 42
Semilla Comunitaria para el Mejoramiento Económico (Community Fund for Economic Improvement) (SECOME) 212
Seruthur village 52–4, 55
settlement planning
    importance of 55
    and risk 23, 35
    traditional 83, 91
Shelter Centre, Geneva 3
'simulation kit' 81, 82fig
social cohesion
    communal spaces 55
    community engagement 34, 139, 147, 198
    relocation and 42
    social infrastructure 23, 33
SofoNic (Sofonias Nicaragua) 187–91, 193–5
'soft invasion' 181
soil block technology 94
solar technology 28, 34, 94, 145, 149
space restriction, effect on livelihoods 12
'squatters' 98, 184
Sri Lanka 97–112

appropriate technologies 102–4
beneficiary targeting 107
centralization of decision-making
   98
community engagement 30,
   100–2
construction targets 99
costs 103–4
disabled people 107
disaster resistant housing 9
end of project situation 104, 105
extensions 106
fishermen 97
follow-up study methods 105, 106
funding for maintenance 106
housing reconstruction 22, 24–35
lessons learned 110–11
livelihoods, empowerment, and
   resilience 109, 110
maintenance handbook 106, 107
Muslim sale of houses 110
participatory approach 100
replication 97, 108, 109
technical performance 108
tourism 98
user satisfaction 106–7
staff, importance of 6
start up fund, small businesses 204,
   211, 236
steel structure houses 213
supervision, and quality 10
Sustainable Livelihoods Framework
   23
'sweat equity' 30, 31
Swiss Agency for Development
   Cooperation 40
Swiss National Science Foundation
   40
Swiss Solidarity 153

Tajikistan 75
Tamil Nadu 50–6
   design as problematic 51
   destruction of habitat 52
   family entitlement re housing 51

fishers 50, 51
health and well-being 51
housing reconstruction 39
increased value housing 55
plot size 51
reduced governmental role 51
relocation rejected 50
targeting rationale, publicized 101
teams, long term memory 132
technical performance, investigation
   into 3, 9–10
Techo Proprio programmes 229
Tegucigalpa 171, 172
temples 48, 49
Thailand 22, 24–9, 31
timber, cost of 66
toilets 27–8, 85, 86, 108, 111
tourism 86, 90, 92, 93, 94
traditional buildings *see* vernacular
   approaches
training 105, 110
transparency 131
transport infrastructure 83, 89, 184,
   195, 211
trauma, psychological 244
tree plantation, importance of 43,
   48, 51, 52, 53, 55
tsunami, Indian Ocean 21–35, 50–6,
   97–112
   access to services 27–8, 29
   community engagement 29–31,
      100–2
   fatalities 50, 98, 137
   house design and construction
      25–7
   relationships with other actors
      32
   site selection and settlement
      planning 23–4
   technologies 102–4
Turner, John 241
Typhoon Pablo 131

UN Habitat 4
unemployment 174, 177, 184

United Nations International
Strategy for Disaster Reduction
(UN-ISDR), 133, 242
Uplink (Urban Poor Linkage)
Indonesia 137, 138–50
achievement and output 140
beneficiary targeting 141, 142,
143
community engagement 148, 149
livelihoods 146–7, 148fig, 149
local culture 149
post-construction assistance
149–50
project intentions and design
138–9
replication 143–4
technical performance 144, 145,
146figs
user satisfaction 140–1
user satisfaction 3, 4-6
house layout 141
'people-centred approach' 78
variation over time 9, 234

Vastu Shilpa Foundation for Studies
and Research in Environmental
Design (VSF) 77, 78, 79, 91
ventilation 26, 27, 108, 109
verandas 49, 51
vernacular approaches
adaptation of 8, 10, 13, 90, 220,
230, 234–5
affordability of 10, 234, 237
agencies' bias against 6, 41, 50
construction 102
extensions 8
importance of 10, 94
loss of confidence in 41, 42
resilience of 80, 81
seismic resistance 66
Vietnam 115–34
beneficiary targeting 123, 124,
126, 127
Binh Dong Commune 124–5

change in building practice 118
community decision re targeting
119
construction regulations 119
construction technique 122
Cyclone Ketsana 119
Dak Tram Commune 125, 126
disaster context 117–18
effect of natural disasters 115,
116
effect of typhoon on livelihoods
117
emergency financial support
governmental 118
fatalities 117
financial assistance 123, 124, 125,
127
flooding 117
health 126
livelihoods 118, 124, 125, 126,
127
Loc Tri Commune 123–4
map 116fig
marginalized women as targets
107
Provincial People's Committee
119
Quang Tho Commune 126–7
replication 124, 125, 126, 127
technical performance 123–4,
125, 126, 127
Thua Thien Hue Province 119
typhoons 115, 116, 117
user satisfaction 125, 126, 127
Vietnam Bank for Social Policies 124,
127, 129, 237
'Village Solidarity Network' (JUB)
139, 140, 149
violence 179
vulnerable groups, targeting of 29

wall reinforcement 65, 66
water
access to 27, 92, 126, 211

for construction 157, 158
management 82, 83
positive effect for women 211, 228
water, sanitation and hygiene,
    integrated approach 34
women
    engagement with 101
    female headed households
        prioritized 119, 127, 184, 219
    gender equity 211, 228
    house design 184
    increase in status 147, 148
    involvement in construction 189
    labour reduced 74
    marginalization of 51
    participatory design 92, 93
    positive effect of water supply
        211, 228
    positive effect reconstruction
        125
    reduction in household chores
        92, 184
    skills training 92
    small businesses 211,
        212
    start-up fund 204
    targeted assistance 12
    traditional needlework 86, 87,
        88fig, 89, 92
    use of sanitation 27
Women's Union 129
workmanship, quality of 9
World Bank, funding for
    reconstruction 7
World Habitat Award (WHA) 2, 129,
    133